THE HIDDEN HANDS OF JUSTICE

The Hidden Hands of Justice: NGOs, Human Rights, and International Courts is the first comprehensive analysis of non-governmental organization (NGO) participation at international criminal and human rights courts. Drawing on original data, Heidi Nichols Haddad maps and explains the differences in NGO participatory roles, frequency, and impact at three judicial institutions: The European Court of Human Rights, the Inter-American Human Rights System, and the International Criminal Court. *The Hidden Hands of Justice* demonstrates that courts can strategically choose to enhance their functionality by allowing NGOs to provide needed information, expertise, and services as well as shame states for non-cooperation. Through participation, NGOs can profoundly shape the character of international human rights justice but, in doing so, may consolidate civil society representation and relinquish their roles as external monitors.

Heidi Nichols Haddad is Assistant Professor of Politics at Pomona College.

T0381905

The Hidden Hands of Justice

NGOS, HUMAN RIGHTS, AND INTERNATIONAL COURTS

HEIDI NICHOLS HADDAD

Pomona College, California

CAMBRIDGE
UNIVERSITY PRESS

CAMBRIDGE
UNIVERSITY PRESS

University Printing House, Cambridge CB2 8BS, United Kingdom

One Liberty Plaza, 20th Floor, New York, NY 10006, USA

477 Williamstown Road, Port Melbourne, VIC 3207, Australia

314-321, 3rd Floor, Plot 3, Splendor Forum, Jasola District Centre, New Delhi - 110025, India

79 Anson Road, #06-04/06, Singapore 079906

Cambridge University Press is part of the University of Cambridge.

It furthers the University's mission by disseminating knowledge in the pursuit of education, learning and research at the highest international levels of excellence.

www.cambridge.org
Information on this title: www.cambridge.org/9781108456852
DOI: 10.1017/9781108557313

First published 2018
First paperback edition 2019

A catalogue record for this publication is available from the British Library

ISBN 978-1-108-47092-6 Hardback
ISBN 978-1-108-45685-2 Paperback

To Naomi and Caroline, who were born during the writing of this book, and to B.J., who supported me throughout.

Contents

Figures

Tables

Acknowledgments

This book rests on the support, generosity, and assistance of so many individuals and groups. I am first and foremost indebted to my dissertation committee – Wayne Sandholtz, Deborah Avant, Diana Kapiszewski, and Christopher Whytock – for encouraging and guiding my untrodden exploration that spanned three international courts over two continents. I am particularly grateful for the mentorship of Wayne Sandholtz, who has always championed and supported me, and who so well models professionalism, research ingenuity, and dedication to students. I would also like to thank my interview subjects who generously shared their time and insights with me, Elisabeth Lambert-Abdalwagat, who granted me institutional affiliation at the University of Strasbourg, and the Institute for European Studies at the University of California, Berkeley and the Centers for Organizational Research, Global Peace and Conflict Studies, and Citizen Peacebuilding at the University of California, Irvine for funding my fieldwork. I am also appreciative of John Berger's stewardship of the book's publication and the thoughtful feedback of the two anonymous reviewers.

Pomona College has been an invigorating and encouraging environment to write this book and I have benefited from the support and feedback of my colleagues, in particular Amanda Hollis-Brusky, and my student research assistants, Margaret Munts, Sarthak Sharma, and Alexandra Goss.

Lastly, I would like to thank my family for accommodating this book in their lives for many years, my parents for their commitment to my education, and my mom for passing on her love of books.

This book is derived in part from an article published in the *Journal of Human Rights* (2012) copyright Taylor & Francis, available online: www.tandfonline.com/doi/abs/10.1080/14754835.2012.648154.

Abbreviations

ACHPR	African Commission on Human and Peoples' Rights
ACtHPR	African Court on Human and Peoples' Rights
APIC	Agreement on Privileges and Immunities
ASF	Avocats Sans Frontières
ASP	Assembly of States Parties – ICC
AU	African Union
CDDH	Council of Europe Steering Committee for Human Rights
CEJIL	Center for Justice and International Law
CICC	Coalition for the International Criminal Court
CofE	Council of Europe
DRC	Democratic Republic of the Congo
ECCC	Extraordinary Chambers in the Courts of Cambodia
ECtHR	European Court of Human Rights
ECOSOC	UN Economic and Social Council
ECOWAS	Economic Community of West African States
EHRAC	European Human Rights Advocacy Centre
EIPR	Egyptian Initiative for Personal Rights
FIDH	International Federation for Human Rights
FNI	National Integrationist Front – Democratic Republic of the Congo (DRC)
GONGO	government-organized non-governmental organization
HRW	Human Rights Watch
IACHR	Inter-American Commission on Human Rights
IACtHR	Inter-American Court of Human Rights
IAS	Inter-American Human Rights System
IBA	International Bar Association
ICB	International Criminal Bar
ICC	International Criminal Court

ICJ	International Commission of Jurists
ICRC	International Committee of the Red Cross
ICTJ	International Center for Transitional Justice
ICTR	International Criminal Tribunal for Rwanda
ICTY	International Criminal Tribunal for the former Yugoslavia
IHRG	International Human Rights Group
IIHR/IIDH	Inter-American Institute of Human Rights
ILC	International Law Commission
IMF	International Monetary Fund
INGO	International non-governmental organization
IRS	Internal Revenue Service – US
KEK	Conference for European Churches
KHRP	Kurdish Human Rights Project
LRA	Lord's Resistance Army
MIND	National Association for Mental Health
NCCL	National Council for Civil Liberties
NGO	Non-governmental organization
NRA	National Rifle Association
OAS	Organization of American States
OSCE	Organization for Security and Cooperation in Europe
OSJI	Open Society Justice Initiative
OTP	Office of the Proscecutor – ICC
PACE	Parliamentary Assembly of the Council of Europe
PGA	Parliamentarians for Global Action
SCSL	Special Court for Sierra Leone
TAN	Transnational Advocacy Network
TVF	Trust Fund for Victims
UN	United Nations
UNCHR	United Nations Commission on Human Rights
UNSC	United Nations Security Council
USAID	United States Agency for International Development
WFM	World Federalist Movement
WIGJ	Women's Initiatives for Gender Justice
WOLA	Washington Office on Latin America
WTO	World Trade Organization
YUCOM	Lawyers Committee for Human Rights

Introduction

The Overlooked Partnerships

On June 15, 2015, Sudanese President Omar al-Bashir – who is wanted for genocide and war crimes by the International Criminal Court (ICC) – narrowly eluded arrest upon leaving South Africa after attending an African Union (AU) summit. A high court in Pretoria had issued an interim order preventing Bashir from leaving South Africa until an application for authorities to arrest him was heard; yet, the government ignored the order and gave Bashir clearance to leave. The government not only violated the high court's order but also shirked its international legal obligations to arrest Bashir under the Rome Statute, the treaty underpinning the ICC. Some media analyses faulted South Africa for embracing the anti-ICC, African bias rhetoric and action promulgated by the AU and Kenyan leaders.[1] Others interpreted the event as another blow to the legitimacy and credibility of a beleaguered institution that relies on state cooperation.[2] Both of these narratives tell a story that pits courts against states, of legalism against power politics. In this instance, politics won out. This narrative of courts and legalism versus states and politics plays out in much scholarship on courts, and international courts in particular. States attempt to insert politics into trials and courts through prosecutorial interference, appointing judges

---

[1] Simon Tisdall, "Omar Al-Bashir Case Suggests South African Foreign Policy Is Going Rogue," *The Guardian*, June 15, 2015, www.theguardian.com/world/2015/jun/15/omar-al-bashir-south-africa-sudan-international-criminal-court-icc; New York Times Editorial Board, "South Africa's Disgraceful Help for President Bashir of Sudan," *The New York Times*, June 15, 2015, www.nytimes.com/2015/06/16/opinion/south-africas-disgraceful-help-for-president-bashir-of-sudan.html. Many of the Courts in this volume are referred to by their acronym ("ECtHR" for the European Court of Human Rights, for example), but in some cases I just refer to them as "the Court."

[2] Eugene Kontorovich, "Sudan's Bashir Is the Palestinians' and Pretoria's Favorite Genocidal Tyrant," *The Washington Post*, June 15, 2015, www.washingtonpost.com/news/volokh-conspiracy/wp/2015/06/15/sudans-bashir-is-the-palestinians-and-pretorias-favorite-genocidal-tyrant/; Somini Sengupta, "Omar Al-Bashir Case Shows International Criminal Court's Limitations," *The New York Times*, June 15, 2015, www.nytimes.com/2015/06/16/world/africa/sudan-bashir-international-criminal-court.html.

with political ties or biases, pulling out of treaties following contentious judgments or choosing not to enforce those judgments.[3]

What is obscured in this narrative – and in the widely circulated story of Bashir eluding arrest in South Africa – is the catalyst behind the high court's order barring Bashir from leaving that made it a near miss. A local, human rights non-governmental organization (NGO), the South African Litigation Center, filed the urgent application to overturn a government decision to grant immunity to all delegates attending the AU summit with the high court.[4] This was not the first time that NGOs had used such a tactic. In November 2011, the local chapter of the International Commission of Jurists (ICJ) initiated proceedings in the Kenyan court that resulted in an order to the government to arrest Bashir if he should enter the country.[5] Behind these lawsuits is a sophisticated network of local and international human rights NGOs that independently, and in coordination, followed Bashir's travel and engaged in advocacy and litigation tactics to bring about his arrest.[6] NGO involvement with the ICC is not limited to pressuring for Bashir's arrest but NGOs participate at the ICC, and its affiliated bodies, in nearly all areas of the Court – from budget, investigations, ratification of the Rome Statute, to working with victims. NGOs support, monitor, and aid the ICC, and in some roles, are critical to the Court's functionality.

NGO interaction with international courts is not unique to the ICC. Although to a lesser extent, NGOs also participate with varying degrees of influence at other international criminal and human rights courts. In 1980, the newly established Inter-American Court of Human Rights set up an affiliated NGO that circuitously provided funding for necessary special sessions for the Court. Currently, the Washington, DC-based NGO, the Center for Justice and International Law

[3] Alison Danner and Erik Voeten, "Who Is Running the International Criminal Justice System?," in *Who Governs the Globe?*, ed. Deborah Avant, Martha Finnemore, and Susan Sell (Cambridge University Press, 2010): 35–71; David Bosco, *Rough Justice: The International Criminal Court in a World of Power Politics*, 1st edition (Oxford and New York, NY: Oxford University Press, 2014); Erik Voeten, "The Politics of International Judicial Appointments: Evidence from the European Court of Human Rights," *International Organization* 61, no. 4 (2007): 669–701; Manfred Elsig and Mark A. Pollack, "Agents, Trustees, and International Courts: The Politics of Judicial Appointment at the World Trade Organization," *European Journal of International Relations* 20, no. 2 (2014): 391–415; Jeffrey K. Staton and Alexia Romero, "Clarity and Compliance in the Inter-American Human Rights System," (2011); Frans Viljoen and Lirette Louw, "State Compliance with the Recommendations of the African Commission on Human and Peoples' Rights, 1994–2004," *The American Journal of International Law* 101, no. 1 (2007): 1–34.
[4] Owen Bowcott and Jamie Grierson, "Sudan President Barred from Leaving South Africa," *The Guardian*, June 15, 2015, www.theguardian.com/world/2015/jun/14/sudan-president-omar-al-bashir-south-africa-icc.
[5] "Kenyan Court Issues Arrest Order for Sudan's Bashir," *Reuters*, November 28, 2011, www.reuters.com/article/2011/11/28/us-kenya-bashir-icc-idUSTRE7AR0YA20111128.
[6] See CICC blog for posts showcasing coordinated civil society action regarding Bashir: http://us2.campaign-archive2.com/?u=8758bcde31bc78a5c32ceee50&id=2713f7bcf9.

(CEJIL) is the driving force behind the Court's overturning of the amnesty laws throughout Latin America and litigates over 60 percent of the cases before the Court, including landmark cases on domestic violence and indigenous rights.[7] At the European Court of Human Rights (ECtHR), NGOs represent petitioners, file amicus briefs, and a coalition of NGOs led by Amnesty International submits informal comments on Court reforms. In contrast to the dominant framework that centers on the interplay between states and international courts, NGOs can also be integral actors. NGOs play a multiplicity of roles vis-à-vis international criminal and human rights courts: from the expected roles in litigation, naming and shaming, and sharing information to the more surprising support-based roles of helping with court administration and capacity building. Through these diverse participatory roles, NGOs have the potential to shape court resources, policies, governance, and jurisprudence.

NGO participation across international criminal and human rights courts is not uniform. NGOs take on different combinations of participatory roles at each court with a varying ability to shape the Court and impact its jurisprudence. The identities, goals, and coordinating strategies of the NGOs also diverge across courts. At the ICC, international and domestic human rights NGOs, often coordinated by the Coalition for the International Criminal Court (CICC), support the Court through the widest range of roles. ICC officials, and even member state diplomats, recognize the benefits of NGO participation, and therefore specific NGOs with channels of access have the ability to substantively shape the Court. At the Inter-American Human Rights System (IAS), NGO participation is long-standing and contributed to the revitalization of the Inter-American Commission in the mid 1970s to address the grave abuses occurring in Latin America. Since the 1970s, NGO participation has centered around a few Washington, DC-based NGOs, most notably Americas Watch, which founded CEJIL. These NGOs focus more on information sharing and litigation strategies than the capacity building of NGOs at the ICC. At the ECtHR, major human rights players and boutique litigation NGOs, mostly based in the United Kingdom, seek to influence the Court through litigation, third-party briefs, and advocacy regarding the reform process but have intermittent success and are often viewed as unnecessary or with skepticism among court officials and member state diplomats.

What explains this variation in NGO participatory roles, frequency, and impact across international criminal and human rights courts? Why do NGOs have such tremendous access and potential influence at the ICC yet are not allowed to make

---

[7] Author interview with a staff member of CEJIL, December 17, 2010. These approximate statistics were confirmed by a personal interview with an official of the Inter-American Commission on Human Rights, December 8, 2010. According to CEJIL's 20 year Activities Report, CEJIL litigated 65 cases at the Court from 1991 to 2001, which comes out to approximately 50% of all of the Court's cases, CEJIL, "CEJIL Activities Report – 20 Years," 2011: 24, http://cejil.org/en/publicaciones/cejil-activities-report-20-years.

formal statements at the meetings on Court reform at the ECtHR? Why does the CICC help with the administrative functions of the ICC while CEJIL mostly engages in litigation at the Inter-American Human Rights System? Unfortunately, the current literature in various disciplines and subfields cannot explain NGO participation at international courts.

This book is the first study to map the breadth and influence of NGO engagement with three international criminal and human rights courts. Using largely original data, it documents NGO participatory roles and measures the frequency of NGO interaction and respective impact on court operations, governance, and jurisprudence. The study also develops a new theoretical framework that explains why NGO participatory roles, frequency, and impact vary at the examined courts. I argue that NGO participation is influenced by three factors: (1) court deficiencies of resources and legitimacy, (2) the institutional history of NGO engagement, and (3) NGO motivation and resources. Combinations of these factors shape whether courts and states grant NGOs access for new or expanded participatory *roles*, the *frequency* at which NGOs choose to utilize the channels of access, and whether this participation results in substantive *impact*.

Most participatory *roles* require decision-makers to grant NGOs some level of formal or informal access, such as a rule change or closed-door policy consultation.[8] The decision-makers are typically courts, commissions, or member states. Courts or commissions that are struggling to fulfill their mandates – either through limited funding, state hostility, hamstrung authority, or loss of legitimacy – are more likely to grant allowance to NGOs to provide formal or informal services for aid. Furthermore, judicial institutions and member states with a prior history of NGO engagement are more likely to allow expanded NGO access because NGOs are viewed as suitable partners. The history of engagement might also condition the ways in which courts or states choose to permit NGOs to provide supplemental services – whether through formal rules of access or informal backchannel networks. NGOs may also contribute to new forms of access by pressuring for, and sometimes manufacturing without state or court consent, opportunities for greater participation.

Once participatory access is granted, the decision to utilize the channels of access largely falls with NGOs. NGOs participate with greater *frequency* when they are motivated and have the financial resources to do so. NGO motivation to engage international criminal and human rights is fairly constant and derives from the unique nature of these judicial institutions. As courts of last resort with enforceable decisions, there are no commensurate alternative venues. As such, NGOs seek to utilize these courts to provide redress to victims and to develop new jurisprudence but are also willing to provide services to aid the courts' ability to function.

---

[8] Some NGO participatory roles require no authorization of access. These typically consist of advocacy roles outside of formal governance institutions or engaging in service provision that would usually be under the purview of the court.

NGO resources to engage with these courts are much more variable. NGO funding streams vary both across judicial institutions and NGOs participating at the same court.

Lastly, the *impact* of NGO participation typically correlates with the reason that courts or member states grant them participatory access. Access granted to mitigate court deficiencies is more likely to result in substantive influence as NGOs are providing much-needed services or information. Conversely, court or member state reticence about NGO participation because of limited historical engagement is more likely to result in shallow or purely symbolic influence. In this situation, the court or states could construct NGO access in a circumscribed way so as to blunt influence or court officials could choose to disregard NGO information or expertise due to negative perceptions of NGOs.

In this introductory chapter, I give an overview of the existing literature on international courts and NGOs and discuss its shortcomings in explaining the phenomenon of NGO engagement with international criminal and human rights courts. I then further detail my argument and specifically define and conceptualize how court deficiencies, history of NGO engagement, and NGO resources and motivation translate to NGO roles, frequency, and impact. The subsequent section articulates why examining the phenomenon of NGO participation at international judicial mechanisms matters theoretically and empirically, particularly for the conceptualization of international courts and human rights NGOs. The final section outlines the plan of study for the remainder of the book.

NGOS AND INTERNATIONAL COURTS: THE OVERLOOKED PARTNERSHIPS

NGOs are increasingly prominent actors in global governance. NGOs contribute to global policy-making at regional and international organizations, institutions, and regimes across a range of issues, from human rights to the environment.[9] A burgeoning literature has begun to explore not only the arenas where NGOs have influence but why the patterns of access and influence across issues and institutions look the way they do.[10] Nevertheless, the relationships and interactions

[9] Thomas George Weiss and Leon Gordenker, eds., *NGOs, the UN, and Global Governance* (Boulder, CO: Lynne Rienner, 1996); Margaret E. Keck and Kathryn Sikkink, *Activists Beyond Borders* (Ithaca, NY and London: Cornell University Press, 1998); Sanjeev Khagram, James V. Riker, and Kathryn Sikkink, eds., *Restructuring World Politics: Transnational Social Movements, Networks, and Norms* (Minneapolis, MN: University of Minnesota Press, 2002); Kal Raustiala, "States, NGOs, and International Environmental Institutions," *International Studies Quarterly* 41, no. 4 (1997): 719–40; Thomas Risse, "Transnational Actors and World Politics," in *Handbook of International Relations*, ed. Walter Carlsnaes, Thomas Risse, and Beth A. Simmons (London: Sage Publications, 2002): 255–74.

[10] Raustiala, "States, NGOs, and International Environmental Institutions"; Jonas Tallberg et al., *The Opening Up of International Organizations: Transnational Access in Global Governance*

between NGOs and international courts – a unique type of international organization – are understudied. This is not to say that *no* scholarship explores these
relationships but that the existing scholarship only captures a slice of what is
occurring: it either looks at one type of participatory role such as filing amicus
curiae briefs or at one court, essentially limiting the ability to judge relative influence and participation across courts.[11] This piecemeal approach is not due to lack of
scholarly attention to either NGOs or international courts, but from disciplinary and
subfield boundaries that cordon off, prioritize, and obscure certain aspects of these
participatory relationships at the expense of viewing the phenomenon as a whole.
For example, the examination of NGOs within international relations highlights
their advocacy roles in establishing new norms or courts, yet typically does not
follow-up on whether NGOs have lasting relationships with established courts.
Conversely, the cause lawyering scholarship in law only examines formal participation in litigation or trials, and therefore misses any informal relationships or the
effects of previous advocacy work on later involvement in litigation. There is a
similar story of disciplinary boundaries with regard to the study of international
courts. Within international relations, the nature of the delegated or contractual
authority to courts by states is the major focus, which can give the impression that
states are the only external actors with the ability to grant participatory access to
NGOs or to influence the court. Scholarship in comparative constitutional courts
and international organizations sees a prominent role for NGOs and civil society in
funneling potentially high-impact cases to courts, yet because of the examination of
constitutional courts, it cannot envision the range of capacity building roles NGOs
play at international courts.

One result of this disciplinary fragmentation is that no existing literature
directly addresses why NGO participation varies across international courts. Therefore, by necessity, my argument pulls from and builds upon the many literatures –
including global governance, constitutional courts, international organizations,
and international law – that speak to possible NGO roles and motivations as well
as institutional and organizational dynamics of international courts. In order to see
how my argument differs from and builds upon these literatures, it is first necessary

(Cambridge University Press, 2013); Jonas Tallberg et al., "NGO Influence in International
Organizations: Information, Access and Exchange," *British Journal of Political Science*,
September 2015: 1–26, https://doi.org/10.1017/S000712341500037X.
[11] Loveday Hodson, *NGOs and the Struggle for Human Rights in Europe* (Hart Publishing, 2011);
Rachel A. Cichowski, "Civil Society and the European Court of Human Rights," in *The
European Court of Human Rights between Law and Politics*, ed. Jonas Christoffersen and
Mikael Rask Madsen (Oxford University Press, 2011): 77–97; Michael J. Struett, *The Politics of
Constructing the International Criminal Court: NGOs, Discourse, and Agency* (New York, NY:
Palgrave Macmillan, 2008); Dinah Shelton, "The Participation of Nongovernmental Organiza-
tions in International Judicial Proceedings," *The American Journal of International Law* 88,
no. 4 (1994): 611–42, https://doi.org/10.2307/2204133; Laura Van den Eynde, "Amicus Curiae
Briefs of Human Rights NGOs at the European Court of Human Rights" (Stanford University
Law School, 2011).

TABLE I.1 *Alternative Theories of NGO Participation*

Type of Theory	Theory	Related Scholarship	How Theory Accounts for NGO Participation	Observable Implications of Theory
NGO Mobilization	NGO Capacity	TANs, Organizational theory	NGO capacity/incentive to participate	NGOs promoting new courts; driven by funding
	NGO Strategy	Cause lawyering, Legal opportunity structure	NGO strategy optimizes reaching normative goals	NGO participation at the most functional courts
Court-Centric	State-driven	International organizations; Rational choice institutionalism	States grant NGO participation and/or push courts to allow NGO participation to advance state interests	NGO participatory access is state-driven; limited unilateral allowance of NGO participation by courts
	Resources (expertise, cases, etc.)	Comparative courts	Courts allow NGO participation to provide resources	NGO participation follows resource needs; resources limited to monitoring and litigation

to articulate what each literature elucidates and obscures with regard to NGO interaction with international courts as well as extrapolate what observable expectations would be predicted from the theory. In this way, I develop plausible alternative explanations in the absence of any established competing explanations. Below, I present four principle bodies of scholarship relating to either NGOs and courts – transnational advocacy networks, cause lawyering and social movements, courts as international organizations, and comparative constitutional courts – and the empirical expectations of NGO participation each body of scholarship would predict (see Table I.1).

An NGO Divided

To engage with international judicial mechanisms, NGOs must be motivated to do so and have the requisite resources. Therefore, a potential explanation for variation in NGO participation across courts is discrepancies in NGO organizational capacity: financial, expert-based, or network resources. Such a capacity-based argument can be derived from both the scholarship on Transnational Advocacy Networks (TANs) and emergent work on NGOs as organizations in global governance.

TANs are networks of principled actors who coordinate efforts and share information in horizontal relationships.[12] The result of this coordination and information sharing is to place new issues on the agenda and pressure for their adoption, which could result in norm change and even "norm cascades."[13] TANs as "norm entrepreneurs" are studied in this way across many issue arenas in international affairs including human rights, the environment, and global regulation.[14] According to this literature, the influence of TANs expanded in the 1980s and 1990s as the number of NGOs grew exponentially and technological advancements allowed for a new range of coordination and tactics.[15] From this insight, it is possible to extrapolate that the supply, or number of NGOs, relates to NGO participation at international courts. This idea merits consideration as greater numbers of more networked NGOs may share or coordinate tactics and approaches. Nevertheless, the TANs literature does not illuminate much more about NGO participation across courts. The scholarship looks at NGOs in a global sense, not at the specific networks that emerge, or do not emerge, around specific courts. The literature also typically envisions NGOs acting as "norm entrepreneurs," pressuring for the establishment of a new court, such as the ICC.[16] This focus overlooks hybridized NGOs that may perform advocacy functions as well as service provision on related issues, such as the recent movement towards NGOs engaging in both human rights advocacy and development service provision.[17]

A more recent vein of global governance research departs from the emphasis on mechanisms and outcomes of governance to consider the types of authority of governors and the relationships between governors.[18] By allowing for governors to have multiple sources of authority and switching the focus from governance

---

[12] Keck and Sikkink, *Activists Beyond Borders.*

[13] Martha Finnemore and Kathryn Sikkink, "International Norm Dynamics and Political Change," *International Organization* 52, no. 4 (1998): 887–917.

[14] Ann Florini, *Third Force: The Rise of Transnational Civil Society* (Washington, DC: Carnegie Endowment, 2000); Keck and Sikkink, *Activists Beyond Borders*; Khagram, Riker, and Sikkink, *Restructuring World Politics: Transnational Social Movements, Networks, and Norms*; Ethan A. Nadelmann, "Global Prohibition Regimes: The Evolution of Norms in International Society," *International Organization* 44, no. 4 (1990): 479–526; Jacqui True and Michael Mintrom, "Transnational Networks and Policy Diffusion: The Case of Gender Mainstreaming," *International Studies Quarterly* 45, no. 1 (2001): 27–57.

[15] Keck and Sikkink, *Activists Beyond Borders*; Steve Charnovitz, "Two Centuries of Participation: NGOs and International Governance," *Michigan Journal of International Law* 18 (1996–1997): 183–286.

[16] Steve Charnovitz, "Nongovernmental Organizations and International Law," *The American Journal of International Law* 100, no. 2 (2006): 348–72; Marlies Glasius, *The International Criminal Court* (London: Routledge, 2006); Struett, *The Politics of Constructing the International Criminal Court.*

[17] Paul J. Nelson and Ellen Dorsey, *New Rights Advocacy: Changing Strategies of Development and Human Rights NGOs* (Washington, DC: Georgetown University Press, 2008).

[18] Deborah D. Avant, Martha Finnemore, and Susan K. Sell, eds., *Who Governs the Globe?* (Cambridge University Press, 2010).

outcomes to governance relationships, this new approach informs research that interrogates the core assumption of NGOs as principled actors working horizontally and cooperatively for universal and cosmopolitan goals. Research in this vein explores why certain issues are picked up by transnational advocacy campaigns and others not, and how the network relationships among NGOs are structured.[19] This literature also looks at networks of non-state actors with principled, but illiberal, goals, such as the National Rifle Association (NRA) promoting the trade in global small arms.[20] Lastly, another body of literature questions the notion that NGOs only act according to their core normative principles with the result of outcomes that further their normative aims. According to this research, NGOs can act both from material and normative interests, the normative goals of NGOs can lead to suboptimal outcomes, and normative goals can become politicized and alter with changing environmental contexts.[21] If one assumes that material interests are a core interest of NGOs, then financial incentive would drive NGO engagement with international judicial mechanisms. In other words, NGO participation would follow donor money.

Focusing on donor money does help explain some of the variation in NGO participation across international courts, as the young ICC was for some time a grant priority for philanthropic foundations and Western European governments. Yet, donor money does not shed light on the initial motivation of NGOs to seek to

---

[19] Clifford Bob, *The Marketing of Rebellion: Insurgents, Media, and International Activism* (Cambridge University Press, 2005); R. Charli Carpenter, "'Women, Children and Other Vulnerable Groups': Gender, Strategic Frames and the Protection of Civilians as a Transnational Issue," *International Studies Quarterly* 49, no. 2 (2005): 295–334; R. Charli Carpenter, "Setting the Advocacy Agenda: Theorizing Issue Emergence and Nonemergence in Transnational Advocacy Networks," *International Studies Quarterly* 51, no. 1 (2007): 99–120; R. Charli Carpenter, "Vetting the Advocacy Agenda: Network Centrality and the Paradox of Weapons Norms," *International Organization* 65, no. 1 (2011): 69–102; David A. Lake and Wendy Wong, "The Politics of Networks: Interests, Power, and Human Rights Norms," in *Networked Politics: Agency, Power, and Governance* (Ithaca, NY: Cornell University Press, 2009), http://papers.ssrn.com/sol3/papers.cfm?abstract_id=1004199; Wendy Wong, *Internal Affairs: How the Structure of NGOs Transforms Human Rights* (Ithaca, NY: Cornell University Press, 2012).

[20] Kenneth Anderson and David Rieff, "'Global Civil Society': A Skeptical View," in *Global Civil Society 2004/5*, ed. Helmut K. Anheier, Marlies Glasius, and Mary Kaldor (Sage Publications, 2004): 26–39; Clifford Bob, "Clashing Interests in Global Arenas: The International Battle over Small Arms Control" (Annual Meeting of the International Studies Association, San Francisco, 2008).

[21] Alexander Cooley and James Ron, "The NGO Scramble: Organizational Insecurity and the Political Economy of Transnational Action," *International Security* 27, no. 1 (2002): 5–39; S. K. Sell and A. Prakash, "Using Ideas Strategically: The Contest between Business and NGO Networks in Intellectual Property Rights," *International Studies Quarterly* 48, no. 1 (2004): 143–75; Aseem Prakash and Mary Kay Gugerty, *Advocacy Organizations and Collective Action* (Cambridge University Press, 2010); Deborah Avant, "Conserving Nature in the State of Nature: The Politics of INGO Policy Implementation," *Review of International Studies* 30, no. 3 (2004): 361–82; Michael Barnett, "Evolution Without Progress? Humanitarianism in a World of Hurt," *International Organization* 63, no. 4 (2009): 621–63.

participate at international judicial institutions when little to no money was available or NGO insistence on continuing to monitor and aid the ICC when donor money is scarcer.

The Myopia of Legalism

The cause lawyering literature in domestic and international law offers another potential explanation that attributes variation in NGO participation to NGOs, not courts. Instead of capacity or funding driving NGO participation, differences in NGO participation across courts is caused by the various strategic motivations of NGOs. Two main questions animate much of this scholarship, which in many ways mirrors the legal opportunity structure in social movement literature.[22] First, why and when do NGOs or social movements utilize international courts as petitioners representing clients or filing amicus briefs? Second, what is the impact of such formal participation on judicial outcomes?[23] This literature views engagement with international courts as one strategic option among many others, including utilizing domestic courts, quasi-judicial institutions, political advocacy, lobbying, or possibly elections.[24] NGO behavior, or the decision to engage with international courts, is based upon a cost-benefit analysis of what would best optimize the desired normative goals of the organization.

---

[22] Ellen Ann Andersen, *Out of the Closets and into the Courts: Legal Opportunity Structure and Gay Rights Litigation* (Ann Arbor: University of Michigan Press, 2009); Chris Hilson, "New Social Movements: The Role of Legal Opportunity," *Journal of European Public Policy* 9, no. 2 (2002): 238–55, https://doi.org/10.1080/13501760110120246; Bruce M. Wilson and Juan Carlos Rodríguez Cordero, "Legal Opportunity Structures and Social Movements: The Effects of Institutional Change on Costa Rican Politics," *Comparative Political Studies* 39, no. 3 (2006): 325–51, https://doi.org/10.1177/0010414005281934.

[23] The results of this research are mixed and significant methodological problems hamper the teasing out of influence on judicial decision-making. See: M. L. Busch and K. J. Pelc, "The Politics of Judicial Economy at the World Trade Organization," *International Organization* 64, no. 2 (2010): 257–79; Laurence Boisson de Chazournes and Makane Moïse Mbengue, "The Amici Curiae and the WTO Dispute Settlement System: The Doors Are Open," *Law and Practice of International Courts and Tribunals* 2 (2003): 205–48; Rachel A. Cichowski, *The European Court and Civil Society: Litigation, Mobilization and Governance* (Cambridge University Press, 2007); Laura Van den Eynde, "Amicus Curiae Briefs of Human Rights NGOs before the European Court of Human Rights" (Stanford University Law School, 2011); Petros C. Mavroidis, "Amicus Curiae Briefs before the WTO: Much Ado about Nothing," 2001; Abdelsalam A. Mohamed, "Individual and NGO Participation in Human Rights Litigation before the African Court of Human and Peoples' Rights: Lessons from the European and Inter-American Courts of Human Rights," *Journal of African Law* 43 (1999): 201–13; Shelton, "The Participation of Nongovernmental Organizations in International Judicial Proceedings."

[24] Austin Sarat and Stuart A. Scheingold, *Cause Lawyering: Political Commitments and Professional Responsibilities* (Oxford and New York, NY: Oxford University Press, 1998); Sidney Tarrow, *Power in Movement: Social Movements and Contentious Politics* (Cambridge University Press, 2011).

Based upon this strategic view of NGOs, one would expect NGOs to engage with well-functioning international courts that have the potential to advance their normative goals, not functionally struggling or fledgling courts. A favorable outcome at a well-functioning court is more likely to be publicized and have compliance with and enforcement of the decision. However, in the three judicial institutions examined, NGO participation seems to negatively correlate with the level of capacity and functionality of the judicial institutions. The ECtHR is highly lauded for its effectiveness and high levels of compliance, yet NGOs play the fewest number of participatory roles and those roles generally have limited to moderate impact.[25] Additionally, this explanation can only account for a few NGO roles at international courts: formal participation representing petitioners or as amicus curiae, who file "friend of the court" briefs. NGOs also informally and formally provide services, share information, and lobby member states. By only concentrating on formal roles in cases, NGOs' impact on court administration, strategy, operations, and functionality is overlooked, even though these can also impact judicial decisions.[26]

In the Shadow of the State

Instead of hypothesizing why NGOs seek participatory relationships with international courts, a second body of theories assumes NGO motivation and articulates why international courts or states would grant these actors access to participate. In international relations scholarship, neither institutional nor organizational approaches to international courts specifically examine questions of NGO participation. Both approaches are state-centered and therefore would not envision potentially influential roles for NGOs at international courts. Institution-based approaches to international courts focus on states using courts to establish credible commitments and how the institutional design of courts can induce compliance, judicial power, or effectiveness.[27] Organizational approaches to international courts study the nature of the relationship between states and operational international courts. The major debate of this literature is the character of the delegated authority to the international court by member states. Principal–agent theories argue that the

---

[25] Laurence R. Helfer and Anne-Marie Slaughter, "Toward a Theory of Effective Supranational Adjudication," *The Yale Law Journal* 107, no. 2 (1997): 273–391.

[26] For the first descriptive accounting of NGO and civil society participation beyond formal litigation, see Tullio Treves et al., eds., *Civil Society, International Courts and Compliance Bodies* (Cambridge University Press, 2005).

[27] Karen J. Alter, "Agents or Trustees? International Courts in Their Political Context," *European Journal of International Relations* 14, no. 1 (2008): 33–63; Helfer and Slaughter, "Toward a Theory of Effective Supranational Adjudication"; Eric A. Posner and John C. Yoo, "Judicial Independence in International Tribunals," *California Law Review* 93, no. 1 (2005): 1–74; Beth A. Simmons and Allison Danner, "Credible Commitments and the International Criminal Court," *International Organization* 64, no. 2 (2010): 225–56; Voeten, "The Politics of International Judicial Appointments."

relationship between international courts and member states is contractual, mean-ing that international courts are agents that work on behalf of the states' interests.[28] If the court does not work on the states' behalf – otherwise known as agency slack – then the states can re-contract with the court thereby reestablishing the terms of the relationship so that their interests can be represented through the court. Trustee theories differ from the principal–agent theories in that they argue that international courts are not agents, but trustees with duties to third-party beneficiaries.[29]

While NGO participation vis-à-vis international courts is not examined in the aforementioned theories – due to the predominant focus on court–state relations – it is possible to extrapolate that NGOs would gain access to international courts because such NGO participation is state sanctioned and advances state interests. Most directly, states could grant NGOs participatory roles that are under their authority – such as observers, consultants, or information providers regarding court governance and compliance. For formal and informal access channels that require judicial allowance or rule changes, states could pressure or coerce the court into permitting NGO participation. State interests could either be different from or the same as the court's interests. Seen in rational-choice terms, member states would weigh the costs and benefits of allowing NGO participation and pressure courts to act based upon the greatest utility. If one assumes that states create these institutions as credible commitments and desire them to operate effectively and efficiently, then NGO participation that boosts a court's functionality would align with state inter-ests.[30] There is evidence this occurs in international governance regimes and organizations. In international environmental governance, NGO inclusion grows as states grapple with ever more transnational and complex issues. As climate problems become more intricate, NGOs become more useful through providing information, monitoring, amplifying state preferences, and placating domestic con-stituencies.[31] On a broader scale, a major driver of the trend of increased access for NGOs across all types of international organizations is member state demand for the resources and services provided by these actors.[32]

The empirical expectations of this theory are difficult to extrapolate because what constitutes state interest is difficult to infer unless it is publically articulated by states. Additionally, states rarely have a consensus of interests and NGO participation may advance or contradict different state values and objectives. Nevertheless, there

[28] Darren G. Hawkins et al., eds., *Delegation and Agency in International Organizations* (Cam-bridge University Press, 2006).
[29] Karen J. Alter, "Delegation to International Courts and the Limits of Re-Contracting Political Power," in *Delegation and Agency in International Organizations*, ed. Darren G. Hawkins et al. (Cambridge University Press, 2006): 312–38; Alter, "Agents or Trustees?"; Giandomenico Majone, "Two Logics of Delegation: Agency and Fiduciary Relations in EU Governance," *European Union Politics* 2 (2001): 103–22.
[30] Simmons and Danner, "Credible Commitments and the International Criminal Court."
[31] Raustiala, "States, NGOs, and International Environmental Institutions."
[32] Tallberg et al., *The Opening Up of International Organizations.*

is mixed evidence that states drive NGO participation at the examined international courts. There is some evidence that states do grant NGOs participatory access and influence because it advances their interest – particularly for roles in which states, not the court, control access. All member states of the Council of Europe (CofE) approved Protocol No. 11 to the Convention for the Protection of Human Rights and Fundamental Freedoms that abolished the Commission and guaranteed individual petition to the Court. At the ICC, member state diplomats stationed in The Hague often do not have the time to keep abreast of all of the administrative developments at the Court, and therefore rely on reputable NGOs to provide information and expertise from which the diplomats can make decisions.[33] Conversely, there is little to no evidence that states pressure courts to allow greater or new forms of NGO participatory engagement. In fact, courts often take unilateral action to allow new forms of NGO participation, some of which states are publically against. This is the case at the Inter-American Court, which established its own NGO to circumvent state interference. In this way, state interests *antithetical* to courts may actually be a catalyst for *courts* allowing expanded forms of NGO participation.

A Court is a Court?

As opposed to the study of international courts in international relations, the scholarship within comparative courts and social movement theory does explore NGO participation at courts, albeit constitutional courts. One major theme within this literature, mostly rooted in social movement literature, discusses the merits of using courts as a means to advance civil or human rights claims. The critical perspective argues that using litigation to advance rights results in a "myth of rights" or that constitutional courts offer "hollow hope" for civil rights.[34] The reasons for this are the high cost of litigation, the court's inability to deliver on dictated reform, litigation detracting from other social movement strategies, narrowing the movement's claims or causing tension within the movement.[35] In response, other scholars have countered and argued that civil society can utilize courts to advance civil or human rights. McCann's typology of legal movement stages posits that legal strategies can have both "direct effects" such as legal precedents or relief to the victims as well as "indirect effects" such as helping to build a social movement or generating public support for the cause.[36] Epp makes an implicit argument about the utility of constitutional courts to advance civil rights through the assertion that

---

[33] Author interview with a diplomat from an ICC member state, August 26, 2010.

[34] Gerald N. Rosenberg, *The Hollow Hope* (University of Chicago Press, 2008); Stuart A. Scheingold, *The Politics of Rights* (New Haven, CT: Yale University Press, 1974).

[35] Michael W. McCann and Helena Silverstein, "Rethinking Law's Allurements," in *Cause Lawyering: Political Commitments and Professional Responsibilities*, ed. Austin Sarat and Stuart A. Scheingold (New York, NY: Oxford University Press, 1998).

[36] Michael W. McCann, *Rights at Work* (University of Chicago Press, 1994).

the "rights revolutions" in the United States and Britain was predicated on the strategic pressure and organization of rights activists.[37] Epp's argument about the importance of activists and civil society speaks to the critical role that non-state actors can play in aiding courts. Activists and legal professionals constituted a "support structure" that was crucial for the dramatic constitutional changes made by the high courts in the United States and Britain. This idea of "support structure" is further supported by studies on the influence of the conservative legal movement at the US Supreme Court and the symbiotic relationship between civil society and the Egyptian Constitutional Court, whereby the Court provided an institutional opportunity to challenge the state and civil society provided the Court services, including monitoring, initiating litigation, and documenting violations.[38]

This literature is useful in theorizing about the reciprocal nature of NGO–court relationships whereby the court is perceived as an instrument to advance NGO claims and NGO participation provides the court with resources or services. Taken one step further, this theory could imply that courts seek out or allow NGO engagement in order to garner resources that NGOs can supply, including information, expertise, and a steady stream of cases. Nevertheless, this literature only studies domestic constitutional courts – not international courts and quasi-judicial institutions – and the kinds of roles civil society actors play to embolden courts are not as extensive as those observed at the three judicial institutions examined. The resources provided by "support structure" civil society groups include providing expertise and financing repeated litigation, not providing or supplementing court resources through service provision.[39]

ARGUMENT

NGO participatory roles, frequency, and impact at the three examined international criminal and human rights courts can be explained by variation in three factors: the extent of *court deficiencies of resources and legitimacy*, the institutional *history of NGO engagement*, and NGO *motivation and resources* (see Table I.2). The participatory *roles* NGOs play is largely a result of access granted by the court, and sometimes member states. The court is more likely to grant NGOs access if it is struggling with resources or legitimacy as NGO engagement can help mitigate those deficiencies. Additionally, the court and member states are likely to allow new avenues of NGO participation if there is an institutional history of NGO engagement. Pre-existing relationships could facilitate new forms of access and past partnerships generally confer upon NGOs the legitimacy of being appropriate, and

---

[37] Charles R. Epp, *The Rights Revolution* (University of Chicago Press, 1998).

[38] Amanda Hollis-Brusky, "Support Structures and Constitutional Change: Teles, Southworth, and the Conservative Legal Movement," *Law & Social Inquiry* 36, no. 2 (2011): 516–36; Tamir Moustafa, "Law versus the State: The Judicialization of Politics in Egypt," *Law & Social Inquiry* 28, no. 4 (2003): 883–930.

[39] Epp, *The Rights Revolution*, 18.

TABLE 1.2 *Theoretical Factors that Shape NGO Participatory Roles, Frequency, and Impact*

Roles (Access)	• Court deficiencies of resources and legitimacy
	• History of NGO engagement
	• NGO motivation and resources
Frequency	• NGO motivation and resources
Impact	• Court deficiencies of resources and legitimacy
	• History of NGO engagement

possibly helpful, participatory actors. Resourced and motivated NGOs can also serve as the catalyst for new participatory channels by pressuring for greater access or establishing new roles that do not require authorization. The *frequency* of NGO engagement is principally determined by the motivation and financial capacity of NGOs to participate in such roles. Driven NGOs with substantial monetary resources will likely participate at much higher rates than those with lesser enthusiasm or capacity. The *impact* of NGO participation is also dictated by the court, or for some roles, member states. Impact tends to correlate with the reasons for granting participatory access. The impact is generally greater for those roles that were permitted in order to grant the court more functionality. Courts with long-standing histories of NGO engagement are also more likely to give weight to the information, services, or expertise provided by NGOs.

This argument builds from and adds new elements to the aforementioned alternative theories. First, it utilizes the general framework developed in the work on NGO inclusion at international organizations to disaggregate participation into roles, frequency, and impact.[40] This allows for a more nuanced understanding of how the three factors influence different aspects of participation – roles, frequency, and impact – often in interconnected ways. Second, the argument uniquely weds together NGO-based theories of resources and motivation with arguments as to why courts, and sometimes member states, consent to participation. Existing theories of NGO mobilization are relevant in highlighting the role of NGO resources – in particular donor funding – in conditioning or limiting the expansion of NGO relationships with international judicial mechanisms. Nevertheless, this argument departs from existing theory on the source of NGO motivation. As opposed to the cause lawyering scholarship, NGO strategy does not target the most functional courts, but NGOs seek participatory roles at all of the examined international courts regardless of functionality. This is because these international judicial mechanisms are not only instruments of justice with the potential to deliver judgments but are ends in themselves. As courts of last resort, NGOs are motivated to provide services or consult on governance issues to enhance the courts' functionality in addition to taking cases before the courts.

[40] Tallberg et al., *The Opening Up of International Organizations*, 8.

TABLE 1.3 *Court Deficiencies and NGO Participatory Roles, Frequency, and Impact*

Roles (Access)	•	Deficiencies represent participatory opportunities for NGOs and prompt courts to allow NGOs participatory access to provide needed information or services
Frequency	–	
Impact	•	Roles granted to mitigate court deficiencies likely to have substantive impact because providing critical information or services

The argument also modifies and adds to the functionalist literature about why international institutions and member states grant NGOs participatory access. The idea of limited court resources prompting judicial institutions to consent or condone NGO participation mirrors the theory of civil society constituting support structures in the constitutional courts scholarship and states utilizing NGOs for functionalist aims at international organizations. Yet, the argument allows for a broader range of participatory roles – including administrative aid and capacity building functions – than theorized in the constitutional courts literature or in the scholarship on international organizations. This is because international courts depend on the complex cooperation and support of multiple member states, which can make their deficiencies greater than domestic courts. Additionally, courts are a unique kind of international organization with independent authority to enforce judgments on states or sitting heads of states. This independent authority potentially allows for courts to grant NGOs participatory access channels that benefit the courts but *contravene* member state interests. Lastly, the argument modifies the functionalist theories as to why states and courts permit NGO participatory access. The pragmatic considerations of states and courts to bring in NGOs to provide needed information, expertise, or services is filtered through the institutional history of NGO engagement. Past experiences, or lack thereof, facilitate expanded NGO participatory access and influence or reinforce existing norms and rules of exclusion.

Court Deficiencies of Resources and Legitimacy

Shortcomings in resources and legitimacy at international judicial mechanisms constitute openings for new or expanded NGO participatory roles (see Table I.3). NGOs wanting greater access or influence at courts can seek out new avenues and functions that help mitigate these deficiencies. In this way, court deficiencies are a form of "political opportunity structure," or an institutional opening, that NGOs can exploit in order to achieve their normative goals.[41] In response, judicial institutions,

---

[41] Heidi Nichols Haddad, "Judicial Institution Builders: NGOs and International Human Rights Courts," *Journal of Human Rights* 11, no. 1 (2012): 126–49, https://doi.org/10.1080/14754835.2012.648154.

and occasionally states, are more likely to provide NGOs participatory access, either through amending rules or tacitly condoning new forms of engagement. New or expanded NGO participatory roles can also come at the instigation of court officials, who recognize their own deficiencies and seek to capitalize on the expertise, information, or legitimacy that NGOs can provide. Court officials may directly or indirectly ask for NGO assistance on certain matters or, in the extreme case, establish their own NGO to service precise institutional needs.

Court deficiencies of resources and legitimacy are particularly problematic for international criminal and human rights courts. These courts are supranational in nature and therefore operate at the whim of member states. The courts are governed by states, are beholden to states for their budgets, and are dependent on states to cooperate with investigations, arrest indicted individuals, and enforce judicial decisions. At international human rights courts, states are the alleged abusers of human rights and if found in violation of the human rights convention must provide restitution to victims and change state policy. At international criminal courts, sitting or former heads of state can be tried for war crimes, genocide, and crimes against humanity. This paradoxical dual role of states – as both the supporters of the judicial institutions and the alleged perpetrators of human rights abuses – creates incentives and channels for states to undermine international judicial mechanisms when decisions are contrary to state interests. The methods available to states to undermine courts range from directly pulling out of the treaty, public shaming, and non-compliance to the subtler forms of non-cooperation with court requests, failure to adopt domestic treaty implementing legislation, restricting the authority of the court, or starving the court of funding. These forms of non-cooperation can damage the legitimacy of the court and financially undercut its ability to fulfill its mandate.

Additionally, the large jurisdictions of international courts – which often span many countries – create logistical difficulties and make them resource-costly to operate. Judicial institutions must fact-find, conduct outreach, transport witnesses across international borders, and function in multiple languages and dialects. Sometimes all of this occurs within conflict zones with tremendous security risks. Fulfillment of the mandates of international judicial mechanisms depends on substantial resources to pay for and coordinate logistics. Helfer and Slaughter's classification of conditions for an effective international court include many conditions that speak to the immense and varied resources necessary for effective international adjudication.[42] The condition of "building a caseload" is facilitated by case information and facts, legitimacy among victims and stakeholders, a large budget, a headquarters with a large library and research staff, and substantial education and public relations staff. The condition of "independent fact-finding capacity" not only relates to the authority given to the court and to state and

---

[42] Helfer and Slaughter, "Toward a Theory of Effective Supranational Adjudication."

victims' cooperation, but the financial resources to repeatedly send investigators to collect evidence and interview witnesses. Even the condition of "quality of legal decisions" can be affected by resources, as the quality of the court library and the workload of the court lawyers and research staff can impact the breadth and depth of judicial decisions. Historical analyses of the International Criminal Tribunals for the Former Yugoslavia (ICTY) and Rwanda (ICTR) demonstrate the critical role of resources for court functionality. The initial lags in investigations, indictments, and trials are partially attributed to the underfunding and understaffing of the tribunals.[43]

Why do deficiencies prompt courts to allow NGO participatory access?[44] Access could take the form of changing the rules of procedure of evidence to participate as amicus curiae or facilitating informal meetings to receive information and expertise. Simply put, courts are more likely to allow NGOs participatory access for roles that help the court function. Member states, on the other hand, are generally less likely to allow greater NGO participatory access as a response to the institutional deficiencies of the judicial institutions. As court deficiencies of resources and legitimacy are often caused by the hostility, non-cooperation, or neglect of member states, it is unlikely that the majority of member states would formally agree to NGO participatory roles that mitigate these problems. However, specific normatively motivated member states or diplomats could choose to engage with NGOs in order to help the struggling court.[45]

[43] Gary J. Bass, *Stay the Hand of Vengeance: The Politics of War Crimes Tribunals* (Princeton University Press, 2000); Chris McGreal, "Second Class Justice," *The Guardian*, April 10, 2002, www.guardian.co.uk/comment/story/0,3604,681623,00.html.

[44] The majority of NGO participatory roles require some level of access from courts or member states. However, some participatory roles do not require access from courts or member states, such as running treaty ratification campaigns or publicly naming and shaming instances of non-cooperation. Even so, many of these roles are ideally done in coordination or cooperation with states or the court.

[45] Potential alternative strategies for courts struggling with resource deficiencies could be to secure funding from non-member states or private foundations. For example, donor countries funded the entire budget of the case of Hissène Habré before the Extraordinary African Chambers in Senegal. Between 1999 and 2012, the Ford Foundation provided $180,000 to the ICC, $600,000 to the Court of Community Justice (ECOWAS Institution), $350,000 to the Special Court for Sierra Leone (SCSL), and $100,000 to the ICTY. The MacArthur Foundation provided $200,000 to the African Court on Human and Peoples' Rights (ACtHPR), $245,000 to the SCSL, $291,000 to the ICTR, and $890,181 to the ICC. Nevertheless, this strategy necessitates reaching out or formally applying to receptive donors, and may be more likely to yield temporary aid for special projects or cases rather than sustained institutional support.
See: Human Rights Watch, "Q&A: The Case of Hissène Habré before the Extraordinary African Chambers in Senegal," Human Rights Watch, May 3, 2016, https://www.hrw.org/news/2016/05/03/qa-case-hissene-habre-extraordinary-african-chambers-senegal. Data on foundations were obtained from author's examination of annual reports by the Ford and MacArthur Foundation and grant searches through Foundation Search.

NGOs are often uniquely positioned to help bolster legitimacy and provide instrumental information and expertise.[46] NGOs – as non-state actors motivated by principles – are frequently seen as representing a larger "public interest."[47] Some scholars argue that they form part of a global civil society that transcends power politics in favor of cosmopolitan and humanistic ideals.[48] This conception of NGOs carries over to the international law arena. A pressing debate in the field centers on whether there should be further legalization of the standing of NGOs as parties that can represent the collective interests of victims at judicial and non-judicial mechanisms.[49] Proponents of this position argue that NGOs should have standing because of the legitimacy NGOs can confer on the international legal system due to their embodiment and representation of the public benefit.[50] Even without formal standing, allowing NGO participation at an international court may augment the court's legitimacy by signaling that it is not a puppet of states and cares about the interests of the wider population. NGOs can also provide quality information and expertise to courts. Supranational judicial institutions with multi-state jurisdictions need on-the-ground information for investigations. Yet, because of the geographical distance of the court from many countries and often-subpar resources for

---

[46] In situations where motivated and resourced NGOs are not available, or the court deems them inappropriate, the court could attempt to address their own institutional inadequacies. A court could choose to limit the number of cases heard to ensure that it could devote adequate resources. It could also engage in "virtual trials," as occurred at the Yugoslav and Rwandan criminal tribunals, whereby court officials undertook shaming and sought outside assistance to coerce or convince states to provide cooperation. For more on "virtual trials" see: Victor Peskin, *International Justice in Rwanda and the Balkans: Virtual Trials and the Struggle for State Cooperation* (Cambridge University Press, 2008).

[47] Sangeeta Kamat, "The Privatization of Public Interest: Theorizing NGO Discourse in a Neoliberal Era," *Review of International Political Economy* 11, no. 1 (2004): 155–76, https://doi.org/10.1080/0969229042000179794; Hans Dieter Wolf, "Private Actors and the Legitimacy of Governance beyond the State," in *Governance and Democracy: Comparing National, European and International Experiences*, ed. Arthur Benz and Ioannis Papadopoulos (London: Routledge, 2006): 200–27.

[48] Mary Kaldor, *Global Civil Society: An Answer to War* (Hoboken, NJ: John Wiley & Sons, 2013).

[49] Anna-Karin Lindblom, *Non-Governmental Organisations in International Law* (Cambridge University Press, 2005); Jacqueline Peel, "Giving the Public a Voice in the Protection of the Global Environment: Avenues for Participation by NGOs in Dispute Resolution at the European Court of Justice and World Trade Organization," *Colorado Journal of International Environmental Law and Policy* 12 (2001): 47–76; Teall Crossen and Veronique Niessen, "NGO Standing in the European Court of Justice – Does the Aarhus Regulation Open the Door?," *Review of European Community & International Environmental Law* 16, no. 3 (2007): 332–40, https://doi.org/10.1111/j.1467–9388.2007.00569.x; Lloyd Mayer, "NGO Standing and Influence in Regional Human Rights Courts and Commissions," SSRN Scholarly Paper (Rochester, NY: Social Science Research Network, April 11, 2012), http://papers.ssrn.com/abstract=2038379; Pierre-Marie Dupuy and Luisa Vierucci, *NGOs in International Law: Efficiency in Flexibility?* (Edward Elgar Publishing, 2008).

[50] Lindblom, *Non-Governmental Organisations in International Law*; Yves Bonzon, *Public Participation and Legitimacy in the WTO* (Cambridge University Press, 2014); Sergey Ripinsky and Peter van den Bossche, *NGO Involvement in International Organizations: A Legal Analysis* (London: British Institute of International and Comparative Law, 2007).

investigations, this information is difficult to ascertain. NGOs are often well suited to supply information because they have an on-the-ground presence or have partnerships with local NGOs. By relying on NGOs, courts may gain crucial information from generally reliable sources at no cost to themselves.[51] Many NGOs are not just information purveyors but are comprised of lawyers and personnel with vast expertise and institutional knowledge of the court. For some long-standing NGO personnel, the institutional knowledge of the court may be longer than that of the court officials, many of which cycle in and out. For the court, NGOs may provide informed evaluations of policies, rules, governance, or legal matters that could aid the functionality of the court.

Although NGOs have the potential to provide courts with legitimacy, their participation is no guarantee of these benefits. In some circumstances, NGO engagement could actually damage the court's legitimacy and credibility. Participation of non-parties in trial proceedings or court operations may constitute, or perceive to constitute, violations of legal impartiality and due process.[52] The court's impartiality could be undermined regardless of the value and objectivity of the NGO-provided information, expertise, or services. Conversely, NGOs may not always share objective information, advice, or expertise with the court. NGOs are not neutral actors but have interests and desired outcomes, even if those outcomes may benefit a larger constituency than the organization. A growing body of scholarship departs from the viewpoint that NGOs are purely normative actors and characterizes them as interest groups, similar to lobbyists or professional associations.[53] When viewed in this way, the services and information provided by NGOs are not necessarily objective or normatively good but represent a particular political perspective. Therefore, undue reliance on NGOs has the potential to politicize the court and jeopardize the court's ability to administer fair and impartial justice.[54]

---

[51] NGOs not only provide valuable information to international courts, but also to intergovernmental and international organizations. See: Jonas Tallberg et al., "NGO Influence in International Organizations: Information, Access and Exchange," *British Journal of Political Science* (September 2015): 4–5, doi:10.1017/S000712341500037X.

[52] This debate is occurring with regard to NGOs as amici curiae in international criminal trials. See: Hannah Woolaver, "The Role of Amicus Curiae Submissions at International Criminal Tribunals" (International Judicial Monitor – Special Report, Spring 2016), www.judicialmonitor.org/spring2016/specialreport2.html.

[53] Kerstin Martens, "Mission Impossible? Defining Nongovernmental Organizations," *Voluntas: International Journal of Voluntary and Nonprofit Organizations* 13, no. 3 (n.d.): 271–85, https://doi.org/10.1023/A:1020341526691; Sell and Prakash, "Using Ideas Strategically"; Elizabeth A. Bloodgood, "The Interest Group Analogy: International Non-Governmental Advocacy Organisations in International Politics," *Review of International Studies* 37, no. 1 (2011): 93–120, https://doi.org/10.1017/S0260210510001051.

[54] For an example of this perspective with regard to the World Trade Organization (WTO) Dispute Resolution Panels, see: J. L. Dunoff, "The Misguided Debate over NGO Participation at the WTO," *Journal of International Economic Law* 1, no. 3 (1998): 433–56, https://doi.org/10.1093/jiel/1.3.433.

Two related sources of motivation can account for the fact that court officials allow, or even seek out, NGO participation. First, court officials are normatively driven and want to effectively utilize the judicial mechanism to advance human rights justice. Partnering with NGOs can increase the ability of the court to fulfill its mandate. Viewing officials of judicial institutions as normative actors is not unprecedented. Normative theories of judging see judicial decision-making as "a sense of obligation to make the best decision possible in light of one's general training and sense of professional obligation" or "judging in good faith."[55] Although these theories singularly focus on judicial decision-making, or the process by which judges make legal decisions, it is not a large leap to assume that judges or other key officials of judicial institutions could approach the non-judicial rule-making aspects of their jobs in similar ways. Moustafa's examination of the Egyptian Constitutional Court demonstrates how civil society groups and the Court are in a symbiotic relationship whereby the Court provides an institutional opportunity to challenge the state and civil society provides the Court with services, including monitoring, initiating litigation, and documenting violations.[56] Conversely and more cynically, court officials could be motivated by institutional survival, or a desire for the court to remain viable. Organizational survival is a core tenet of organizational theory and even institutions with normative agendas such as courts are not above strategically acting to preserve the reputation and continued existence of the organization.[57] Court officials may also be individually motivated to sustain their employment and advance their professional promise through a successful judicial enterprise.

It is possible that these normative and rational motivations operate simultaneously and in mutual cooperation. Utilizing NGO participation in order to maintain a more functional and effective judicial mechanism would help provide continued justification for the existence of the court, and therefore advance the careers of those working for the institution. Yet, it is also possible these motivations could function in conflict. Overreliance on NGOs to keep a court operational could erode the impartiality and legitimacy of the judicial institution and raise questions about its organizational viability. Additionally, allowance of NGO participation to supplement the insufficient cooperation and resources provided by states could further antagonize member states, whose buy-in is required for operational survival.

If NGOs are granted participatory access as a response to court deficiencies, and NGOs choose to assertively engage in these roles, then it is very likely that the

---

[55] Steven J. Burton, *Judging in Good Faith* (Cambridge University Press, 1994); Howard Gillman, "What's Law Got to Do with It? Judicial Behavioralists Test the 'Legal Model' of Judicial Decision Making," *Law & Social Inquiry* 26, no. 2 (2001): 465–504, https://doi.org/10.1111/j.1747-4469.2001.tb00185.x.

[56] Moustafa, "Law versus the State."

[57] Neil Fligstein, "Organizations: Theoretical Debates and the Scope of Organizational Theory," in *Handbook of International Sociology*, ed. C. Calhoun, C. Rojek, and B. Turner (London: Sage, 2005).

impact of NGO participation will be substantive. This is because NGOs will be consistently providing information, expertise, or services to the court that the court needs to increase its functionality.

The court's reliance on NGOs implies that the information, expertise, and services provided by NGOs is at a minimum taken into consideration and at a maximum critical to the operation of the court.

History of NGO Engagement

Institutional deficiencies represent opportunities for new forms of NGO engagement: NGOs galvanize around these gaps to increase their presence and potential influence and courts are more likely to respond positively to augment the court's functionality. Yet, courts are not only organizations concerned about functionality but are also cognizant of *how* they should operate. Process and procedure are foundational to a court's legitimacy. Therefore, the unprecedented inclusion of NGOs – which are non-state, and sometimes non-party, actors – in trials, court administration, or governance could be seen by the court or member states as a delegitimizing violation of process. Consequently, the history of NGO engagement, or whether courts and states view NGOs as appropriate participatory partners, also factors into the decision to allow NGO participatory access (see Table I.4). Even functionalist claims to allow NGO participation as a means to increase the functionality of the court are mediated through the existing norms, practices, and rules regarding NGO engagement.

In general, a history of NGO engagement increases the likelihood of courts and states granting access to new participatory relationships. This is the case for two reasons. First, pre-established relationships between NGOs and court officials or member state diplomats facilitate future relationships. Past interactions can build trust, professional relationships, or reputations that could positively contribute to the decision to allow new forms of NGO access. These past relationships may actually pre-date the establishment of the court if NGOs were involved with the advocacy efforts to create the judicial institution. Second, the history of NGO participation informs whether courts and member states view NGOs as appropriate participatory

TABLE I.4 *History of NGO Engagement and NGO Participatory Roles, Frequency, and Impact*

Roles (Access)	•	Prior history of NGO engagement generally increases likelihood of courts or states granting access for new or expanded participatory roles
Frequency	–	
Impact	•	Robust history of NGO engagement increases likelihood that participation is impactful

partners. Court and member state perspectives on the appropriateness of NGO participation are determined both by the encoded rules and norms of the court and the governance body and current circumstances.[58] The rules and norms, developed over the lifetime of the court, dictate whether, and to what degree, NGOs have formal and informal channels of participatory access. A history of past NGO engagement likely shapes views on NGO interaction as appropriate and possibly even a customary aspect of court functioning. When combined with profound deficiencies in resources or legitimacy, new or expanded forms of NGO participation are even more likely. In this situation, courts can readily accept and rely on the services provided by actors that are generally viewed as legitimate and appropriate.

Conversely, a history of NGO exclusion or restriction may make court officials and member states hesitant to include outside actors that have historically and purposefully been kept at a distance. Even in situations where courts have institutional needs that NGOs could mitigate, long-standing exclusionary norms may inhibit NGO access or reliance on NGO services. This is not determinative but depends on calculations by court officials over the benefits of NGO partnerships versus the perceived loss of legitimacy. Nonetheless, it is becoming increasingly difficult for courts to completely shut out NGOs. Since the late 1990s, there have been calls for greater civil society involvement and influence at global institutions and organizations.[59] Many international organizations responded and granted NGOs greater access, in particular those relating to human rights.[60] This emerging norm or practice of civil society inclusion makes it less likely that courts will completely exclude NGOs, even if they feel NGOs are inappropriate actors. In this case, courts could allow very circumscribed or restricted access with little to no influence. This is especially likely to be the case when a court has little functional need for NGOs.

In general, a robust history of NGO participation makes future NGO participatory access more likely. However, this is not determinative and there could be instances where courts or states restrict participatory access because of prior negative effects. Courts or states could restrict a specific NGO participatory role if such a role

[58] The literature on "new institutionalism" supports the claim that institutional features – rules, norms, and identities – can shape the behavior of actors working within the institution. See: B. Guy Peters, *Institutional Theory in Political Science* (London and New York, NY: Continuum International Publishing Group, 2005): 19.

[59] Miles Kahler, "Global Governance Redefined" (The Conference on Globalization, the State, and Society, Washington University School of Law, 2004), https://law.wustl.edu/centeris/Papers/globalization/KAHLERMilesFINALPAPER.pdf; Francesca Bignami, "Civil Society and International Organizations: A Liberal Framework for Global Governance," SSRN Scholarly Paper (Rochester, NY: Social Science Research Network, 2005), http://papers.ssrn.com/abstract=2031012.

[60] NGOs have some form of access at nearly all UN bodies, the World Bank, the International Monetary Fund (IMF), WTO, and in many environmental treaties. See Tallberg et al., *The Opening Up of International Organizations*, 3–5.

violated court procedures such as due process or equality of arms. Pulling back NGO access could also happen for specific NGOs if that NGO provided misinformation or politicized the court in a way costly to its legitimacy.

A robust history of NGO participation not only makes future access more likely but also increases the chances that the participation will be substantive and impactful. When courts and member states see NGOs as normal and appropriate partners in court governance, trials, and administration, then it is logical that those actors would utilize their information and services. On the other hand, if states and court officials are wary of NGOs and question their place in court affairs, then the fruits of their participation will also likely be viewed as circumspect.

NGO Motivation and Resources

Even if courts or states grant NGOs participatory access, NGOs must choose to engage with international judicial mechanisms. NGO participation therefore requires NGOs with the motivation and financial capacity to utilize those roles (see Table I.5). Consequently, variation in NGO motivation and resources most directly and significantly shapes the frequency in which NGOs utilize channels of participatory access. It is also possible that NGOs can contribute to the expansion of NGO participatory roles. For those roles that do not require state or court permission, determined and well-financed NGOs could expand their work and take on these new duties. For new or expanded roles that require states or courts to grant NGOs participatory allowance, NGOs may serve as instigators of the expanded roles by envisioning and pressuring for such roles.

The principal motivation for NGOs to participate at international criminal and human rights judicial mechanisms is that these are distinctive courts. They are permanent, supranational courts of last resort with the authority to enforce their judgments for human rights violations. There are no commensurate alternatives. National courts do not serve as viable substitutes because in order for cases to have reached these supranational courts, national remedies must have been exhausted or domestic courts were unable or unwilling to try the cases. For human rights cases, the United Nations (UN) human rights treaty monitoring bodies do not have equivalent

TABLE I.5: *NGO Motivation and Resources and NGO Participatory Roles, Frequency, and Impact*

Roles (Access)	• NGOs imagine and take up new roles and/or pressure courts (or states) for new forms of participatory access
Frequency	• Motivated and well-resourced NGOs engage with courts at higher incidence
Impact	–

enforcement powers and can only recommend state action.[61] In social movement or advocacy terms, human rights NGOs cannot "venue shop" among judicial and non-judicial mechanisms and expect similar remedies.[62] In practice, the distinct character of the examined international judicial mechanisms means that the overall motivation of human rights NGOs to seek influence at these courts is fairly strong and constant.[63] NGO motivation does not significantly wax and wane depending on case outcomes or the impact of previous participatory engagement. Avenues for NGOs to seek influence are also broader than formal involvement in trials and can include shaping court processes and rules through service provision and governance roles. This is not to say that all human rights NGOs choose to engage these courts in all roles, but there exists a core group of motivated NGOs continually seeking greater influence at each of the examined courts. As such, NGO motivation – while a necessary condition for NGO participation – does not explain the levels of frequency of NGO participation at the examined courts. Different levels of frequency are more a result of NGO funding and capacity to participate.

The ability of NGOs to engage with international judicial mechanisms is inexorably tied to NGO funding. Formal participation in litigation requires expert legal research and analysis and often necessitates international travel to document evidence or take statements from witnesses. Informal participation can also be costly, particularly the roles that help build the capacity of the judicial institution by providing services such as outreach, advocacy, information sharing, or administrative aid. Donors are thus essential for NGOs to initiate, sustain, and expand NGO participation. Changes in donor receptiveness to judicial tactics or work on specific courts profoundly impact the ability of individual and networks of NGOs to participate at international courts and the scope of the roles that they can assume.

Human rights NGOs typically receive funding from two types of donors: states and private philanthropic foundations.[64] While information on historical state contributions to human rights NGOs is not available, data from philanthropic foundations show sizeable contributions devoted to human rights. In 2010, the grants to human rights projects by the ten foundations with the largest grant dollars totaled $581.1 million.[65] With these large grant figures, it would be easy to assume that

---

[61] For a list of the human rights treaty monitoring bodies, see: United Nations Human Rights Office of the High Commissioner, "Human Rights Treaty Bodies," accessed September 13, 2016, http://www.ohchr.org/EN/HRBodies/Pages/WhatTBDo.aspx.

[62] Keck and Sikkink, *Activists Beyond Borders*; Charles Tilly and Sidney Tarrow, *Contentious Politics* (Oxford University Press, 2015).

[63] It is possible, and even likely, that the advent of new institutions with comparable legal remedy could significantly alter the motivation of human rights NGOs to seek participatory relationships with these courts.

[64] Amnesty International is an exception to this trend and receives a portion of its funding from membership fees and donations.

[65] Foundation Center, "Advancing Human Rights: The State of Global Foundation Grantmaking," 2013: 8, http://foundationcenter.org/gainknowledge/humanrights/.

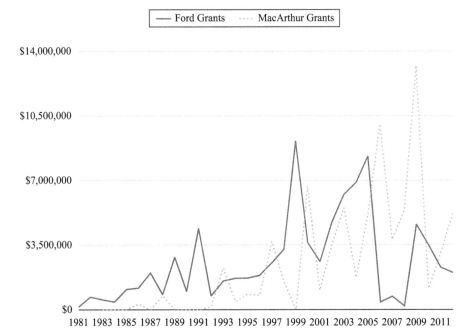

FIGURE I.1: Ford and MacArthur Foundation Funding of NGO Projects Relating to
International Judicial Mechanisms (1981–2011)
Note: The data highlight the Ford and MacArthur Foundations because these private
philanthropic foundations are prominent human rights funders with publically available
historical funding data. Data are triangulated from two sources: (1) from searches of grant
descriptions from IRS filings compiled in the Foundation Search database. The search
criteria used include: Africa human rights, African Court, special court, ECOWAS
(limited to those grants related to human rights), strategic litigation, ICC, European
Court, Inter-American, Tribunal, ICTY, and ICTR. All search results were then
examined to make sure that the project description did pertain to an international
judicial mechanism; (2) from Ford Foundation annual reports from 1981–2011. Data
appear more volatile than they actually may be as funding is sometimes allocated one
year (as seen in the data) but given out over three years in various segments.

foundations have always had close relationships with human rights NGOs. In fact,
the consistent financial support of human rights NGOs by large foundations is a
more recent phenomenon that developed in tandem with the exponential growth of
NGOs in the mid 1970s. Prior to 1975, there were only a few major foundations and
these foundations rarely funded international human rights projects because their
work was antithetical to the dominant ethos of foundations to build state capabilities.[66]
    In the late 1970s and early 1980s, two factors converged which shifted the
attention to human rights grants. First, the Ford Foundation reversed its prior policy

---

[66] Keck and Sikkink, *Activists Beyond Borders*, 98.

and added human rights to its funding criteria following its work with Latin American NGOs over the issue of academic freedom.[67] Second, new foundations were established during this period, including the MacArthur Foundation, the Open Society Institute (later retitled as the Open Society Foundations), and the Oak Foundation, which all eventually adopted a human rights focus. During the 1990s, many foundations – including the major human rights funders, the Ford and MacArthur Foundations – adopted a decidedly legal and judicial approach to human rights that emphasized international human rights justice and the promotion, capacity building, and use of international judicial mechanisms (see Figure I.1).[68] The expansion of donor funding during this time allowed, and in a few cases may have motivated, NGOs to seek out new participatory relationships or increase the frequency of existing engagement with international courts.[69] In the case of the Ford and MacArthur Foundations, even though historical grants related to international judicial mechanisms rose in aggregate, the amount of funding varied across the examined judicial mechanisms.[70] This suggests that some NGO funding environments related to specific judicial mechanisms are more competitive and volatile than others. In the past few years, however, the overall donor enthusiasm for international justice appears to have cooled. Even though a 2010 report on the state of philanthropic allocation calls for a three-fold increase in funding for human rights and international justice projects, foundations such as MacArthur have shifted toward funding domestic, as opposed to international, judicial accountability mechanisms for atrocity crimes.[71]

IMPLICATIONS

This research fundamentally expands understandings of both international courts and NGOs. For international courts, it provides insights into how courts behave and how courts are conceptualized. The research demonstrates that court officials are strategic actors that can utilize NGOs to help fulfill the court's institutional

---

[67] Keck and Sikkink, *Activists Beyond Borders*, 98–101.

[68] Jonathan Fanton and Zachary Katznelson, "Human Rights and International Justice," 2010, www.atlanticphilanthropies.org/sites/default/files/uploads/HumanRightsandInternationalJustice_ChallengesandOpportunitiesatanInflectionPoint_0.pdf.

[69] It is possible that donor funding priorities could spur NGOs not previously utilizing judicial tactics to adopt them. If foundations continually fund projects or establish funding categories relating to the development and utilization of judicial mechanisms for human rights enforcement, then NGOs may respond and expand existing projects or begin new projects in these areas. See: Cooley and Ron, "The NGO Scramble."

[70] I do not disaggregate the funding data by individual NGO because I cannot obtain a complete or near-complete assessment of NGO funding sources, as NGOs are not required to disclose such information. Author interviews with NGO personnel in the empirical chapters do give evidence about the state of NGO funding for specific organizations.

[71] Fanton and Katznelson, "Human Rights and International Justice," 39; MacArthur Foundation, *Protecting Freedom of Expression and Enhancing Criminal Justice*, 2013, www.macfound.org/videos/379/.

mandate. The strategic use of NGO participatory services has positive implications for court functionality but also raises questions about politicization, funding sustainability, and the erosion of state responsibility. Secondly, courts should be conceptualized as complex institutions with structures, rules, and procedures apart from formal trials and judicial decision-making processes. When the scholarship on international courts is limited to judicial elections, decision-making, and outcomes, courts are seen as more impervious to external influence than is the case.

This research also contributes to the theoretical conceptualization of human rights NGOs in several ways. First, it broadens the conceptualization of human rights NGOs by documenting the seamless transitions between advocacy and service provision. When NGOs see international courts as ends in themselves because they are courts of last resort, then NGOs are willing to horizontally or vertically expand their activities to provide needed services and, in doing so, further shape the court in their vision. Second, it identifies "insider" NGOs, which relinquish their roles as objective monitors and critics due to their special positions vis-à-vis international courts. Lastly, it details a new kind of NGO "gatekeeping" whereby some NGOs have inordinate formal or informal access to courts or member states due to pre-established relationships and brand recognition. This phenomenon broadens the conception of NGO gatekeeping from issue emergence to the constitution of civil society voices heard at international courts.

Courts and the Strategic Use of NGO Participation

Existing scholarship acknowledges that courts are political entities that act strategically to enhance functionality and address problems of state cooperation. Prosecutors at the ICTR and ICTY tribunals conducted "virtual trials" of state cooperation over sharing information and executing arrest warrants. These "virtual trials" consisted of both conciliatory and adversarial tactics, including the tribunal prosecutors making media appearances, urging other states to provide incentives, and engaging in private diplomacy.[72] At the Egyptian Constitutional Court, judges developed mutually beneficial relationships with civil society actors. Activists were granted access to bring forward important cases, and in exchange, would defend the court's independence from the ruling regime.[73] Building on previous work, this research demonstrates that international courts have another strategic tool in the perennial struggle for state cooperation: allowing, requesting, or manufacturing NGO participation. Often times, utilizing NGO participation is a more attractive option than court officials conducting "virtual trials" and pressuring states directly. NGOs can shame states for non-cooperation, typically in more acerbic or controversial language than court officials could use because of the court's need to maintain perceptions of

---

[72] Peskin, *International Justice in Rwanda and the Balkans*.

[73] Moustafa, "Law versus the State"; Tamir Moustafa, *The Struggle for Constitutional Power: Law, Politics, and Economic Development in Egypt* (Cambridge University Press, 2007).

impartiality and independence. Yielding this role to NGOs allows the court to appear to be apolitical and shields it from state blowback. Additionally, NGO participation usually requires limited effort by court officials. On the whole, NGOs want greater channels of participatory access and influence at international criminal and human rights courts because they view these courts as critical courts of last resort. Allowance of NGO participation often requires little to no action at all. Minor efforts include allowing backchannel communications with court officials or making rule changes within the purview of the court itself. Only in the case of the Inter-American Court did the Court undertake the major effort of establishing its own NGO in order to reap the benefits of NGO participation. Lastly, NGO participation is particularly attractive to courts with substantial deficiencies in financing and state support because NGOs can provide critical services that compensate for institutional needs.

Courts strategically employing NGO participation can increase their institutional capacity, and therefore enhance the potential for international human rights accountability. Without NGOs, some victims would have never utilized the judicial institutions, received redress, and the resulting jurisprudence would likely be less wide-reaching. For judicial institutions besieged by state hostility, lack of authority, or little to no financing, NGO participation could constitute the difference between actualizing their mandate to provide human rights accountability and existing purely as a symbolic, but non-functional, institution.

On the other hand, if NGOs are providing these crucial and resource-intensive services then states or the court are not providing them. This could lead to several unintended and problematic situations. First, high levels of NGO service provision to courts could inadvertently relieve states from their obligation to provide sufficient financial resources and cooperation to judicial institutions. The fact that NGOs are already shouldering some of the costs may change state incentives to provide more funding or support, as the judicial institutions will function regardless. Second, international courts could become dependent on NGO actors to provide key functions of the court, as occurred in the early years of the ICC. This raises questions of potential politicization by private actors and threatens courts' independence and impartiality, even if NGOs do not have relationships with court judges. Although NGOs are motivated by principles, the organizational goals and tactics of NGOs may not always align with fundamental judicial values and processes. For example, due process considerations for defendants at the ICC – who have lengthy trials and the right to know the source of the evidence used against them – have largely been absent from the efforts of the major NGO players. Instead, NGOs push for greater victims' services, additional indictments for crimes of sexual violence, execution of arrest warrants, and on-the-ground outreach in situation countries. Third, for international courts that are perpetually and dramatically underfunded, NGOs and courts could end up competing for funding from the same international donors. This is the case with the Inter-American Court and the court-created NGO, the Inter-American Institute of Human Rights (IIHR). As the Organization of American

States (OAS) does not provide the Court with a sufficient budget in order for it to operate, the Court has approached European countries and international foundations to supplement its budget. The Inter-American Institute, which receives no support from the OAS, relies exclusively on donor foundations and states for its budget. Because of the limited number of donor countries and foundations willing to fund projects on international justice, the Court and the Institute compete with one another for the same funding. As of 2010, the Institute was more successful in its pursuit of donor funding and had a greater budget than the Court.[74]

Courts as Institutionally Complex and Porous Institutions

The myriad ways in which NGOs influence the rules, procedures, governance, and jurisprudence of international criminal and human rights courts implies that international courts are more institutionally complex and porous to external actors than much of the scholarship depicts. The conceptualization of what a court is and how it operates needs rethinking and broadening. Currently much of the literature examines ways in which states politicize international courts through institutionalizing state preference, judicial nominations, and non-compliance with judgments.[75] Courts are more than judicial decision-making bodies that release decisions, and over time, develop jurisprudence. Prior to the step of judicial decision-making, many non-legal factors already influence the case: whether a viable legal aid program exists, the procedures for submitting a case, prosecutorial strategy, the financial and logistical abilities of the court to conduct on-the-ground outreach or investigations, state cooperation to share information, and the workload and budget of the court staff to conduct extensive legal research. These rules, procedures, and resource and informational needs all constitute opportunities for NGOs to build the capacity of the court, shape it in their normative vision of how the court should operate, and indirectly influence court jurisprudence. In the three judicial institutions examined, NGOs did not have relationships or influence with judges, but NGOs were still able to have considerable impact and influence on the ways the institutions functioned and ultimately the judicial outcomes.

NGO Hybridization

The diverse participatory roles NGOs play at international criminal and human rights courts suggests that NGOs are versatile and strategic in different ways than

---

[74] Personal interview with an official of the Inter-American Court of Human Rights, November 22, 2010.

[75] Alter, "Agents or Trustees": 33–63; Elsig Pollack, "Agents, Trustees, and International Courts": 391–415; Voeten, "The Politics of International Judicial Appointments": 669–701; Courtney Hillebrecht, *Domestic Politics and International Human Rights Tribunals: The Problem of Compliance* (Cambridge University Press, 2014).

much of the NGO literature theorizes. While there is an emerging literature that explores the "hybridization" of NGOs, or NGOs engaging in both service provision and advocacy, much of the literature still demarcates NGOs into advocacy NGOs or humanitarian NGOs.[76] Advocacy NGOs are "norm entrepreneurs" that use pressure, persuasion, and shaming to raise attention to issues and push states to change behavior and create new institutions.[77] Humanitarian NGOs are NGOs associated with humanitarian causes or development and provide vital services that states are unable or unwilling to provide.[78] This theoretical classification of NGOs has implications for how scholars think about NGOs' motivations, behavior, and strategies. Advocacy NGOs are viewed as normatively driven and choose the targets of their activism based on political opportunity structures or perceived impact.[79] Humanitarian NGOs are increasingly viewed as juggling multiple motivations – normative and opportunistic – based upon competition for funding and shifting political environments.[80]

Existing theories characterize advocacy NGOs as versatile or flexible in that NGOs have organizational structures capable of switching issue areas, missions, or campaigns. This study suggests that advocacy NGOs are versatile not because they can shift issues, but because they can hybridize and take on service provision or governance roles. Advocacy NGOs not only pressure for new norms or institutions but can morph into providing services or doing both simultaneously.[81]

Similarly, NGOs are also strategic in the way they recognize and capitalize upon opportunities for new or expanded participatory roles. NGOs with participatory roles at functional international criminal or human rights courts, recognize areas in which the court is struggling – based on limited resources or state cooperation – and strategically craft roles that allow them to help fulfill the needs of the judicial institution.

---

[76] Nelson and Dorsey, *New Rights Advocacy: Changing Strategies of Development and Human Rights NGOs*.

[77] Florini, *Third Force: The Rise of Transnational Civil Society*; Keck and Sikkink, *Activists Beyond Borders*; Thomas Risse, Steve C. Ropp, and Kathryn Sikkink, *The Power of Human Rights* (Cambridge University Press, 1999); Kathryn Sikkink, "Transnational Advocacy Networks and the Social Construction of Legal Rules," in *Global Prescriptions*, ed. Yves Dezalay and Bryant G. Garth (Ann Arbor: University of Michigan Press, 2002): 37–64.

[78] Abby Stoddard, "Humanitarian NGOs: Challenges and Trends," February 27, 2009, http://dspace.cigilibrary.org/jspui/handle/123456789/22644.

[79] Alison Brysk, "From Above and Below: Social Movements, the International System, and Human Rights in Argentina," *Comparative Political Studies* 26, no. 3 (1993): 259–85; Keck and Sikkink, *Activists Beyond Borders*; Khagram, Riker, and Sikkink, *Restructuring World Politics: Transnational Social Movements, Networks, and Norms*; Audie Klotz, "Norms Reconstituting Interests: Global Racial Equality and U.S. Sanctions Against South Africa," *International Organization* 49, no. 3 (1995): 451–78.

[80] Barnett, "Evolution Without Progress?"; Cooley and Ron, "The NGO Scramble"; Sell and Prakash, "Using Ideas Strategically."

[81] Heidi Nichols Haddad, "After the Norm Cascade: NGO Mission Expansion and the Coalition for the International Criminal Court," *Global Governance: A Review of Multilateralism and International Organizations* 19, no. 2 (2013): 187–206.

The strategic motivations for these expansions may be normative – or driven by the desire to see these judicial institutions function and administer justice – but factors of financial resources and organizational survival are not completely absent. In order to successfully adopt new or expand existing participatory roles, NGOs must successfully match donor support to the new or expanded roles. New or expanded participatory roles can also help ensure NGOs' organizational survival as these new roles may be permanent governance or service provision roles and the judicial institution may depend on NGO participation in these roles for functionality.

"Insider" NGOs and Court Monitoring

The current understandings of NGOs only allow for instrumentalization by states. Government-organized NGOs (GONGOs) promote national interests and agendas through civil society channels. NGOs can also become captured by states through repression or dependence on state funding.[82] This research suggests that NGOs with inordinate or special access at international criminal and human rights courts are also susceptible to self-censorship or capture, particularly in their roles as public monitors and critics.

This occurs at both the IAS and the ICC. At the IAS, the judicial institutions and the Court-created Inter-American Institute of Human Rights (IIHR) enjoy a close relationship whereby many former commissioners, officials, and judges have prominent positions at the Institute. This club environment contributes to the unwillingness of the Institute to publically criticize the work of the Commission or Court, even though the Institute regularly produces a publication about the status of the work of the IAS.[83] At the ICC, the relationship dynamic between NGOs and the Court is incredibly congenial. ICC officials speak highly of NGOs and are generally grateful for NGO support and services.[84] Similarly, NGOs often provide court officials the courtesy of constructive criticism behind closed doors and only resort to public criticism if backdoor channels to do not produce results.[85] These examples stand in contrast to the traditional model of transnational advocacy, which assumes NGOs have outsider status and NGOs are independent and objective monitors.

---

[82] David Lewis, *Non-Governmental Organizations, Management and Development* (London: Routledge, 2014): 204; Moses Naim, "What Is a GONGO?," Foreign Policy, October 13, 2009, https://foreignpolicy.com/2009/10/13/what-is-a-gongo/.

[83] Author interview with a former official of the Inter-American Commission and Court of Human Rights, November 25, 2010.

[84] Author interviews with ICC officials, August 12, 13, and 17, 2010.

[85] Human Rights Watch, "Unfinished Business," 2011; Human Rights Watch, "ICC: Course Correction," June 16, 2011, www.hrw.org/news/2011/06/16/icc-course-correction; Richard Dicker, "Throwing Justice Under the Bus Is Not the Way to Go | Human Rights Watch," *Open Democracy*, January 6, 2015, www.hrw.org/news/2015/01/06/throwing-justice-under-bus-not-way-go.

In the case of the ICC, NGOs are independent from states, which allows them both to "name and shame" states and to request help for the Court in ways that would violate the Court's objectivity, such as focusing on the plight of victims. Yet, the tremendous access NGOs have to the Court coupled with its dependence on NGOs to operate, raises questions about how independent NGOs really are from the ICC. NGOs claim that they are not "flag wavers of the Court" and that their commitment is to the Rome Statute, not the Court.[86] But NGOs also state that they don't need "neutrality like the ICRC," highlight their "unconditional support" for the Court, and some tread lightly on issues that could appear to publically criticize the Court.[87] This can make it difficult to see a distinction between support for the Rome Statute and support for the ICC. NGOs, while claiming objectivity, are not outsiders. Prominent NGOs are part of the ICC system and some have insider channels of access and influence with key court and state stakeholders. Insider access is not inherently problematic – and it may actually engender NGO success in reaching its goals – but it does raise questions about whether NGOs are playing a true public monitoring role if the public only hears partial criticisms when insider channels fail.

NGO Gatekeepers

This research also contributes to greater understanding of how power differentials in reputation and access play out among international and domestic human rights NGOs. Building from the scholarship on NGO gatekeepers whose buy-in is neces-sary for an issue to gain international salience, NGO gatekeepers also exist at international criminal and human rights courts.[88] These NGO gatekeepers regulate the access of other NGOs to consultative court forums.

In two of the three examined courts, specific NGOs have inordinate access due to pre-established relationships and NGO brand recognition. These NGOs are in essence a type of "gatekeeper," who control whether and which NGOs can seek to influence key court officials and member states. At the ECtHR, only three NGOs – Amnesty International, the ICJ, and the International Federation for Human Rights (FIDH) – have observer status at the meetings of the Steering Committee for Human Rights of the Council of Europe (CDDH), which drafts new protocols to the European Convention on Human Rights. Unless the CDDH

---

[86] Author interview with a CICC staff member, August 20, 2010.

[87] Author interview with Deborah Ruiz Verduzco, Senior Programme Officer, PGA, September 8, 2010. The ICRC is the International Committee of the Red Cross.

[88] Clifford Bob, *The Marketing Of Rebellion: Insurgents, Media, And International Activism* (Cambridge University Press, 2005); R. Charli Carpenter, "Setting the Advocacy Agenda: 99–120; R. Charli Carpenter, *"Lost" Causes: Agenda Vetting in Global Issue Networks and the Shaping of Human Security* (Ithaca, NY: Cornell University Press, 2014).

specifically requests the presence of non-observer NGOs, all other NGOs must channel their voices through these three NGOs. To counteract their exclusive status and to include NGOs that represent petitioners at the ECtHR – none of which the three gatekeeping NGOs do – Amnesty and the ICJ created a wider coalition of NGOs who submit joint statements to the CDDH. At the ICC, the CICC serves as the Court's NGO gatekeeper by selecting domestic NGOs from situation countries or countries under investigation to attend the annual civil society meetings with the organs of the Court and the Secretariat of the Assembly of States Parties (ASP). The CICC also certified which NGOs officially participated at the "People's Space" at the 2010 Kampala Review Conference.

NGO gatekeepers exist because they simplify civil society consultations with international courts. One or several reputable NGOs can vet other NGOs, which court officials or member states do not have the time or knowledge to do. Yet, this arrangement privileges prominent, international NGOs who invariably take on the gatekeeping functions. It also begs the question about whose voices are transmitted through those channels, whose interests those voices represent, and whether critical civil society perspectives are left out or muffled in the process. Some scholars believe that NGOs, by virtue of their normative drive and non-state status, are key players in civil society and represent broader societal interests and civil society.[89] The existence of NGO "gatekeepers" casts doubt on these general characteristics of NGOs. In the examined courts, the major NGOs with the most access, and therefore the most influence, were all well-funded, international NGOs with headquarters in major North American or Western European cities. These NGOs do not have permanent headquarters in the countries experiencing the gravest human rights violations, but serve as middlemen or intermediaries, choosing to connect local actors with international courts. Even though these NGOs operate by normative principles, their views or strategies are not ascertained by consensus from a larger constituency of civil society actors, but are their own. Many of these "gatekeeper" NGOs choose to liaise with civil society actors, but these consultations are not mandated and the gatekeepers are under no imperative to take into consideration the needs of these smaller, domestic, more resource-poor actors.

PLAN OF THE BOOK

Chapter 1 details the research methods of the book and maps NGO participation at the three examined judicial institutions using a typology of NGO participatory roles with respective measures of frequency and impact. The subsequent four chapters (Chapters 2–5) represent in-depth case study examinations of three judicial institutions: The ECtHR (and Commission pre-1998), the IAS, and the ICC. Each

---

[89] Cichowski, *The European Court and Civil Society*; Lindblom, *Non-Governmental Organisations in International Law.*

chapter traces how court resources and legitimacy, history of NGO engagement, and NGO motivation and financial capacity translate into specific and varied NGO roles, frequency, and impact.

Chapter 2 examines NGO engagement with the European System of Human Rights (the Court and Commission pre-1998). It demonstrates that the relatively lower levels of NGO access and influence stem from two complementary factors. First, the Court is well funded and supported – despite its ever-increasing caseload – and generally does not need the expertise, services, or information provided by NGOs to effectively function. Second, because of the long-standing historical exclusion of NGOs, member states and court officials view NGO engagement as unnecessary and in some situations, inappropriate. Even so, motivated NGOs have continually sought greater access, particularly with regard to court governance and reforms.

By capitalizing on rule changes and demanding the inclusion of civil society voices, NGO efforts yielded a few inroads in obtaining avenues of participation. Yet, as this access was often quite circumscribed and NGO funding could never match the enormous caseload, NGO participation never reached high levels nor led to considerable impact on court functionality and jurisprudence.

Chapter 3 analyzes NGO participation at the IAS and shows that the precipitous explosion of NGO access, engagement, and influence in the mid 1970s resulted from chronic underfunding of the judicial institutions combined with NGOs galvanizing around the Commission as a means to address the human rights abuses occurring throughout the region. The deficiencies of the Inter-American Commission and Court have consistently been large, including negligible funding, treaty renunciation, and hamstrung authority. These deficiencies were so great that Commission officials were willing to overlook any previous exclusionary norms or rules to allow NGOs to aid their cause. NGO resources to devote to building the capacity of these institutions were substantial but were more constrained than at the ICC. In the mid 1970s, a small group of Washington, DC-based NGOs provided critical money and information to the Commission that revitalized it and allowed it to begin to document and publically shame Latin American states for their human rights records. This advocacy eventually took permanent form with the establishment of CEJIL, an offshoot of Americas Watch, devoted to litigating before the IAS and now the greatest NGO player at the Court. Prior to CEJIL's establishment, NGO engagement centered on the Commission in Washington, DC, which left the Costa Rica-based Court without the NGO support services enjoyed by the Commission. This prompted the Court to take the unprecedented step of establishing its own independent NGO, the IIHR, that supplied the Court with money and political cover during its early years.

Chapters 4 and 5 explore the broad participatory access, robust engagement, and critical impact of NGOs at the ICC. It illustrates that these strong relationships and channels of access were facilitated by pre-established relationships and legitimacy born from the prior advocacy work of NGOs coupled with the fledgling Court's need for greater resources and state cooperation. NGOs play the most roles and have the greatest impact because of the tremendous deficiencies of the young Court struggling to establish itself and the well-resourced, thousands-strong coalition of NGOs that views the Court as its child and wishes it to grow into the court that they fought to bring into existence. The ICC needs the expertise, advocacy, and institutional support of NGOs to operate. The CICC and other prominent international NGOs – financially buoyed by the outpouring of monies from foundations – proactively sought to fill the needs of the ICC and through its role as central coordinator of NGO activity, effectively became the Court's eyes and ears of civil society.

The Conclusion explores the application of the central argument to two additional courts: The African Court on Human and Peoples' Rights (ACtHPR) and the Khmer Rouge trials at the Extraordinary Chambers in the Courts of Cambodia (ECCC). The ACtHPR represents a test case for the argument, as the case fits with the scope of the cases examined in the book, but only recently became operational. The Khmer Rouge trials are outside of the scope of the cases examined due to its temporal and conflict-specific nature as well as its hybrid structure. Preliminary research on these courts shows similar patterns of NGO interaction and suggests that aspects of the book's argument may be more generalizable and could apply to a wider universe of human rights or criminal courts.

1

Mapping NGO Participation

The research method utilized in this study is case studies of three international criminal and human rights judicial institutions: The European System of Human Rights (pre-1998 commission and the ECtHR), the Inter-American Human Rights System (IAS), and the International Criminal Court (ICC). Case studies are an appropriate research method because of the understudied nature of the examined phenomenon. There are no existing studies that exhaustively map the many forms of NGO participation at these judicial institutions. Nor are there well-developed theories that explain why NGO participation may vary in scope, intensity, and impact across courts. Case studies provide empirical richness and facilitate the identification and tracing of relevant causal factors, which is necessary when inductively developing causal explanations.[1] Such an exploratory method is not without precedent; inductive approaches to examining understudied phenomena have a rich history in institutional scholarship.[2] Nevertheless, this method is not without qualification. While case studies allow for rich empirical documentation of NGO participation at the examined courts, the theoretical scope of the explanatory factors derived from the cases is limited. These explanatory factors constitute an initial attempt to build theory through inductive analysis and therefore it is not possible to confidently ascertain their broader applicability to other international courts or the comparative weight of each factor. The project does begin to assess the question of broader applicability through preliminary examinations of the African Court on

---

[1] To clarify, the study is *not* utilizing the comparative method and therefore the cases were not selected based on their analytic leverage in testing causal explanations but as a means to map the understudied phenomenon of NGO participation and generate factors that explain such participation.

[2] Robert H. Bates et al., *Analytic Narratives* (Princeton University Press, 1998); Theda Skocpol, "Bringing the State Back In: Strategies of Analysis in Current Research," in *Bringing the State Back In*, ed. Peter B. Evans, Dietrich Rueschemeyer, and Theda Skocpol (New York, NY: Cambridge University Press, 1985): 3–37.

Human and Peoples' Rights (ACtHPR) and the Extraordinary Chambers in the Courts of Cambodia (ECCC) in the Conclusion. Further research is needed to systematically test and refine the explanatory factors.

Although NGOs have some form of engagement with many different types of international courts, this project examines one subset: international criminal and human rights courts.[3] International criminal and human rights courts are studied because NGO participation is relatively long-standing and includes the greatest scope of roles and frequency of any subset of international courts. While selecting cases based upon high values of NGO participation within a larger field of cases can be viewed as a selection bias, this selection is justified because of the lack of existing theory relating to the divergence in NGO participation at international courts. According to Collier and Mahoney, at the early stages of a research program it can be advantageous to examine subsets of a larger universe of cases in order to identify causal pathways and variables that lead to the examined outcome.[4] Studying this subset of cases can elucidate factors that shape differences in NGO participation, even if the argument is not generalizable to the larger universe of international courts.

Some may also question the decision to combine international criminal and human rights courts into one category due to their fundamental structural, procedural, and legal differences. International criminal courts hold *individuals* criminally accountable for violations in international criminal law, such as war crimes, crimes against humanity, and genocide. International human rights courts are venues for individuals to seek remuneration and policy change from *states* for violations of human rights articulated in regional conventions. International human rights courts may also give advisory opinions to states on questions of whether state practice violates the underlying human rights conventions. The institutions are structurally distinct and these differences do account for some minor variation in the participatory roles NGOs can play vis-à-vis these courts. For example, NGOs can liaise, provide information, and advocate to the Office of the Prosecutor at criminal courts – whereas no such office exists at the civil human rights courts. These differences do not warrant dismissing the comparison. There are profound similarities, particularly in the central and complementary role of both types of courts in how NGOs seek and promote international human rights justice. Both international human rights and criminal courts are courts of last resort that provide judicial remedy for human rights violations. Increasingly, both types of courts address human rights violations – including

---

[3]   Chazournes and Mbengue, "Amici Curiae and the WTO Dispute Settlement System"; Cichowski, *The European Court and Civil Society*; Treves et al., *Civil Society, International Courts and Compliance Bodies*.

[4]   David Collier and James Mahoney, "Insights and Pitfalls: Selection Bias in Qualitative Research," *World Politics* 49, no. 1 (1996): 56–91.

grave abuses such as murder, disappearances, and torture – in conflict situations.[5] The fact that human rights courts, usually seen as upholders of rights during peacetime, can hold states accountable for abuses during conflict is representative of the larger trend of the blurring between international humanitarian and human rights law.[6] Human rights NGOs imagined and pushed for this legal trend as it could help bridge legal gaps and afford greater rights protection.[7] This idea of creating an encompassing "humanity's law" is reflected in the organizational strategies of many large international NGOs, such as Amnesty International and Human Rights Watch (HRW), that participate at both kinds of courts within a larger normative agenda of international human rights justice.

Why examine the ECtHR, the IAS, and the ICC? The entire subset of international human rights and criminal courts is comprised of six courts: the ECtHR, the Inter-American Court, the ACtHPR, the ICTY, the ICTR, and the ICC.[8] The Yugoslav and Rwandan Tribunals are excluded from this analysis because of their ad hoc and conflict specific nature, which disincentivizes NGOs from seeking participatory relationships in favor of permanent, treaty-based courts.[9] In fact, with the advent of the ICC, many large advocacy NGOs, including Amnesty International, chose to focus on the ICC because of the larger potential impact on the future character of international criminal law.[10] The ACtHPR is not included in the main body of this study because it became operational after the main research for this project was conducted. Because it falls within the scope of the cases examined, I consider the case in the Conclusion as a means to conduct a preliminary test of this book's argument. In addition to examining courts, I also include international human rights commissions that are linked to courts in the main analysis.

---

[5] The Inter-American Court has addressed cases of disappearances, torture, and extrajudicial killings. The ECtHR has cases related to the conflicts in Chechnya and Southern Turkey. For an examination of the interplay between transitional justice and post-Cold War cases before the ECtHR, see: James A. Sweeney, *The European Court of Human Rights in the Post-Cold War Era: Universality in Transition* (London: Routledge, 2013).

[6] ICRC, "International Humanitarian Law and International Human Rights Law," n.d., www .icrc.org/Web/Eng/siteeng0.nsf/htmlall/57JR8L/$File/IHL_and_IHRL.pdf; Kirby Abbott, "A Brief Overview of Legal Interoperability Challenges for NATO Arising from the Interrelationship between IHL and IHRL in Light of the European Convention on Human Rights," *International Review of the Red Cross* 96, no. 893 (2014): 107–37, 8.

   Another example of the merging of international humanitarian and human rights law is the plan to establish criminal chambers at the ACtHPR. This court would then serve as both a human rights and criminal court.

[7] Ruti G. Teitel, *Humanity's Law* (Oxford University Press, 2011).

[8] See www.pict-pcti.org/publications/synoptic_chart.html for the synoptic chart on all international courts and tribunals.

[9] Hybrid tribunals such as the Special Court for Sierra Leone, "Regulation 64" Panels in the courts of Kosovo, Serious Crimes Panels in the District Court of Dili, or the Extraordinary Chambers in the Courts of Cambodia are also excluded because they are ad hoc and conflict specific in nature.

[10] Dean Zagorac, "International Courts and Compliance Bodies: The Experience of Amnesty International," in *Civil Society, International Courts and Compliance Bodies*, ed. Tullio Treves et al. (The Hague: T.M.C. Asser Press, 2005): 11–39.

International human rights commissions not only negotiate settlements of human rights grievances but are also the filtering mechanisms that decide which cases are heard at the respective international human rights courts. Because of these quasi-judicial and gatekeeping roles, NGOs often engage both the courts and commissions and therefore an examination of NGO participation at human rights courts would not be exhaustive without including these commissions.

What constitutes NGO participation with regard to the examined international courts? This study takes a broad but consistent view of NGO participation and maps all formal and informal NGO participatory roles that *directly pertain* to judicial process, functionality, or outcomes.[11] In other words, the NGO activities must primarily relate to court operations, cases before the court, or the court's ability to fulfill its mandate. Participatory roles included within these parameters not only include activities at the judicial institution but also court-related activities directed at governance bodies, states, and victim communities.[12] For example, NGO activities such as running campaigns for treaty ratification, advocating to member states for a larger court budget, or conducting outreach in situation countries are examined because these actions *directly pertain to* the court. Treaty ratification expands the court's jurisdiction, larger budgets increase court functionality, and outreach shapes victim and witness participation in court proceedings.

This study purposefully adopts a broader scope of NGO participation at international courts than the existing scholarship, which focuses on legal standing and formal roles in trials. The reasons are two-fold. First, a more expansive participatory scope better captures and reflects the multi-faceted nature and activities of many international human rights NGOs. NGOs not only utilize judicial institutions but

---

[11] Formal roles are those specified in court or governance body rules or procedures. Informal roles are all other forms of engagement that occur outside of the channels specified in institutional rules or procedures.

   In excluding NGO activities that *indirectly* relate to the examined courts, this study does not negate the possibility that NGOs engage in activities that have secondary or peripheral effects on international courts. Future research could build on this study and explore such activities. Nevertheless, this study only maps NGO participatory roles that directly pertain to the courts because this demarcation allows for richer theoretical analysis. A critical and understudied aspect of explaining patterns of NGO participatory roles, frequency, and impact at international courts is understanding *why* NGOs seek to engage with international courts. If NGO activities that either directly and incidentally relate to international courts are combined in one analysis, then NGO motivation and funding becomes too broad and varied to ascertain any court-related patterns.

[12] With regard to NGO participation targeting court governance bodies, *only* those activities that directly pertain to judicial process, functionality, or outcomes fall within the scope of this study. This means that for organizations with broader mandates than court governance and enforcement – such as the Council of Europe and the Organization of American States (OAS) – this study is not exhaustive of all NGO participatory activity vis-à-vis these institutions, only those aspects of the institutions that have authority on court governance issues. At the Council of Europe, this is the Committee of Ministers and its affiliated subcommittees. At the OAS, it is the Permanent Council and the General Assembly. At the ICC, it is the Assembly of States Parties (ASP).

   This book uses the phrase "NGO participation at the [court]" for readability, although this does not imply that the participatory roles are limited to those that engage with the court.

are also experts and normative advocates and entrepreneurs of the human rights standards adjudicated at international judicial institutions. Second and relatedly, judicial decisions do not occur in an institutional vacuum but may be influenced by court rules and procedure, functionality, and state cooperation. Taken together, many international human rights NGOs possess the capacity and legitimacy to successfully develop and utilize potential channels of influence vis-à-vis international courts in addition to formal roles in trials.

Why focus on NGO participation as opposed to participation by a broader group of non-state actors including individuals, law firms, social movements and professional associations? The main reason is pragmatic: an exploratory project of the many forms of civil society participation at three international courts is too large and unwieldy in scope.[13] To make the project feasible, I had to reduce its scope and focusing on NGOs is a logical demarcation. NGOs, while part of a larger conception of civil society, constitute a distinct organizational form. NGOs are characterized as formal non-profit organizations with staff, mission statements, and external funding (usually from philanthropic foundations, individual contributors, and governments) working on behalf of a societal goal.[14] Even though there is tremendous diversity across NGOs, this distinct organizational form allows for the cross-court study of NGO-specific variables – such as funding and motivation – that may impact NGO engagement with international courts. Choosing to exclusively focus on NGOs is not a novel demarcation. There is a rich precedent in the scholarship, particularly with regard to topics related to human rights, human security, and humanitarianism.[15] Furthermore, since the end of the Cold War, NGOs are increasingly influential actors in the global promotion of human rights norms and institutions.[16] Nevertheless, exclusive attention to NGO participation is not without drawbacks. Most obviously, it only captures the participatory roles, frequency, and impact of one aspect of civil society. Other groups within civil society may have prominent participatory engagement with the examined international courts that

---

[13] Examining participation of all non-state civil society actors at a single, or possibly two, courts represents a fruitful area for future research.

[14] Martens, "Mission Impossible?," 282.

This definition departs from Marten's definition by substituting "societal goal" for "societal good" as what constitutes and who delineates a societal or common good is often contested. A societal goal is one that benefits members of society other than the advocate but does not assume that it would benefit a majority of society or is normatively positive.

[15] Nelson and Dorsey, *New Rights Advocacy: Changing Strategies of Development and Human Rights NGOs*; Amanda Murdie, *Help Or Harm: The Human Security Effects of International NGOs* (Stanford University Press, 2014); Wong, *Internal Affairs*; Sarah S. Stroup, *Borders among Activists: International NGOs in the United States, Britain, and France* (Ithaca, NY: Cornell University Press, 2012); R. Charli Carpenter, "Studying Issue (Non)-Adoption in Transnational Advocacy Networks," *International Organization* 61, no. 3 (2007): 643–67, https://doi.org/10.1017/S0020818307070221X.

[16] Risse, Ropp, and Sikkink, *The Power of Human Rights*; Keck and Sikkink, *Activists Beyond Borders*; Thomas Risse and Kathryn Sikkink, *The Persistent Power of Human Rights: From Commitment to Compliance* (Cambridge University Press, 2013).

may supplement or even replace NGO participation. Therefore, this book makes no claims about *civil society* participation at the three courts, only NGO participation.

To construct the case studies, I use a variety of sources, many of which are original data. I conducted interviews with dozens of court or commission officials, diplomats, academics, NGO personnel that participate at the judicial institutions, and a journalist that covers international courts for a major European news outlet (see Appendix A). The majority of these interviews were conducted between August 2010 and January 2011 during fieldwork I undertook at each respective court and commission – in The Hague, the Netherlands; Strasbourg, France; San José, Costa Rica; and Washington, DC – as well as in London, England, where many human rights NGOs that work on the ECtHR are headquartered. A second set of interviews was conducted during a follow-up fieldwork trip to The Hague in June 2015. All interview subjects were guaranteed anonymity and identifiers of name, organization, and position are only attached to those individuals that approved of such identifiers. These interviews constitute the bedrock of the case studies as the information gleaned from inquiries about the range of NGO engagement, how and why those roles came about, the major NGO players, and the impact of such roles constitute the basic map of NGO participation at the examined courts and suggest explanatory factors that shape such participation. To substantiate and triangulate the interview data, I draw on a range of sources including internal and public NGO documents, court documents and case databases, governance body documents and publications, archived records of third-party participation from the library of the ECtHR, as well as secondary analyses and datasets. In order to quantify the funding environment for human rights NGOs, I constructed an original dataset of NGO grants relating to international courts by two major human rights donors, the Ford and MacArthur Foundations. The dataset is limited to the Ford and MacArthur Foundations, even though the donor pool for human rights NGOs is much larger, because these foundations are the only major human rights funders with publically available historical funding data. States and private philanthropic foundations are not required to share their granting information publically and only some of the NGOs I interviewed were willing to share their donors and financial situations. This dataset does not give an exhaustive picture of the funding environment for human rights NGOs but likely represents broad trends, many of which are mirrored in NGO interview data. Lastly, to see the courts in operation, I observed trial proceedings before the ICC and the ECtHR.[17]

---

[17] At the ICC, I observed portions of the trial of *The Prosecutor* v. *Germain Katanga and Mathieu Ngudjolo Chui* in August 2010 and the status conference proceedings of *The Prosecutor* v. *Bosco Ntaganda* in June 2015. I also observed the Grand Chamber hearing of *Giulliaini and Gaggio* v. *Italy* (no. 23458/02, ECtHR 2011) at the ECtHR in September 2010.

TYPOLOGY OF NGO PARTICIPATION

In order to categorically map the variations in NGO participation at the three examined courts, I construct a typology (see Table 1.1). This first factor of the typology is the participatory *roles*, or what NGOs do. The literature on transnational advocacy, humanitarian NGOs, and international law provide empirical examples of the types of roles that NGOs play at operational international courts including advocacy, expert consultations, monitoring, information sharing, service provision, representing petitioners, and acting as amici curiae.[18] I sort these roles into three typological categories: (1) consultations/advocacy, (2) information sharing and operational support, and (3) formal participation in litigation/ trials.

Consultations/advocacy include all non-trial activities wherein NGOs provide expertise and advocate for policy changes that promote principles, norms, or causes.[19] I combine consultations and advocacy activities into one category because expertise is often a source of authority that aids advocacy efforts.[20] Many human rights NGOs – especially those utilizing legal and judicial strategies – have influence both because of their commitment to normative principles as well as their strong technical and expert legal knowledge.[21] Information sharing and operational support are non-trial roles that could aid the court's functionality through providing information or services. I merge information sharing with operational support because much of the information sharing vis-à-vis international courts constitutes a type of service provision. Information sharing – which includes providing investigative information or evidence of non-compliance – supplements, or is in lieu of, the investigative and compliance functions of courts and commissions. Formal participation in litigation/trials consists of all the roles that NGOs could play in trials or litigation as articulated by the rules of evidence and procedure of the respective courts. These include serving as

---

[18] Alan Fowler, "PVO and NGO Futures: A Framework for Reflection and Dialogue," 2004, www .usaid.gov/our_work/cross-cutting_programs/private_voluntary_cooperation/conf_fowler.pdf; Keck and Sikkink, *Activists Beyond Borders*; Sarat and Scheingold, *Cause Lawyering*; Shelton, "The Participation of Nongovernmental Organizations in International Judicial Proceedings"; Treves et al., *Civil Society, International Courts and Compliance Bodies*; Weiss and Gordenker, *NGOs, the UN, and Global Governance.*

[19] This definition of advocacy is drawn from Keck and Sikkink's description: "they [NGOs] are organized to promote causes, principled ideas, norms, and they often involve individuals advocating policy changes that cannot be easily linked to rationalist understanding of their 'interests.'" Keck and Sikkink, *Activists Beyond Borders*, 8.

[20] Emanuel Adler and Peter M. Haas, "Conclusion: Epistemic Communities, World Order, and the Creation of a Reflective Research Program," *International Organization* 46, no. 1 (1992): 367–90.

[21] Deborah Avant, Martha Finnemore, and Susan Sell, "Who Governs the Globe?," in *Who Governs the Globe?* (Cambridge University Press, 2010): 12–13.

TABLE 1.1 *Typology of NGO Participatory Roles, Frequency, and Impact Across Judicial Institutions*

	Types of Roles/NGO Participatory Roles	Frequency/ Impact of NGO Participation
European System of Human Rights (includes Commission prior to 1998)	**Formal roles in litigation/trials**	
	• Representing petitioners	Low/Medium
	• Filing amicus curiae briefs	Low/Low
	Court-directed advocacy/consultative roles	
	• Biennial meeting with Court Registry	Medium/Low
	State-directed advocacy/consultative roles	
	• Observing and advocating in reform process	Medium/Low
	Information sharing and operational support	
	• Communications to the Committee of Ministers about execution of judgments	Low/Unknown
Inter-American Human Rights System (Commission and Court)	**Formal roles in litigation/trials**	
	• Representing petitioners/Providing information on the execution of judgments*	High/High
	• Filing amicus curiae briefs	High/High
	State-directed advocacy/consultative roles	
	• Advocating for funding and treaty ratification	Low/Medium
	• Consultants and advocates at the OAS	Medium/ Medium
	Information sharing and operational support	
	• Sharing information on human rights abuses	Medium/High
	• Aiding Commission in investigations and cases	High/High
	• Providing funds for court special sessions	Low/High
International Criminal Court	**Formal roles in litigation/trials**	
	• Filing amicus curiae briefs	Medium/ Medium

| | Frequency/ Impact of NGO Participation |
Types of Roles/NGO Participatory Roles	
Court-directed advocacy/consultative roles	
• Formal meetings with each organ of Court and ASP Secretariat	High/Low
• Informal meetings with Court organs	High/Medium
State-directed advocacy/consultative roles	
• Advocating for the universality of Rome Statute	High/High
• Lobbying the ASP	High/Medium
• Enforcement of decisions/warrants	High/Low
Information sharing and operational support	
• Article 15 communications to the ICC Prosecutor	High/Medium
• Intermediaries and sharing information	High/High
• Communications and outreach	High/High
• Organizing legal counsel for victims and defense	Medium/ Medium

* The role of providing information on the execution of judgments is merged with representing petitioners because at the Inter-American Court, the compliance process is more closely aligned with the trial and is performed by the Court. This is in contrast to the ECtHR, where a member state governance body decides issues of non-compliance.

legal counsel, a third-party intervener through filing amicus curiae briefs, or an expert witness.

The typology also demarcates the underlying *target* of the NGO activity for advocacy/consultative roles. Both the scholarship on transnational advocacy and social movements highlight the importance of strategic target selection for advocacy efforts.[22] The typology only includes two targets – states and courts/commissions – because these are the only actors with the authority to change policies regarding international courts. Which actor has the authority depends on the specific policy. For example, elections of judges and prosecutors lie with member states whereas court officials organize victims' programs or draft prosecutorial strategies. States are the only entities that can sign and ratify the treaties or protocols relating to

---

[22] Keck and Sikkink, *Activists Beyond Borders*; David S. Meyer, *The Politics of Protest: Social Movements in America* (Oxford University Press, 2007).

international courts. Thus, states and courts constitute the fundamental targets of NGO advocacy efforts. This does not preclude the fact that NGOs may engage in public advocacy, such as generating societal support for human rights, which could indirectly benefit the courts under examination. However, as these activities could only indirectly affect judicial process, functionality, or outcomes, they are excluded from the analysis.

The typology also includes approximate measures of the *frequency* and the *impact* of NGO participatory roles. *Frequency* consists of the rate of occurrence of the NGO participatory role or how often NGOs are engaging in the role relative to the access granted. Frequency is measured as high, medium, or low. Low means infrequent participation, medium means some participation, and high means sustained and intense participation. This measurement encompasses as best as possible both the intensity of frequency relative to access and the duration of such participation over time. For example, NGOs acting at amici curiae would be measured as the average percentage of all cases for the years that such participation was allowed, barring available data. High frequency of participation would require a preponderance of the cases to have NGO participation as amici curiae for the better part of the years allowed. If either the rate of occurrence was consistently lower or spiked and dropped over time, then the frequency would be measured at a medium level. Low frequency of participation would mean that NGOs generally act as amicus curiae in few cases. Data used to measure frequency of participatory engagement are specific to each particular NGO role but often consist of a combination of interviews with NGOs and court and commission officials and quantitative or qualitative measures using court archives or NGO documents (see Appendixes B, C, and D for specific data and measures). *Impact* assesses the influence of NGO participation on the strategies, administration, functioning, governance, or decisions of the judicial institutions, member states, or non-member states. Impact is also scored as low, medium, or high. Low means mostly symbolic effect, medium means general substantive effect, and high means essential for functionality. Scores of "low" on impact mean that NGO influence is mostly limited to their presence or involvement in the process, such as boosting legitimacy through adherence to norms of civil society inclusion. Scores of "medium" on impact would necessitate NGOs substantively and directly shaping court functionality, governance, or outcomes. Scores of "high" on impact must meet the threshold that the NGO engagement be critical to the court's functionality. Without NGOs engaging in the role, the court would be unable or substantially less able to fulfill its mandate. Data used to measure impact include interview responses from court or commission officials, NGO staff, or member state diplomats. When possible, these personal assessments of impact are verified and triangulated with quantitative or qualitative analyses or statistics (see Appendixes B, C, and D for specific data and measures).[23] The measures of frequency and impact are approximate, as they include only three rough levels and rely on data that are not always comprehensive for all pertinent NGOs across time. Even with these limitations, the measures provide an important metric to evaluate how much NGO participation is occurring and how such participation matters for the examined international courts.

When NGO participation is mapped according to the typology, it is possible to see the disaggregated variation in the facets of NGO participation – roles, frequency, and impact – across the judicial institutions. First, there are differences in the breadth of participatory access afforded to NGOs, which is represented in the absolute number of roles NGOs play across courts. NGOs play five participatory roles at the ECtHR, seven participatory roles at the IAS, and ten participatory roles at the ICC. Looking further, there are also differences in the types of NGO participatory roles across the judicial institutions. NGOs have more avenues to share information and provide various types of operational support at the IAS and the ICC than at the ECtHR. At the ICC, NGOs are significantly more involved with advocacy towards member and non-member states than at the other two judicial institutions. Second, the typology suggests a positive relationship between the number of participatory roles and the associated measures of frequency and impact. At the ICC, NGOs not only interact with the Court, and member states, in the most varied and broad ways, but on average they do so with sustained regularity and in ways that strongly shape, and sometimes are necessary for the viability of, the Court. At the IAS, NGOs also interact with the Court and Commission in multiple ways but the frequency of interaction is less sustained and the impact more variable. At the ECtHR, NGOs have the fewest avenues of participatory engagement with the Court, and this engagement is more infrequent and less substantive.

---

[23] Measuring the impact of strategic litigation (representing petitioners and filing amicus briefs) is particularly difficult. For NGOs representing petitioners, all cases in which a violation, or violations, are found are not equally influential. Some case judgments substantially expand the jurisprudence of the courts, and are often preceded by similar cases in which no violation is found. For NGOs filing amicus briefs, influence on the decision or judgment is also hard to ascertain as the decisions or judgments typically only mention the brief in a cursory manner and the decision-making processes of the judges are not known. The data and measures utilized in this study attempt to mitigate these limitations. To measure the impact of NGOs representing petitioners, the study utilizes both interviews with court officials and analysis of NGO involvement in most important cases (Grand Chamber cases of the Highest Importance at the ECtHR). To measure the impact of NGOs acting as amici curiae, the study largely depends on interviews with court officials as well as content analysis of amicus briefs with chamber's decisions. These measures offer insights into the conditions under which judges take into account the information and arguments provided by NGO amicus briefs.

2

Seeking Voice at the European Court of Human Rights

It was surely Pascal who wrote of his own times: "Not being able to ensure that what was just would have force, one made what was forceful just"... May the member countries of the Council, sharing a patrimony compounded of idealism and political traditions, of respect for freedom and for the rule of law, deserve one day to have said of them: "They succeeded in giving force to what was just."[1]

INTRODUCTION

According to William Schabas, an eminent scholar of international law, the Nobel Peace Prize Committee erred in granting the European Union the 2012 Nobel Peace Prize. Schabas acknowledged that granting the European Union the Nobel Peace Prize was an "inspired choice," but one that leaves out the tremendous contributions of the Council of Europe (CofE) and the European System of Human Rights (Commission and Court or ECtHR) to the long-standing peace in Europe.[2] Schabas is not alone in his praise of the European System of Human Rights. The ECtHR is lauded as "quasi-constitutional," as "effective as a domestic court," and "a far more important body than either the International Court of Justice or even the International Criminal Court."[3] The jurisdiction of the Court

---

[1]   Léon Marchal, Secretary General of the Council of Europe (Inaugural speech at the European Commission of Human Rights, July 12, 1954).

[2]   William A. Schabas, "Why Didn't the Council of Europe Get the Nobel?," *PhD Studies in Human Rights* (blog), October 13, 2012, http://humanrightsdoctorate.blogspot.com/2012/10/why-didnt-council-of-europe-get-nobel.html.

[3]   Ed Bates, *The Evolution of the European Convention on Human Rights: From Its Inception to the Creation of a Permanent Court of Human Rights* (Oxford University Press, 2009): 4; Helfer and Slaughter, "Toward a Theory of Effective Supranational Adjudication"; Eric Metcalfe, "The Birth of the European Convention on Human Rights," in *The Conscience of Europe: 50 Years of the European Court of Human Rights* (London: Third Millennium Publishing, 2010): 16.

is expansive and ensures the human rights of over 800 million people in 47 countries. The Court has delivered over 10,000 cases, which constitute a sophisticated body of jurisprudence that shape and refine individual human rights standards.[4] The European System also served as the institutional model for the Inter-American and African Human Rights Systems.[5]

Recent scholarship lauds NGOs and civil society as foundational to the human rights gains made by the ECtHR. According to Hodson, "much of the momentum of the Court's jurisprudence emerges from the 'struggle for rights', the impetus for which derives from NGO activity."[6] Similarly, Cichowski states: "comparatively speaking, no other international court possesses such a rich history of engagement with and reliance on civil society and public interest representatives."[7] From these accounts, one might assume that NGOs constitute crucial participatory actors with multiple channels of access and influence vis-à-vis the Court. However, when compared with NGO participation at the other examined international and criminal human rights courts, NGO engagement and influence at the ECtHR is relatively limited.[8] NGOs participate in several roles with regard to the Court: representing petitioners, filing amicus curiae briefs, acting as observers in the reform process and consultants to the court registry, and sharing information on the execution of judgments (see Table 2.1). This is not insignificant participation, yet in comparison to the other examined courts, the scope of participatory access available to NGOs at the ECtHR is much narrower and the roles tend to be more formal, demarcated, and restrictive. For the greater part of the existence of the judicial institutions, NGOs have not provided any information sharing or operational support roles outside of formal roles in trials. NGOs monitoring and sharing documentation on the execution of judgments with the Committee of Ministers of the CofE is a recent development that only began in 2010. In tandem with the fewer and more formal roles, the impact of these roles is modest. Except for specific circumstances such as providing comparative law or bringing cases from conflict zones, NGO participation is often more symbolic than substantive. NGOs do bring important cases to the Court, yet NGOs are not the driving force of jurisprudential development nor are customarily responsible for providing crucial services, resources, expertise, or information.

---

[4] Council of Europe, *The Conscience of Europe: 50 Years of the European Court of Human Rights* (London: Third Millennium Publishing, 2010): 162.

[5] Metcalfe, "The Birth of the European Convention on Human Rights."

[6] Hodson, *NGOs and the Struggle for Human Rights in Europe*, 9.

[7] Cichowski, "Civil Society and the European Court of Human Rights," 95.

[8] A focus on NGOs does not discount the potential contributions of *other* non-NGO civil society members such as public interest lawyers, professional associations, and academic institutions. It is possible, and even likely given the thousands of petitions drafted by individual lawyers, that civil society participation at the ECtHR is quite robust but that NGO participation is limited. Future research could measure and evaluate the relative participation of different groups within civil society across international courts.

TABLE 2.1 *NGO Participatory Roles, Frequency, and Impact at the European System of Human Rights*

Types of NGO Participation	Roles	NGO Participatory Frequency*	NGO Participatory Impact*
Formal roles in trials	• Representing petitioners	Low	Medium
	• Filing amicus curiae or "friend of the court" briefs	Low	Low
Court-directed advocacy/ consultative roles	• Biennial meeting with Court Registry	Medium	Low
State-directed advocacy/ consultative roles	• Observing and advocating in reform process	Medium	Low
Information sharing/operational support roles	• Communications to the Committee of Ministers about execution of judgments	Low	Unknown

* Note: For frequency, low means infrequent participation, medium means some participation, and high means sustained and intense participation. For impact, low means mostly symbolic effect, medium means general substantive effect, and high means essential for functionality. For the specific measures and data of each participatory role, see Appendix B.

NGOs play fewer roles at the European System of Human Rights because of a long history of NGO exclusion coupled with the fact that the Court has not needed NGO services to supplement institutional deficiencies. The European Commission and Court were established in the 1950s, a time when NGOs were few and not a dominant form of non-state political action.[9] Even though the European movement – comprised of various voluntary organizations drawn from government, political parties, churches, trade unions, and professionals – sparked the idea of a distinctly European human rights convention, once the idea was taken up by the CofE member states, civil society involvement ceased.[10] As such, NGOs were not

[9] In 1948, only 41 NGOs held consultative status with the UN Economic and Social Council (ECOSOC). In Britain during this period, political parties and trade unions were the dominant organizational forms of political action. See William Korey, *NGOs and the Universal Declaration of Human Rights: A Curious Grapevine* (New York, NY: Palgrave Macmillan, 1998): 2; M. Hilton et al., *A Historical Guide to NGOs in Britain: Charities, Civil Society and the Voluntary Sector since 1945* (New York, NY: Springer, 2012).

[10] Campaign members included European Union of Federalists, United Europe Movement, Economic League for European Co-Operation, French Council of United Europe, Nouvelles Équipes Internationales, and Socialist Movement for United States of Europe. See Mouvement européen (Brussels), *European Movement and the Council of Europe* (London: Hutchinson & Co., 1949): 33–4; Bates, *The Evolution of the European Convention on Human Rights*, 8.

afforded any participatory access, either formal or informal. Over time, these exclusionary rules bred a general norm of exclusion that questioned the motivations of NGOs and their self-identified role as the protectors of human rights – a role Western European states saw for themselves. Even as human rights NGOs grew in number and prominence, and had sufficient resources and motivation to participate with greater frequency or in new roles, these rules and norms of exclusion proved difficult to overcome. In tandem, there was little demand for greater functionality by the judicial institutions. Throughout its lifetime, the European System has had adequate financial resources, state support, and a well-organized administration. Because it is well-run, supported, and financed, there have been fewer opportunities for NGOs to request greater access to assist the Commission, Court, or member states with resources, information, expertise, or services. Few opportunities to seek participation based on functionalist claims resulted in NGOs largely making claims to greater participation based on representing victims and making sure the voices of claimants inform the judicial processes. In some cases, these claims resulted in greater participatory access but the impact of this participation was often more symbolic than substantive.

ORIGINS AND STRUCTURE OF THE EUROPEAN SYSTEM OF HUMAN RIGHTS

The Convention for the Protection of Human Rights and Fundamental Freedoms ("European Convention on Human Rights" or "the European Convention") both enumerates the rights owed to individuals by member state governments and establishes the Commission and Court as monitoring and enforcement bodies of those rights.[11] The treaty opened for signature in 1950 and came into force in 1953 (see Figure 2.1). Even though the Universal Declaration of Human Rights – adopted in 1948 by the UN General Assembly – articulated many of the same rights as the European Convention, the member states of the CofE wanted a specifically European convention that included enforcement mechanisms, which the Universal

---

[11] The individual rights enumerated in the original Convention are: the right to life; the prohibition of torture, slavery and forced labour; the right to liberty and security; the right to a fair trial; no punishment without law; the right to respect for private and family life; freedom of thought, conscience, and religion; freedom of expression; freedom of assembly and association; right to marry; right to effective remedy; and the prohibition of discrimination. Subsequent amendments to the Convention have added additional rights, including the protection of property, the right to education and to free elections, the prohibition of imprisonment for debt, freedom of movement, the prohibition of the expulsion of nations from their state and the collective expulsion of aliens, the abolition of the death penalty, the right of appeal in criminal matters, compensation for wrongful conviction, the right not be tried or punished twice for the same offense, equality between spouses, and a general prohibition on any type of discrimination.

1950	European Convention on Human Rights signed
1953	European Convention comes into force
1954	European Commission on Human Rights established
1959	European Court of Human Rights established
1963	Legal aid program established
1978	First NGO petition for third party intervention submitted and denied
1981	First non-state actor (trade union) granted leave as third party intervener
1982	Amnesty International granted observer status at the CDDH
1983	Revised Court Rule 37(1)—allows Court President discretion to allow third party observations
1994	Protocol 9 adopted—changed standing at Court to include individuals and their legal representation
1998	Protocol 11 adopted—abolished the Commission and made individual petition mandatory
2010	Interlaken Ministerial Conference (meeting on Court reform)
2011	High Level Conference on the Future of the European Court of Human Rights in Izmir, Turkey (meeting on Court reform)
2012	Brighton Ministerial Conference (meeting on Court reform)
2012	Protocol 14 adopted—permits NGOs to share information about state noncompliance

FIGURE 2.1 Historical Timeline of the European System of Human Rights.

Declaration lacked.[12] The desire for such a collective treaty arose from the threat of communism in Eastern Europe and the Soviet Union. Western European countries wanted to enshrine their values of human rights and promote unity and solidarity.[13] The opening declaration of the Convention reads: "Being resolved, as governments of European countries which are like-minded and have a common heritage of political traditions, ideals, freedom and the rule of law, to take the first steps for the collective enforcement of certain of the rights stated in the Universal Declaration."[14] Sir David Maxwell Fyfe, one of the founders of the Convention, described the Convention as a "light" that would be "a beacon to those at the moment in totalitarian darkness and will give them a hope of return to freedom."[15] The Convention was also viewed as a deterrent to potential large-scale human rights abuses occurring within one of the CofE member states.[16] Deterrence would be achieved by states referring one another to the Commission. Even though the Convention included enforcement mechanisms, the member states of the CofE

---

[12] Bates, *The Evolution of the European Convention on Human Rights*; Martyn Bond, *The Council of Europe and Human Rights: An Introduction to the European Convention on Human Rights* (Strasbourg: Council of Europe Publishing, 2010): 6.

[13] Bond, *The Council of Europe and Human Rights*; M. R. Madsen, "From Cold War Instrument to Supreme European Court: The European Court of Human Rights at the Crossroads of International and National Law and Politics," *Law & Social Inquiry* 32, no. 1 (2007): 137–59; Andrew Moravcsik, "The Origins of Human Rights Regimes: Democratic Delegation in Postwar Europe," *International Organization* 54, no. 2 (2000): 217–52.

[14] Council of Europe, "The European Convention on Human Rights," 5, accessed April 11, 2013, www.echr.coe.int/NR/rdonlyres/D5CC24A7-DC13-4318-B457-5C9014916D7A/0/Convention_ENG.pdf.

[15] Bates, *The Evolution of the European Convention on Human Rights*, 5.

[16] David Harris et al., *Law of the European Convention on Human Rights* (New York: Oxford University Press, 2009).

believed that human rights were protected in Western Europe and therefore did not imagine that the enforcement mechanisms would be used against themselves.[17] This idea is reflected in former Court President Wildhaber's statement that during the 1950s and 1960s "the most frequent justification [for not ratifying individual petition] given was that the ratification of the Convention was only an act of pan-European solidarity anyway, as the individual state concerned did not in fact need an international control mechanism, because its national courts had long fulfilled the task of protecting human rights."[18] A focus on symbolic protection and pan-Europeanism is also reflected in the key roles that French and British personnel played in drafting the Convention, although simultaneous to the drafting, both countries were experiencing unrest and human rights concerns within their respective colonies.[19]

The enforcement mechanisms articulated in the European Convention are the Commission and Court, established in 1954 and 1959, respectively. These mechanisms are a means to ensure the legal obligations of states to guarantee the individual rights espoused in the European Convention. The Commission is a quasi-judicial institution that determines admissibility, investigates facts, secures friendly settlements, files reports on breaches of the Convention to the Committee of Ministers of the CofE, and serves as a filtering mechanism for the Court. In the circumstance that no friendly settlement is reached by the Commission, a case can go the Court if referred by a state party or the Commission, granted the respondent states signed the optional declaration to submit to the Court's jurisdiction. From 1953 until the adoption of Protocol 11 in 1998, neither the jurisdiction of the Court or the right of individuals to file petitions with the Commission were mandatory components of the Convention. States could sign optional declarations that submitted to the Court's jurisdiction or allowed individual petition by its citizens.

The CofE is the regional body from which member states are eligible to join the European Convention.[20] It is an intergovernmental body of member states established in 1949 in the aftermath of the Second World War to promote the values of human rights, democracy, and rule of law.[21] It cannot make law but sets standards for the European continent through conventions, or treaties, that member states then sign and ratify. In 1949, there were ten member states of the CofE, but it has since expanded to 47 members and includes Central and Eastern European states as well as Turkey and Russia. The CofE comprises multiple institutional bodies including the Secretary General, Committee of Ministers, Parliamentary Assembly, Congress

---

[17] Alfred William Brian Simpson, *Human Rights and the End of Empire: Britain and the Genesis of the European Convention* (Oxford University Press, 2004).

[18] Bates, *The Evolution of the European Convention on Human Rights*, 11.

[19] Madsen, "From Cold War Instrument to Supreme European Court."

[20] The CofE is distinct from the European Union, and is comprised of a different subset of member states. Protocol 14 allows for the accession of the European Union to the European Convention on Human Rights.

[21] Bond, *The Council of Europe and Human Rights*.

of Local and Regional Authorities, ECtHR, Commissioner for Human Rights, and Conference of International Non-Governmental Organizations (INGOs). The Committee of Ministers – the decision-making body made up of Foreign Affairs Ministers of each member state – is the main body whose authority and institutional purview directly relates to the Court.[22] The Committee of Ministers chooses members of the Commission, elects members of the Court, and determines the budget of the Commission and Court. Subcommittees that work under the Committee of Ministers – particularly the Steering Committee for Human Rights (CDDH) – draft Convention protocols that articulate new reforms to the Convention and the Committee of Ministers takes final action on these protocols. Prior to 1998, the Committee of Ministers had a quasi-judicial role and could determine whether a state had committed a violation of the Convention if the case was not resolved at the Commission level or referred to the Court. Lastly, the Committee of Ministers supervises the execution of judgments reached by the Commission and Court.

The European System of Human Rights – comprising the Commission and Court – has gone through many institutional reforms and differs quite drastically from its inception. As with many treaties, these take the form of protocols, or amendments to the original treaty that must be signed and ratified by member states. With the European Convention, early protocols focused on expanding the rights enumerated in the treaty.[23] However, in the 1990s, the European System began a series of structural and procedural reforms in response to the exponential growth in individual petitions to the Commission. The most notable reform is Protocol 11, which came into force in 1998, and dissolved the Commission in order to make the Court a permanent institution with mandatory individual petition. This means that individual petitions are directly evaluated by the Court and do not need to be referred to the Court by the Commission. The most recent set of reforms is Protocol 14, which came into force in 2010 and was prompted by the substantial caseload and backlog at the Court. From 1999 to 2009, the number of pending applications before the Court rose from 8,400 to 57,200.[24] Protocol 14 adds new admissibility criteria, allows single judges to decide admissibility in certain cases,

---

[22] The other relevant body is the Parliamentary Assembly of the Council of Europe (PACE), which plays an advisory role in approval of the Court's budget. While seemingly relevant, the INGO Conference is not included in this analysis because the collective work of the Conference does not pertain to the ECtHR. As the mandate of the Council of Europe is broader than governance of the ECtHR, there are other issues around which these NGOs collectively mobilize. Because this NGO advocacy could only *indirectly* relate to the ECtHR, it is excluded. The study *does* examine the engagement of NGOs – who may also be members of the INGO Conference – in their roles that *directly pertain to* the ECtHR. For example, the study documents the participatory roles of Amnesty International, a member of the INGO Conference, as amicus curiae in trials and as a consultant in the court reform process.

[23] Protocols 1, 4, 6, 7, 12, and 13.

[24] Council of Europe, "Reform of the European Court of Human Rights," accessed December 8, 2015, www.coe.int/t/DGHL/STANDARDSETTING/CDDH/REFORMECHR/.

TABLE 2.2 *Theoretical Factors that Shape NGO Participatory Roles, Frequency, and Impact at the European Court of Human Rights*

Roles (Access)	• History of NGO exclusion and skepticism
	• Minimal deficiencies of court resources and legitimacy
	• Motivated NGOs seeking new participatory roles
Frequency	• Motivated but variably resourced NGOs
Impact	• History of NGO exclusion and skepticism predominantly resulting in modest or symbolic impact

and adopts measures to deal more efficiently with repetitive cases.[25] Currently, Protocols 15 and 16 are open for signature and consist of additional procedural changes intended to limit the caseload and encourage domestic remedies.

NGOS AND THE EUROPEAN SYSTEM OF HUMAN RIGHTS

A network of human rights and strategic litigation NGOs fervently believes in the premise of the ECtHR as an enforceable court of last resort that can hold states to account and provide redress to victims of human rights abuses. With moderate but competitive funding, these NGOs seek to utilize the Court, influence its jurisprudence, and believe that NGOs should have a formidable voice in shaping how it functions. Nevertheless, NGOs play fewer roles with lesser engagement and impact than at the IAS or the ICC. NGOs only have formal participatory access as participants in trials, observers in the reform process, consultants to the court registry, and purveyors of information on the execution of judgments.

NGO participation at the Court is circumscribed largely because of historical exclusion and diminished necessity. The fact that the judicial institutions operated without NGO engagement for so long made member states and court officials question the appropriateness of NGO inclusion and their principled claims to protect human rights and serve the public interest. The Court and Commission have also enjoyed high levels of state support and adequate funding, which limited the opportunities for NGOs to provide critical services or information that could bolster the institutions and provide new or expanded channels of access (see Table 2.2). All of the NGO participatory roles at the ECtHR came about through non-needs-based avenues, either where NGOs capitalized on rule changes made for other purposes or where NGOs made claims to greater access based on principles. NGOs were able to represent petitioners at the Court and file amicus briefs as third parties because the Court wanted to better take into account the views of applicants and non-party states. States granted NGOs consultative status and the ability to share

---

[25] Council of Europe, "Protocol 14: The Reform of the European Court of Human Rights," accessed April 2, 2013, http://www.echr.coe.int/NR/rdonlyres/57211BCC-C88A-43C6-B540-AF0642E81D2C/0/CPProtocole14EN.pdf.

information on the execution of judgments to satisfy the emergent standard of civil society inclusion at international human rights institutions. Yet with engrained skepticism towards NGOs and the lack of need for NGO information or services, NGO participation often ends up serving as a symbolic demonstration of democratic involvement rather than a driver of court functionality, governance, or outcomes. Only in a few situations where NGOs provide important, but difficult to gather, information or bring conflict-related cases to the Court is NGO participation strongly impactful.

A History of NGO Exclusion and State Support

Both the Commission and the Court were established in the 1950s, a time when NGOs were not global players. NGOs did exist but their numbers and global impact were small.[26] In 1952, NGOs were allowed consultative status at the CofE but NGOs were not involved in the formal drafting of the European Convention and were not afforded any participatory roles at the Commission, Court, or the Committee of Ministers.[27] Even though a European human rights convention was first proposed by the European Movement – an organization of governmental and non-governmental actors campaigning for European unity – the drafting process only included state diplomats and the resultant convention largely operated at the state level.[28] The right of individual petition and the jurisdiction of the Court were both optional and the Commission's reports only operated as non-binding opinions with the final determination made by the Committee of Ministers.[29]

This early exclusion of NGOs from the European System of Human Rights created future difficulties for NGOs when they were able and sought to participate to a greater extent. Two main obstacles impeded NGO access. First, NGO access was written out of the institutional rules and therefore reforms or work-arounds were necessary in order for NGOs to participate through formal channels. Second, the absence of NGOs from the system for so long reinforced the notion that the human rights institutions were inherently *state-based* and that member states, through establishing and abiding by these institutions, were the primary protectors of human rights. This manifested in states and court officials expressing skepticism about the

---

[26] According to Charnovitz "Two Centuries of Participation," the period from 1950 to 1971 was a time of NGO "underachievement" due to Cold War politics and weakness of the United Nations (UN). Additionally, the numbers of international human rights NGOs have grown from less than 50 in the late 1940s to more than 400 in the early 2000s with the largest increase in growth occurring after 1980: Tarrow, *Power in Movement*.

[27] Council of Europe, "Participatory Status | At a Glance," accessed January 9, 2013, www.coe.int/ t/ngo/particip_status_intro_en.asp; Lindblom, *Non-Governmental Organisations in International Law*.

[28] Bates, *The Evolution of the European Convention on Human Rights*, 8, 46.

[29] Bates, *The Evolution of the European Convention on Human Rights*, 8–9.

motivations and appropriateness of NGOs when NGOs sought greater participation based on their principled commitment to human rights.[30]

NGOs have also faced few opportunities to expand participatory channels by providing the Court or Commission vital services, expertise, support, or information. Although the Court and Commission were originally intended to act as symbols of pan-European commitment to human rights and democracy more than operational enforcement mechanisms, the institutions have been historically well-funded and supported. The members of the CofE – in particular Britain and France – strongly supported the institutions of the European Convention from their inception. According to Madsen, the European Convention was the "crown jewel of the Council of Europe and more generally postwar Europe."[31] The United Kingdom, the Netherlands, and Denmark even expanded the Convention to cover many of their colonies and dependencies.[32] By the time NGOs began to see strategic litigation at the European Commission and Court as an avenue to advance their goals in the 1970s and 1980s, the European Commission and Court were well-functioning institutions with adequate funding, administration, and governmental support.[33] In fact, the Commission and Court budget has steadily increased over time and continually occupies a larger percentage of the overall CofE budget (see Figure 2.2). In 1989, the combined Court and Commission's budget represented 10 percent of the CofE budget, in 2001 it represented 15.8 percent, and by 2011 it represented nearly one-third of the overall budget.[34] This is substantially higher than at the IAS, whose combined Commission and Court budget comprise only 6–7 percent of the OAS budget.[35] The exponential caseload increase of the 1990s, and the subsequent case backlog, placed tremendous pressure on the budget but also justified budget increases. PACE made it a priority that the Court was sufficiently

---

[30] Even though the eminent ECtHR judge and President, René Cassin (1959–1968), headed multiple NGOs and established his own NGO, the International Institute of Human Rights (now the René Cassin Foundation) with his Nobel Peace Prize monies, the Court made no efforts to expand participatory access for NGOs during his tenure.

[31] Madsen, "From Cold War Instrument to Supreme European Court," 148.

[32] Simpson, *Human Rights and the End of Empire*.

[33] Madsen, "From Cold War Instrument to Supreme European Court."

[34] These statistics have not been adjusted for the scope of the jurisdiction or the changes in the caseload.

[35] Andreas Føllesdal, Birgit Peters, and Geir Ulfstein, *Constituting Europe: The European Court of Human Rights in a National, European and Global Context* (Cambridge University Press, 2013): 293.

  This comparison is limited by the fact the OAS and the CofE have distinct mandates that differ in breadth. The main pillars of the CofE's mandate are human rights, democracy, and rule of law promotion while those of the OAS are human rights, democracy, security, and development. Nevertheless, the monetary apportionment across these pillars does give some insight into their comparative institutional value.

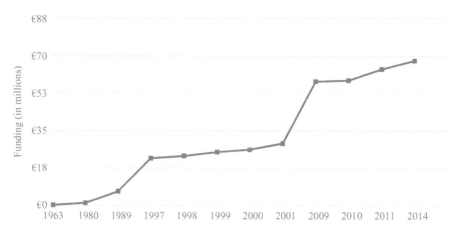

FIGURE 2.2: Historical Funding of the European System of Human Rights (1963–2014)
Source: Annual reports of the ECtHR and the CofE. Funding in French Francs (FRF) has been
converted into Euros at the rate of 1 EUR = 6.55957 FRF to standardize pre-Euro and post-Euro time
periods.

funded even as the CofE budget experienced zero growth during the recent
economic downturn.[36]

State support for the European human rights institutions extends beyond funding.
State compliance with judgments, particularly with respect to financial reparations,
occurs at a very high degree – much higher than at the Inter-American Court.[37] Western
European and EU member countries have rates of full compliance of judgments near or
above 50 percent.[38] Although state obligations have continually ratcheted up
through additional protocols, not a single country has left the European Convention

---

[36] Føllesdal, Peters, and Ulfstein, 293.
[37] Darren Hawkins and Wade Jacoby, "Partial Compliance: A Comparison of the European and
Inter-American Courts of Human Rights," *Journal of International Law & International
Relations* 6 (2010): 35–85.
    Financial reparations to victims is only one kind of measure mandated by the Court. Other
kinds of measures include general measures, such as changing policy or law, which often have
much lower levels of compliance. See: Sergei Golubok, "The Achilles' Heel of the European
Court of Human Rights," OpenGlobalRights, accessed October 27, 2017, www.openglobal
rights.org/the-achilles-heel-of-the-european-court-of-human-rights/?lang=English.
[38] Courtney Hillebrecht, "The Power of Human Rights Tribunals: Compliance with the
European Court of Human Rights and Domestic Policy Change," *European Journal of
International Relations*, March 18, 2014, 12, https://doi.org/10.1177/1354066113508591.
    According to Gerards and Fleuren, the legitimacy of the Court and its judgments is steadfast
even though states occasionally express criticism relating to specific judgments. See: Janneke
Gerards and Joseph Fleuren, *Implementation of the European Convention on Human Rights
and of the Judgments of the ECtHR in National Case Law*, 2014, http://intersentia.com/en/
implementation-of-the-european-convention-on-human-rights-and-of-the-judgments-of-the-
ecthr-in-national-case-law.html.

on Human Rights.[39] Both Russia and the United Kingdom have threatened to leave and have taken steps to empower domestic courts over Strasbourg.[40] Nevertheless, simultaneous to the threats, the countries have mostly complied with Court judgments and have integrated elements of the Convention or the Court domestically.[41]

The Rise of NGO Strategic Litigation

Sustained NGO engagement with the judicial institutions first occurred in the 1970s and 1980s. It was during this time that the stature of NGOs as advocates, monitors, and generators of new human rights law solidified.[42] NGOs also began to see strategic litigation – or the use of the judicial system for social change through test cases – at the European Commission and Court as an avenue to advance their goals.[43] This turn towards strategic litigation largely occurred among civil rights NGOs based in the United Kingdom. Prior to the 1970s, few NGOs utilized strategic litigation strategies and very little information was available about civil rights in British law.[44] UK-based NGOs first began this practice, as opposed to NGOs in continental Europe, for two reasons. First, the UK ratified the optional protocol

---

[39] Member states have withdrawn or been suspended from the Council of Europe for serious violations of human rights and the rule of law (Article 3). Greece withdrew in 1969 (prior to being suspended) and was readmitted in 1974, Turkey was suspended from 1980 to 1984, and Russia was suspended from 2000 to 2001. See: CVCE, "Withdrawal, Expulsion and Suspension of a Member State of the Council of Europe," www.cvce.eu/en/about-us/accessed April 10, 2017, www.cvce.eu/obj/withdrawal_expulsion_and_suspension_of_a_member_state_of_the_council_of_europe-en-f9b31f98-f1a1-407c-97ad-7e92363117fd.html.

[40] BBC News, "UK 'Should Cut Links to the European Court of Human Rights,'" *BBC News*, February 7, 2011; Courtney Hillebrecht, "The Rocky Relationship between Russia and the European Court of Human Rights," *The Washington Post*, April 23, 2014, www.washingtonpost.com/news/monkey-cage/wp/2014/04/23/the-rocky-relationship-between-russia-and-the-european-court-of-human-rights/; "Putin Enables Russia to Overturn European Court of Human Rights Decisions," *The Moscow Times*, December 15, 2015, www.themoscowtimes.com/news/article/putin-enables-russia-to-overturn-european-court-of-human-rights-decisions/552855.html.

[41] The Russian Supreme Court is working to incorporate the European Court's jurisprudence into its rulings. See: Hillebrecht, "The Rocky Relationship between Russia and the European Court of Human Rights."

   The United Kingdom incorporated the entire European Convention into a Bill of Rights known as the Human Rights Act, which enables domestic courts to interpret and rule on human rights violations. See: "Human Rights Act 1998," accessed December 21, 2015, www.legislation.gov.uk/ukpga/1998/42/contents.

[42] Tarrow, *Power in Movement*, 249.

[43] Epp, *The Rights Revolution*; Carol Harlow and Richard Rawlings, *Pressure through Law* (London: Psychology Press, 1992); Austin Sarat and Stuart A. Scheingold, *The Worlds Cause Lawyers Make: Structure And Agency In Legal Practice* (Stanford University Press, 2005): 29.

[44] Epp, *The Rights Revolution*, 141.

allowing for individual petition in the United Kingdom and Northern Ireland in 1966.[45] Second, the UK-based common law legal system is more conducive to strategic litigation than the civil law system. In civil law France: "Most NGOs and activist groups 'despise' the use of Law to fight against exclusion and consider media and political lobbying much more effective."[46]

NGO participation as legal representatives grew as NGOs took advantage of the expansion of individual petition and the rule change that gave individuals standing before the Court. Prior to 1998, states could select whether or not to allow individual petition by their citizens by choosing to declare under Article 25 of the Convention. Individual petition is the ability of an individual to directly file a petition at the Commission or Court claiming a violation of the Convention. If states did not ratify the optional protocol, then the state could only appear before the Commission if another state submitted an inter-state petition. In 1998, Protocol 11 made individual petition mandatory for all member states. Prior to 1983, individuals that filed petitions to the Commission, and had their case subsequently referred to the Court, did not have standing before the Court. This meant that the individual did not have their own legal counsel at the Court proceedings, but was represented by the Commission. In 1983, individuals were given de facto standing before the Court and in 1991, individuals were granted full standing.[47]

The expansion of individual standing at the Court was not a result of NGO pressure and was not meant to specifically grant NGOs access to Court proceedings. The changes were first discussed in the 1960 *Lawless* v. *Ireland* case (no. 332/57, ECtHR 1961) in the context of the Court feeling that because the rights of the individual are at stake, the Court should take into account the applicants' view.[48] Subsequent case law further reinforced this notion, which eventually resulted in revision of the Court Rules in 1983 and amendment to the Convention in 1991 to allow individuals full standing before the Court.[49] NGOs serving as legal counsel to petitioners did not significantly alter the long-standing skepticism of NGO

---

[45] For text of the declaration see: http://conventions.coe.int/Treaty/Commun/ListeDeclarations
.asp?PO=UK&NT=005&MA=999&CV=0&NA=Ex-25&CN=999&VL=1&CM=5&CL=ENG.

[46] Amaya Ubeda de Torres, "Strasbourg Court Jurisprudence and Human Rights in France: An Overview of Litigation, Implementation and Domestic Reform," JURISTRAS State of the Art Report, February 2007: 17, www.juristras.eliamep.gr/?cat=7.
    An example of this can be seen in the approach of French NGOs to disability rights. Even as reforms expanded the opportunity for individuals and associations to bring legal action about discrimination, French NGOs remain adverse to using litigation as a means to pursue their policy goals. R. Daniel Kelemen, *Eurolegalism: The Transformation of Law and Regulation in the European Union* (Cambridge, MA: Harvard University Press, 2011): 229.

[47] Jean Monnet Center for International and Regional Economic Law & Justice, "Access of Private Parties to International Dispute Settlement: A Comparative Analysis – Part IV: The European Convention on Human Rights (ECHR)," accessed December 12, 2012, http://centers.law.nyu.edu/jeanmonnet/archive/papers/97/97-13-Part-4.html#Heading48.

[48] Jean Monnet Center for International and Regional Economic Law & Justice.

[49] Jean Monnet Center for International and Regional Economic Law & Justice.

motivations and principles held by the Court and member states. In an interview, a court official stated: "the Court does not see NGOs as representing victims, it sees them as having an interest."[50] This mistrust about NGOs' motivations is also apparent in the limitations in the rules of standing for NGOs: NGOs only having standing at the Commission or Court if they act as legal representatives to petitioners or if the organization itself has been an alleged victim of a human rights violation. The Court has developed case law that prohibits NGOs from submitting petitions to the Commission or Court on behalf of the public interest and the Court has continuously rejected cases brought forward by NGOs when NGOs could not prove direct harm.[51] This approach to NGO standing by the European System is much more restrictive than at the IAS or the European Court of Justice, which both give NGOs greater standing based on representation of public interests.[52]

By the 1990s and 2000s, the momentum among NGOs towards utilizing strategic litigation in the European System intensified and a network of mostly UK-based human rights NGOs that employed strategic litigation emerged.[53] This network included long-standing NGOs such as Liberty, Justice, and Interights, as well as more recently established organizations that focus on specific groups or issues such as Redress, the Kurdish Human Rights Project (KHRP), the European Human Rights Advocacy Centre (EHRAC), and the AIRE Centre.[54] I refer to this grouping of NGOs as a network because of the connectivity and general characteristics across NGOs. In terms of connectivity, individuals revolve through positions at many of these NGOs and some of the newer organizations were formed by experts who spun-off from more renowned firms to establish their own boutique NGOs.[55] These NGOs also employ similar strategic litigation tactics and join together in a coalition to submit NGO comments on court reforms.[56] Undergirding these shared judicial tactics is a consensus on both the value of the ECtHR as a necessary court of last resort and the need for NGO voices in ensuring it remains accessible and helpful to victims.[57] NGOs continually utilize and seek greater access at the ECtHR because it

[50] Author interview with a Court official, September 27, 2010.
[51] Cichowski, "Civil Society and the European Court of Human Rights," 85.
[52] Lindblom, *Non-Governmental Organisations in International Law*, 272; Mario Mendez, *The Legal Effects of EU Agreements* (Oxford University Press, 2013): 256.
[53] Exceptions to the UK-based trend include the European Roma Rights Centre, Open Society Justice Initiative, and Russian Justice Initiative.
[54] Liberty was founded in 1934; Justice in 1957; Interights in 1982; Redress and the KHRP in 1992; the AIRE Centre in 2002.
[55] For example, the KHRP, the AIRE Centre, and EHRAC were established by individuals who had previously worked at other human rights NGOs that engaged in strategic litigation.
[56] The coalition includes Amnesty International, the AIRE Centre, EHRAC, Interights, the ICJ, Justice and Redress.
[57] Author interviews with a staff member of the AIRE Centre, September 3, 2010, a staff member of a UK-based human rights organization, September 3, 2010, and Catriona Vine of the KHRP, September 9, 2010.

is a "very clear and defined court" with enforcement mechanisms.[58] In other words, the fact that the Court does not have a commensurate alternative drives NGOs to utilize the Court. NGOs also unanimously feel that their organizations should have a more pronounced role because they are representatives of the victims that use the system.[59]

NGO motivation to participate at the ECtHR is strong and consistent, yet donor funding is variable. Resources are more stable and ample for larger, more prominent NGOs involved with the reform process such as Amnesty International, the International Commission of Jurists (ICJ), and the International Federation for Human Rights (FIDH). For smaller, boutique firms that specialize in litigation before the ECtHR, funding has generally been adequate to sustain their work, although at a no-frills level. These firms typically comprise only a few lawyers and interns and they compete with one another for private foundation grants.[60] Funding is not always assured. In May 2014, the long-established strategic litigation NGO, Interights, shut its doors due to lack of funding. Interights was a casualty of a donor trend to favor more short-term tactics such as filing amicus briefs over the gradual gains from representing petitioners.[61] The financial capacity of NGOs to formally participate in trials has also never been remotely commensurate to the astronomical caseload of the Court. In comparative terms, grants by the Ford and MacArthur Foundations to NGOs engaging with the ECtHR have been consistently lower than those provided to NGOs engaging with the IAS, yet in the 2000s, the ECtHR decided on average 10,000 percent more cases than the Inter-American Court.[62]

NGO participation as legal representatives to petitioners occurs with limited frequency and moderate impact. NGOs serve as legal counsel to petitioners in less

---

[58] Author interview with Catriona Vine of the KHRP, September 9, 2010.

[59] Author interviews with a staff member of the AIRE Centre, September 3, 2010, a staff member of a UK-based human rights organization, September 3, 2010, and Catriona Vine of the KHRP, September 9, 2010.

[60] Many of these NGOs receive funding from the same private philanthropic foundations, including the Sigrid Rausing Trust and the Oak Foundation.

[61] Author interview with Helen Duffy, former Legal Director of Interights, September 18, 2014.

[62] In the 2000s, the court decided approximately ten cases per year. Inter-American Court of Human Rights, "Inter-American Court of Human Rights Annual Report," 2009: 7, www.corteidh.or.cr/docs/informes/eng_2009.pdf. Between 2000 and 2008, the ECtHR decided approximately 1,000 cases per year. European Court of Human Rights, "Ten Years of the 'New' European Court of Human Rights 1998–2008 Situation and Outlook," 80, accessed September 20, 2016, www.echr.coe.int/Documents/10years_NC_1998_2008_ENG.pdf.

It is important to note that this comparison is limited by the fact that the MacArthur and Ford Foundations are not the only major donors to strategic ligation NGOs engaging with the ECtHR. Major donors for these NGOs also include European states and European headquartered foundations such as the Sigrid Rausing Trust and the Oak Foundation. However, funding information for these other donors is not available. Even though using the Ford and MacArthur Foundation grant data likely underestimate the financial capacity of NGOs working on the ECtHR, the funding per caseload spread is so dramatic that it would not be greatly reduced with complete donor grant information.

than 1 percent of all of the cases before the Court.[63] Some scholars argue that frequency is not important, but that NGOs have substantial impact in the cases that they bring forward.[64] This is partially true. Court officials credit NGOs with picking good cases that are admissible.[65] With 90 percent of cases deemed inadmissible, getting cases to trial is an accomplishment, and most NGO cases do make it through admissibility requirements.[66] Yet, the overall impact of the cases that NGOs bring forth is moderate when viewed within the context of the entire case history of the ECtHR. In terms of the ECtHR finding violations of the Convention in cases in which NGOs represent petitioners, NGO cases fall below the average (see Table 2.3). Hodson's sampling of 149 ECtHR cases (all levels of importance) with judgments in the year 2000 also finds that NGO cases are less likely than the average to result in a finding of at least one violation of the Convention.[67]

It is possible that this measure of the ECtHR finding violations of the Convention in cases in which NGOs represent the petitioner may not capture the full impact of NGO participation as legal representatives. NGOs could bring forward cases that push the boundaries of the case law of the ECtHR, but which are more likely to be dismissed or not have violations found. To measure this cutting-edge component to NGO cases, I compiled the percentage of the highest importance Grand Chamber cases where NGOs represented the petitioner from 2002 to 2012.[68] In these cases, NGOs represent petitioners in approximately 8 percent of cases and the major NGOs that repeatedly engage in strategic litigation make up 5 percent of the cases (see Table 2.4). As NGOs represent petitioners in less than 1 percent of all cases before the ECtHR, NGOs representing petitioners in 8 percent of the highest importance Grand Chamber cases demonstrates that NGO cases do tend to push forward the jurisprudence of the ECtHR. This is particularly true for the UK-based NGO, Liberty, which has a less than 50 percent rate of success in its cases in judgments finding violations of the Convention, yet represented petitioners in three

---

[63] Author interviews with Court officials, September 21 and 27, 2010. This figure was estimated based upon personal experiences working with petitions and cases. This figure corroborates with data from the ECtHR Database, which include 15,136 judgments spanning the years 1960–2014. During this time period, 60 out of 15,136 cases (0.4 percent of cases) were brought by organizations that could be designated NGOs. The coded designation of these organizations included: rights organizations, women's rights organizations, minority rights, freedom of speech organizations, community organizations, environmental organizations, health organizations, and legal aid organizations. Rachel A. Cichowski and E. Chrun, "European Court of Human Rights Database, Version 1.0 Release," http://depts.washington.edu/echrdb/.

[64] Cichowski, "Civil Society and the European Court of Human Rights"; Hodson, *NGOs and the Struggle for Human Rights in Europe.*

[65] Author interview with a Court official, September 27, 2010.

[66] Author interview with a Court official, September 27, 2010.

[67] *NGOs and the Struggle for Human Rights in Europe,* 63.

[68] All cases in the court's database, HUDOC, are coded by importance. There are four levels of importance ranging from low to medium to high to case reports, which have highest importance.

TABLE 2.3 *Comparison of Cases where NGOs Represent Petitioners to Court Average in Terms of Violations to Convention Found in Judgments*

NGO representing petitioner	Years of cases	percent of cases with judgments where at least one violation of the Convention found
Liberty	1970s–2010	<50
EHRAC	2003–2010	72
The AIRE Centre	1993–2012	78
Average for all cases with judgments	1959–2009	<83

Source: The three aforementioned NGOs were selected because these NGOs had the most reliable data available. The data pertaining to Liberty came from an author interview with a staff member of Liberty on September 15, 2010. This Liberty staff member estimated this percentage based upon their long-standing personal experience at Liberty. Liberty does not have compiled statistics to verify this number. The data pertaining to EHRAC were provided by internal statistics compiled by EHRAC. The data about the AIRE Centre were compiled by triangulating the data from the AIRE Centre's 15 year Report (1993–2008) found at www.google.com/url?sa=t&rct=j&q=&esrc=s&source=web&cd=2&cad=rja& ved=oCDgQFjAB&url=http%3A%2F%2Fwww.airecentre.org%2Fdata%2Ffiles%2Fresources%2F7% 2FThe_AIRE_Centre_Report.pdf&ei=FYXHULnLH5CUigKt2oHgAQ&usg=AFQjCNFWNRrMmw zyfFMioHxMvvKaEoQ3CA&sig2=9B6MaZkdty5ljVt7KIGv6w&bvm=bv.1354675689,d.cGE and a search on the Court's HUDOC database of cases that listed the AIRE Centre as representing the petitioner. I did not rely exclusively on searching HUDOC because during my fieldwork the Court's librarian informed me that the information about legal representatives and third parties are not often accurately inputted into HUDOC. Therefore, I rely more heavily on NGO statistics. The data on the average cases were obtained on page 5 of a Court report entitled, "50 Years of Activity: The European Court of Human Rights: Some Facts and Figures," found at: www.google.com/url?sa=t&rct=j&q=&esrc=s&source=web&cd=1&cad=rja&ved= oCDUQFjAA&url=http%3A%2F%2Fwww.echr.coe.int%2FNR%2Frdonlyres%2FACD46AoF-615A-48B9- 89D6-8480AFCC29FD%2Fo%2FFactsAndFigures_EN.pdf&ei=vojHUJSUE4SdmQW-soCYDg&usg= AFQjCNEg7Z2NxXFGi-D7vcApOJ89r29Jvw&sig2=Qvhjf7TtkeWXyzv8342GEQ&bvm=bv.1354675689,d .dGY.

TABLE 2.4 *Percentage of Grand Chamber Cases of the Highest Importance where NGOs Represent Petitioners (2002–2012)*

All NGOs	8%
Major Human Rights Strategic Litigation NGOs (Liberty, European Roma Rights Centre, EHRAC, KHRP)	5%

Source: The universe of cases was determined by selecting the following criteria on HUDOC: (1) Grand Chamber cases with judgments, (2) case reports' importance and (3) cases decided in the past ten years. The number of cases with these criteria was 129. I selected Grand Chamber cases because cases are relinquished to the Grand Chamber if they raise serious questions about the interpretation of the Convention or risk inconsistency with previous ECtHR judgments. Case reports comprise those cases that are the highest level of importance to the ECtHR and are published in the ECtHR's official reports series.

highest importance Grand Chamber cases in the examined period – the greatest number of any NGO.[69] Nevertheless, these high importance Grand Chamber judgments are not always in favor of the NGOs; in two out the three of Liberty's cases, no violations of the Convention were found.[70]

NGOs do bring forward important cases deemed of high importance to the ECtHR's jurisprudence, yet the vast majority of cases deemed of high importance are not brought by NGOs. In the highest importance Grand Chamber cases, non-NGO lawyers represented the petitioner in 92 percent of cases (see Table 2.4). NGOs do not have greater representation in these Grand Chamber cases of high importance because generally the ECtHR does not need NGOs to supply important and admissible cases. NGO representation is not necessary for individual petitioners because the ECtHR procedures for petition are not arduous and do not require extensive or expert legal knowledge. Individuals can and do utilize legal representatives from their hometown or city.[71] Additionally, since 1963, the Court grants legal aid to needy petitioners, so individuals do not have to seek out NGOs that will take their case on a pro bono basis. A JURISTRAS report on ECtHR jurisprudence regarding Austria confirms the minimal presence of NGOs as legal representatives for petitioners in many CofE countries: "NGOs do not seem to be very actively involved in cases taken to the ECtHR. We [the researchers] tried to conduct a survey among lawyers that have taken relevant cases to Strasbourg and ask them whether they had co-operated with NGOs; only two of the respondents answered this question in the affirmative ... Therefore, no pattern of support by NGOs can be traced ..."[72]

In one circumstance the ECtHR does rely on NGOs to bring important cases: representing petitioners from conflict or post-conflict zones, such as Chechnya, Georgia, Moldova, and South-Eastern Turkey.[73] In conflict zones, there may not be sufficient numbers of lawyers to file petitions on behalf of individuals or state repression may make working with NGOs based in other countries easier and safer. A JURISTRAS report on ECtHR jurisprudence regarding Turkey highlights the collaborative relationship between UK-based NGOs and Kurdish lawyers:

---

[69] The cases are: *Roche v. The United Kingdom* (no. 32555/96, ECtHR 2005), *O'Halloran and Francis v. The United Kingdom* (no. 15809/02, ECtHR 2007), and *Austin and Others v. The United Kingdom* (no. 39692/09, ECtHR 2012).

[70] A violation of Article 8 was found in the judgment of the *Roche* case. No violations were found in the *O'Halloran and Francis* and *Austin and Others* cases.

[71] Local public interest lawyers are also increasingly being trained on how to take cases to the ECtHR. The training is typically conducted by NGOs or universities and is funded by governments or prominent private philanthropic foundations.

[72] Hannes Tretter et al., "Strasbourg Court Jurisprudence and Human Rights in Austria: An Overview of Litigation, Implementation and Domestic Reform," JURISTRAS State of the Art Report, March 2007: 12, www.juristras.eliamep.gr/?cat=7.

[73] Author interview with a Court official, September 27, 2010.

When national remedies were *de facto* inaccessible under the state of emergency regime, Kurdish lawyers sought justice in Strasbourg. Lawyers associated with the bar associations of Diyarbakir and Istanbul, the Istanbul-based Foundation on Social and Legal Studies (Toplumsal ve Hukuk Arastirmalari Vakfi-TOHAV), Human Rights Association and the Human Rights Foundation of Turkey became the pioneers of litigating in Strasbourg and developed the expertise in this regard. In this process, they developed a close cooperation with lawyers in Europe, particularly those affiliated with the Human Rights Centre at the University of Essex and the Kurdish Human Rights Project, both in the United Kingdom. British lawyers associated with these organizations filed scores of petitions, alone or in cooperation with Kurdish lawyers.[74]

Collaboration between Dutch and UK-based NGOs and their Russian counterpoints were also instrumental in bringing cases before the ECtHR on widespread human rights violations during the Chechen wars. Nearly all of the Chechen cases before the ECtHR were taken by human rights NGOs with international connections, most notably the UK-based EHRAC (often in coordination with Memorial) and the Stichting Russian Justice Initiative, an offshoot of Human Rights Watch with offices in Moscow but officially registered in the Netherlands.[75] Both the Chechen and Kurdish cases consider some of the gravest violations of the Convention, including disappearances, torture, and widespread displacement.[76]

Capitalizing on Rule Change: NGOs as Third Parties

Amicus curiae, or "friend of the court" briefs, are a means for third parties to submit information in a case. These briefs consist of written observations meant to influence the outcome of the case either through providing facts, comparative data, or legal rationale. Since NGOs do not have standing at the Commission or Court – unless they are victims themselves – third-party interventions are a means for NGOs to potentially influence important cases in which they do not serve as legal representatives to the petitioners. Similar to representing petitioners before the ECtHR, NGOs as third parties emerged because NGOs were able to capitalize on a rule

---

[74] Dilek Kurban, "Strasbourg Court Jurisprudence and Human Rights in Turkey: An Overview of Litigation, Implementation and Domestic Reform," JURISTRAS State of the Art Report, 20, accessed December 13, 2012, www.juristras.eliamep.gr/?cat=7.

[75] Ole Solvang, "Chechnya and the European Court of Human Rights: The Merits of Strategic Litigation," *Security & Human Rights* 19, no. 3 (2008): 211; Freek Van der Vet, "Seeking Life, Finding Justice: Russian NGO Litigation and Chechen Disappearances before the European Court of Human Rights," *Human Rights Review* 13, no. 3 (2012): 303–25, https://doi.org/10.1007/s12142-012-0226-2.

[76] 69 percent of the 2010 Chechen cases before the Court concerned disappearances. See: Van der Vet, "Seeking Life, Finding Justice," 309. For information on the Kurdish cases, see: Kurban, "Strasbourg Court Jurisprudence and Human Rights in Turkey: An Overview of Litigation, Implementation and Domestic Reform."

change that was implemented for purposes other than allowing expanded NGO participatory access. Participation as third parties was not allowed in the original rules of procedure and evidence of the Commission or Court, but manifested at the Court because member states wanted an avenue for their own interests to be heard in cases in which they were not a party. Third-party participation was never allowed at the Commission, although petitioners could incorporate NGO reports into their submissions.[77] Amicus briefs were not allowed at the Court until 1979 when the United Kingdom wanted to submit written comments in a case against the Netherlands – a case in which it was not a party. In *Winterwerp* v. *The Netherlands*, the Court allowed the United Kingdom to submit comments, but did not officially change their rules of procedure with regard to third-party comments. Prior to the *Winterwerp* case, the British NGO, the National Council for Civil Liberties (NCCL, later renamed "Liberty"), sought to submit information to the Court as a third party in the 1978 *Tyrer* v. *the United Kingdom* case, but was refused without explanation.[78] In 1980, the Court allowed the first non-state actor, the Trade Union Congress, to submit written comments at the request of the United Kingdom in *Young, James and Webster* v. *the United Kingdom*.[79] In 1983, the Court formalized the practice of allowing third-party comments and revised its Rules of Procedure and Evidence to allow the President of the Court discretion to request or allow states or persons to submit written comments within a specific time period and on specific issues.[80] This rule change did not specifically address third-party comments from NGOs, but left open the possibility that NGOs could submit comments, if approved or requested by the President of the Court. In 1984, the Post Office Engineering Union in the *Malone* case was the first non-state actor to submit observations under this new rule. This non-state actor did so with the help of two UK-based NGOs, Justice and Interights.[81] In 1985, the first NGO, the National Association for Mental Health (MIND), was granted leave by the ECtHR to submit third-party comments

---

[77] Lindblom, *Non-Governmental Organisations in International Law*, 328.
[78] Lindblom, *Non-Governmental Organisations in International Law*, 329.
[79] Lindblom, *Non-Governmental Organisations in International Law*, 329.
[80] Rule 37(1) of the 1983 Revised Rules states: "The President may, in the interest of the proper administration of justice, invite or grant leave to any Contracting State which is not a Party to the proceedings to submit written comments within a time-limit and on issues which he shall specify. He may also extend such an invitation or grant such leave to any person concerned other than the applicant." Since the 1983 Revised Rules, the rules regarding third-party comments have been further revised (in 2003 and 2006) to include the possibility that a third party could take part in a hearing (in exceptional cases) and to further refine the time limit specifications for third-party comments. Currently, there is a 12-week window in which third-party comments must be filed and the comments must be limited to ten pages. See: Rule 44(3) of the current Rules of Procedure and Evidence. With the adoption of Protocol 11 in 1998, the rules allowing third-party intervention were incorporated in the Convention.
[81] Andrew Drzemczewski, "The Role of NGOs in Human Rights Matters in the Council of Europe," *Human Rights Law Journal* 8, no. 2–4 (1987): 273–82.

in the *Ashingdane* case.[82] Even though NGOs were successful in establishing a participatory role as third parties, member state and court officials still view NGO and non-party participation as third parties with some suspicion. From 1990 to 2012, the Court denied approximately 46 percent of requests to submit amicus curiae without specifying a cause.[83]

NGO participation as third parties occurs in less than 1 percent of all cases before the ECtHR.[84] NGOs do submit third-party comments more in Grand Chamber cases of high importance. From 2002–2012, NGOs submitted third-party comments in 28 percent of Grand Chamber cases of the highest importance.[85] Even though NGOs strategically choose to request to submit third-party comments in cases of the highest importance and with the most pressing legal questions, the impact of NGO third-party comments is generally minimal and often symbolic in nature. Van den Eynde's comprehensive study of NGO third-party comments determined that the ECtHR found a violation less often in cases in which NGOs submitted third-party comments than the general docket.[86] Lindblom observes that the ECtHR recently adopted a formulaic approach to NGO third-party interventions: the contents of the NGO observations are described in a discrete section of the judgment but the observations are not mentioned in the evaluative section.[87] According to Court officials, NGO third-party comments are regarded as only occasionally helpful.[88]

---

[82] European Court of Human Rights, "SURVEY: Forty Years of Activity (1959–1998)," 134, accessed December 14, 2012, www.echr.coe.int/NR/rdonlyres/66F2CD35-047E-44F4-A95D-890966820E81/0/Surveyapercus_19591998.pdf.

[83] These statistics do not parse out what percentage of the requests are from NGOs; however, it is likely that a good portion are from NGOs. From 1985 to 1998, the ECtHR rejected 29 percent of amicus curiae requests by NGOs and post-1998 there has been an upward trend in NGOs seeking amicus intervention. See: European Court of Human Rights, "SURVEY: Forty Years of Activity (1959–1998)"; Nicole Bürli, *Third-Party Interventions Before the European Court of Human Rights: Amicus Curiae, Member-State and Third-Party Interventions* (Cambridge: Intersentia, 2017): 116.

[84] Author interviews with Court officials, September 21 and 27, 2010. This figure was estimated based upon personal experiences working with cases. This figure corroborates with data from the ECtHR Database, which include 15,136 judgments spanning the years 1960–2014. During this time period, 93 out of 15,136 cases (0.6 percent of cases) included third-party submissions by organizations that could be designated NGOs. The coded designation of these organizations included: rights organizations, women's rights organizations, minority rights, freedom of speech organizations, community organizations, environmental organizations, health organizations, and legal aid organizations. Cichowski and Chrun, "European Court of Human Rights Database, Version 1.0 Release."

It is not possible to ascertain how often the Court refuses leave to NGO third-party comments because after 1998 the Court no longer compiles those statistics.

[85] This statistic was determined by looking through judgments in the following cases on HUDOC: (1) Grand Chamber cases with judgments, (2) case reports' importance, and (3) cases decided in the years 2002–2012. The number of cases with these criteria was 129 and 37 of them had NGOs submit third-party comments.

[86] "Amicus Curiae Briefs of Human Rights NGOs before the European Court of Human Rights."

[87] *Non-Governmental Organisations in International Law*, 343.

[88] Author interviews with Court officials, September 21 and 27, 2010.

In their view, many of the comments often reiterate facets of international law that the registry lawyers already know. A Court official stated that with regard to NGO third-party observations: "Sometimes there is a feeling that NGOs are preaching to the choir – especially if they are not bringing forth any new information."[89] Another ECtHR official stated: "We [the Court] don't need to be lectured by NGOs about general human rights information."[90]

NGO comments can also serve as "argumentative representation" or symbolic representation of a particular viewpoint.[91] This often occurs in polemical cases, such as when dealing with contentious issues like abortion.[92] In these cases, judges may allow an NGO amicus brief for each different viewpoint; however, the comments do not figure in the judicial reasoning or decisions. For example, in the *Pretty* v. *United Kingdom* case about assisted suicide, the ECtHR allowed two NGOs with opposing views to submit third-party comments: The Voluntary Euthanasia Society and the Catholic Bishops' Conference of England and Wales. In this situation, the judge wanted everyone's interest represented as well as a "balance of interest." Therefore, the judge allowed these two NGOs to submit comments and refused leave to other groups that represented either of the same opinions as the allowed briefs.[93] It is important to note that this philosophy on third parties does not extend to states submitting third-party comments – member states are always granted leave to submit comments.[94]

According to ECtHR officials, NGO comments only have impact when they provide novel information, either factual or legal. This is often well-researched, objective, comparative law or technical knowledge.[95] Because Court registry lawyers are overworked with a large caseload, the lawyers do not have time to meticulously gather comparative law research, such as compiling the domestic laws of multiple European countries. In the same vein, registry lawyers are not experts in specific human rights or technical fields, such as Roma rights or global health. Therefore, NGO observations that either articulate comparative law or provide specific expertise can provide a crucial service to the ECtHR and have substantial impact. For example, in the Grand Chamber *D.H. and Others* v. *the Czech Republic* case, multiple NGOs filed third-party observations that included comparative studies and

---

[89] Author interview with a Court official, September 27, 2010.

[90] Author interview with a Court official, September 21, 2010.

[91] Bürli, *Third-Party Interventions Before the European Court of Human Rights*, 31.

[92] Bürli asserts that these types of briefs are a "crude barometer of public opinion" and are most common in cases that relate to three issues: beginning and ending of life; the rights of lesbian, gay, bisexual, and transgender people; and relations between religion and the state. See: Bürli, *Third-Party Interventions Before the European Court of Human Rights*, 31.

[93] Author interview with a Court official, September 27, 2010.

[94] Author interview with a Court official, September 27, 2010.

[95] Author interviews with Court officials, September 21 and 27, 2010.
      This idea corresponds to Bürli's typological categories of the roles of amicus curiae at the ECtHR as "knowledge production" through providing legal expertise and "contextualization," or providing factual information, often on national law or practice. See: Bürli, *Third-Party Interventions Before the European Court of Human Rights*.

statistics about conditions of the Roma population in Central and Eastern Europe. These NGO observations were referenced in the evaluative section of the judgment and were important to the legal outcome.[96] In *Kiyutin* v. *Russia*, Interights submitted a third-party observation documenting the consensus among public health experts and international organizations that restricting the travel of HIV positive individuals is ineffective in preventing the spread of HIV. The judgment referenced this technical information as "undoubtedly relevant" to establishing the common standard from which the ECtHR determined discrimination. In one unprecedented case, the ECtHR even requested that the NGO, Liberty, submit third-party comments in order to ascertain the latest comparative data on laws regarding transsexuals.[97]

Seeking Voice in the Process

Concurrent to rule changes that allowed NGOs to participate in formal litigation at the European System, NGOs sought a voice in court governance. Instead of taking advantage of rule changes, NGOs claimed the right of participation based on their groundbreaking work documenting abuses at the United Nations Commission on Human Rights (UNCHR) in the 1970s and 1980s. Because of the important strides NGOs were making in the promotion and protection of human rights worldwide, states allowed NGOs to have a limited presence at the CDDH. The CDDH – and its predecessor, the Committee of Experts on Human Rights – works directly under the Committee of Ministers to set standards to develop and promote human rights in Europe and to improve the effectiveness of the mechanisms established by the European Convention on Human Rights.[98] The CDDH performs much of the research on possible reforms to the Court and drafts new protocols to the European Convention.[99] As with many of the CofE meetings, CDDH meetings are private and occur behind closed doors. Outside observers, including NGOs, are not allowed access to these meetings unless they are either granted formal observer status or their presence is requested to provide expertise in oral hearings on an ad hoc basis.[100]

In 1982, the CDDH granted observer status to the first NGO, Amnesty International.[101] In a 1982 meeting of the CDDH, Martin Ennals, the Secretary-

[96] Author interview with a Court official, September 21, 2010.
[97] See: *Goodwin* v. *The United Kingdom*, no. 28967/95, ECtHR 1996.
[98] The name of the Committee was changed in 1976.
    The CDDH is composed of high-ranking national officials of each member state and is assisted by a Bureau and a Secretariat. The CDDH also has non-permanent subcommittees created to perform specific functions that relate to issues of the CDDH's work.
[99] The CDDH assisted in the elaboration and coming into force of the additional protocols to the Convention as well as the adoption of the European Convention for the Prevention of Torture and Inhuman or Degrading Treatment or Punishment.
    See: Andrew Drzemczewski, "The Work of the Council of Europe's Directorate of Human Rights," *Human Rights Law Journal* 11, no. 1–2 (1990): 105.
[100] Drzemczewski, "The Role of NGOs in Human Rights Matters in the Council of Europe," 277–8.
[101] Drzemczewski, "The Role of NGOs in Human Rights Matters in the Council of Europe," 277.

General of Amnesty International, was permitted to speak on the contributions of NGOs to human rights. The response of the CDDH to Ennals' speech reflects both suspicion of NGOs as well as an acknowledgment of their critical role in publicizing human rights abuses. The skepticism of NGOs appears to stem from NGOs' work on human rights threatening the prevailing identities of states as the protectors of human rights in Europe:

> Mr. Ennals reminded us that, because they are poor, non-governmental organisations are sometimes perhaps more efficient than governmental organisations and institutions. This may be true; at any rate, there is no doubt that they are poor! It is of course, necessary to bear in mind the particular nature and role of states and their representatives. Clearly, the fact that state representatives are obliged to act cautiously means that they operate quite differently from non-governmental organisations, which can be outspoken. As we all know, diplomatic secrecy has secured the release of many people in the human rights field, and the presence of Mr. Pahr[102] is enough to remind us of this if necessary.[103]

Following the deprecating remarks about NGOs being poor, the same CDDH report acknowledges how instrumental NGOs were in uncovering widespread human rights atrocities in the 1970s and 1980s:

> In connection with the debate about NGOs – bearing, of course, in mind the difference of approach between government experts and NGOs – it is surely impossible to forget, on a day when our main concern is human rights, the decisive role played by NGOs in cases of torture and with regard to missing persons. Despite the coalition of states – which nevertheless belong to opposing blocs – in the United Nations, NGOs – and it may said – they alone, have provided the Commission on Human Rights with crucial evidence which has sometimes led to reprisals, as some states, although guilty, have had no hesitation in demanding the withdrawal of consultative status from the NGOs concerned, such as Amnesty International, the International Movement of Catholic Jurists, and the International Federation for Human Rights and many others, so as to exclude them from this type of intervention. Unfortunately, not until common graves were discovered did the NGOs' accusations come to be considered and fully believed.[104]

Interestingly, two of the three NGOs granted observer status are mentioned in this 1982 CDDH report – although FIDH was not granted observer status until much later. Additionally, all three of the NGOs granted observer status at the CDDH held consultative status with the Council of Europe prior to their admission as observers.

---

[102] This is in reference to Willibald Pahr, Austrian Minister of Foreign Affairs from 1976 to 1983.

[103] L.E. Pettiti, "Seminar on Extra Judicial Means of Protecting and Promoting Human Rights" (Siena, Italy: Council of Europe, October 28, 1982): 8, CDDH (82) 36 def.

[104] Pettiti, "Seminar on Extra Judicial Means of Protecting and Promoting Human Rights," 8.

Both the ICJ and Amnesty International also won the CofE's first two human rights prizes in 1980 and 1983, respectively.[105]

Simultaneous to recognizing the important contributions of NGOs to the world-wide protection of human rights, the CDDH remained wary of NGOs and kept them at a distance from decision-making. Despite the fact that the ICJ received the Council of Europe's first human rights prize in 1980, the CDDH did not approve the ICJ's request for observer status until 1985, when the objections of the Legal Advisor to the Netherlands were resolved.[106] The rules of access for NGOs with observer status are quite restrictive. NGOs can only attend those meetings deemed appropriate by the CDDH, have no voting privileges, and can only submit oral or written comments with CDDH approval.[107] In general, NGO relations with the CDDH are more distant and the CDDH's decision-making is much more difficult to influence than other intergovernmental bodies, such as the UN.[108] Other NGOs have also requested observer status at the CDDH, but have all been denied.[109] In 2004, the NGO, the Conference for European Churches (KEK) requested observer status but the CDDH did not consider it appropriate "so as to not create a precedent which would encourage other organisations, notably representing religious faiths or philosophies, to request the same status."[110] Even though the CDDH specifically mentions the religious nature of this organization as a reason to deny it observer status, the CDDH also denies secular organizations and prefers NGOs attending specific CDDH meetings on an ad hoc basis, rather than granting them observer status.

Representatives of the three NGOs with observer status – Amnesty, the ICJ, and FIDH – are allowed to observe CDDH meetings and the subcommittee meetings on court reform (DH–GDR) as well as attend and request to submit comments to the ministerial-level meetings on court reform. NGOs have submitted comments on the Group of Wise Persons' Report on court reform and have attended and submitted comments at the high-level ministerial meetings in Interlaken, Izmir, and Brighton.[111] NGOs can also lobby, share information, and engage in advocacy

---

[105] Drzemczewski, "The Role of NGOs in Human Rights Matters in the Council of Europe," 277.

[106] Hilde Reiding, "The Netherlands and the Development of International Human Rights Instruments" (Utrecht University, 2007): 64, http://igitur-archive.library.uu.nl/dissertations/2007-0316-202014/index.htm.

[107] Drzemczewski, "The Role of NGOs in Human Rights Matters in the Council of Europe." See also Article 9 of the Rules of Procedure for Council of Europe committees, Appendix 2 to Resolutions (76) 3 adopted by the Committee of Ministers on February 18, 1976.

[108] Reiding, "The Netherlands and the Development of International Human Rights Instruments," 64.

[109] Council of Europe, "Steering Committee for Human Rights (CDDH)," 59th Meeting (Strasbourg, France, November 23, 2004), CDDH(2004)030.

[110] Council of Europe, 18.

[111] Amnesty International et al., "Recommendations to Strengthen the Draft Declaration for Interlaken Ministerial Conference," 2010, www.londonmet.ac.uk/londonmet/fms/MRSite/Research/HRSJ/EHRAC/Advocacy/Joint%20NGO%20Comments%20on%202013%20Jan%202010%20draft%20Interlaken%20Declaration%20250110.pdf; Amnesty International et al.,

outside of the CDDH or the Committee of Ministers meetings. According to a staff member of Amnesty International, even though they do not have a vote, NGOs make their positions known, and are "doing everything to inform and influence the debate."[112] Amnesty was also active in the ratification efforts of Protocols 6, 12, and 13, which relate to the death penalty and non-discrimination.[113] Amnesty urged ratification not only through CofE channels but also through the Organization for Security and Cooperation in Europe (OSCE), the UN Universal Periodic Review, and its national chapters.[114] Amnesty's ratification efforts were limited to these specific protocols and did not extend to new member ratification of the European Convention or significant work on state declaration under Article 25 to allow individual petition.[115]

"Joint Statement for the High Level Conference on the Future of the European Court of Human Rights, Izmir, Turkey, 26–27 April 2011," 2011, www.londonmet.ac.uk/londonmet/fms/MRSite/Research/HRSJ/EHRAC/Advocacy/Joint%20NGO%20Statement%20Izmir%20confer ence%20FINAL%2019%20APRIL%202011.doc; Amnesty International et al., "NGO Comments on the Group of Wise Persons' Report," in *Reforming the European Convention on Human Rights* (Strasbourg: Council of Europe Publishing, 2009): 265–74; Amnesty International et al., "Recommendations Regarding the Draft Declaration for Interlaken Ministerial Conference of 11 December 2009," 2009, www.londonmet.ac.uk/londonmet/fms/MRSite/Research/HRSJ/EHRAC/Advocacy/NGOJointcommentsInterlaken.pdf; Amnesty International et al., "Joint NGO Input to the Ongoing Negotiations on the Draft Brighton Declaration on the Future of the European Court of Human Rights," 2012, www.amnesty.org/en/library/asset/IOR61/005/2012/en/b721f975-c545-4087-90d8-4cbc1501a5d4/ior610052012en.pdf; Amnesty International et al., "Reform of the European Court of Human Rights: Open Letter to All Member States of the Council of Europe Consideration of the Drafts of the Brighton Declaration Must Include Civil Society," 2012, www.amnesty.org/en/library/asset/IOR61/003/2012/en/24bb4499-eaeb-4381-a57b-70b912ba023c/ior610032012en.pdf.

[112] Author interview a staff member of Amnesty International, September 24, 2010.

[113] Amnesty International, "Amnesty International Annual Report 1985," May 1, 1984, 11, www.amnesty.org/en/documents/document/?indexNumber=pol10%2f0004%2f1984&language=en; Amnesty International, "Amnesty International Report 1985," May 1, 1985, 15, www.amnesty.org/en/documents/document/?indexNumber=POL10%2f002%2f1985&language=en; Amnesty International, "Amnesty International Annual Report 1986," January 1, 1986, 16, www.amnesty.org/en/documents/document/?indexNumber=pol10%2f0003%2f1986&language=en; Amnesty International, "Amnesty International Annual Report 1987," January 1, 1987, 19, www.amnesty.org/en/documents/document/?indexNumber=pol10%2f0002%2f1987&language=en; Amnesty International, "Amnesty International Annual Report 1988," January 1, 1988, 18, www.amnesty.org/en/documents/document/?indexNumber=pol10%2f0001%2f1988&language=en; Amnesty International, "Amnesty International Annual Report 2002," May 27, 2002, 293, www.amnesty.org/en/documents/document/?indexNumber=pol10%2f0001%2f2002&language=en.

[114] Amnesty International, "OSCE Human Dimension Implementation Meeting 2006," October 4, 2006, www.osce.org/odihr/21108?download=true; Amnesty International, "Austria: Amnesty International Submission to the UN Universal Periodic Review," January 2011, http://lib.ohchr.org/HRBodies/UPR/Documents/Session10/AT/AI_Amnesty%20International_eng.pdf; Amnesty International UK, "Council of Europe: A Step Closer to a Death Penalty-Free Zone," February 25, 2002, /press-releases/council-europe-step-closer-death-penalty-free-zone.

[115] A review of Amnesty International's annual reports from 1961 to 2002 yielded no discussion of international or national chapter ratification campaigns on new member treaty ratification of the European Convention on Human Rights. Only Amnesty International's 1987 annual report mentions state declarations under Article 25 of the European Convention. The 1987 report

The fact that only three NGOs have observer status at the CDDH – with limited ability to influence decision-making – frustrates excluded NGOs and brings up questions about whether NGO presence is substantive or more symbolic. According to a staff member of an NGO not granted observer status:

> I think the system should be different though. I think civil society should have much more leverage, much more say in the system ... When you think that these NGOs are effectively representing the users of the Court. For states to be able to get together and dream up new ideas without any real engagement of the users, victims are unaccept-able. But this is international relations. We have to muscle our way in. Amnesty has got observer status on the Steering Committee on Human Rights, which is the intergov-ernmental body that meets, and the ICJ and maybe a couple of others. I've been there under the Amnesty hat before ... do they really listen to you? Or actually change their views? Or change their outputs as a result of observer status? It is difficult.[116]

Because only three NGOs have observer status, Amnesty International coordinates with mostly London-based NGOs that represent petitioners before the ECtHR (Amnesty does not represent petitioners) in order to "feed the advocacy."[117] Amnesty and the ICJ report on the CDDH and ministerial-level meetings and coordinate jointly drafted NGO comments on court reforms.

The impact of NGOs acting as observers to the CDDH and providing comments on court reform declarations and protocols is difficult to measure with certainty, but appears limited. The instance where NGOs may have had considerable influence was Amnesty International's early work on Protocol 6. Prior to receiving observer status at the CDDH, Amnesty had long pressured for an optional protocol to the European Convention that would abolish the death penalty under all circum-stances. In 1982, Amnesty was granted observer status and the CDDH brought up and drafted an optional protocol – what would become Protocol 6 to the European Convention – that abolished the death penalty for peace time offenses.[118] Apart from

---

    mentions urging states to seek declarations under Article 25 but does not elaborate on the advocacy methods.

[116] Author interview with a staff member of a UK-based human rights organization, September 3, 2010.

[117] Amnesty and the ICJ work with the AIRE Centre, EHRAC, Interights, Justice, Liberty, Redress, Human Rights Watch, and most recently, Open Society Justice Initiative and the Helsinki Foundation for Human Rights.

    Author interview with a staff member of Amnesty International, September 24, 2010.

[118] The extent of Amnesty's influence in the CDDH taking up, and subsequently drafting, a protocol on the death penalty at this time is uncertain. There is no public record of Amnesty submitting recommendations on the draft protocol. However, it is unlikely that Amnesty's advocacy and subsequent admittance to CDDH meetings would be purely coincidental to the CDDH taking up the issue. See: Amnesty International, "Amnesty International Annual Report 1983," January 1, 1983: 13, www.amnesty.org/en/documents/document/?indexNumber=pol10%2f0001%2f1983&language=en.

Amnesty's advocacy relating to Protocol 6 in the 1980s, there is no record of significant NGO involvement in the drafting of subsequent protocols until the institutional reform protocols of the 2000s.[119]

According to Jill Heine, the Legal Advisor for Amnesty International, NGOs were not successful in shaping Protocol 14, which was drafted by the CDDH in 2004.[120] NGOs also have limited influence at the ministerial-level meetings on court reform.[121] Written NGO comments on the draft declaration of the 2010 ministerial-level meetings on court reform in Interlaken proposed two main recommendations. First, civil society should be consulted on generating new reform proposals and implementing these reforms. Second, access to petitioners should not be inhibited in any way, such as mandating petitioners to use lawyers or by establishing fees to file a petition.[122] The resulting Interlaken declaration was in line with NGO recommendations: discussion of future civil society consultation was included and specific references mandating lawyers and fees were excluded.[123] Nevertheless, the ministerial-level meeting in Izmir, Turkey in 2011 reversed many of the NGO gains at Interlaken. The Izmir declaration proposed fees and other procedures that could limit court access by petitioners.[124] Additionally, only NGOs with observer status at the CDDH were allowed to attend at Izmir – no further civil society consultation occurred. NGOs also had mixed success in influencing the court reform process at the subsequent 2012 ministerial-level meeting in Brighton. Open Society Justice Initiative (OSJI) made a public declaration lambasting the Brighton meetings for not including any representatives of civil society from Russia

---

[119] A review of publicly available annual reports from the ICJ – 1986–1988 and 1995 – uncovered no mention of the ICJ's work at the CDDH. A review of Amnesty International's annual reports from 1961 to 2000, yields only one other instance of Amnesty's involvement in drafting court reforms at the CDDH apart from its work on Protocol 6. In 1993, Amnesty submitted recommendations for a protocol on the "rights of people deprived of their liberty" that ultimately failed, and to which Amnesty discouraged states from signing. See: Amnesty International, "Amnesty International Annual Report 1994," January 1, 1994, 42, www.amnesty.org/en/documents/document/?indexNumber=pol10%2f0002%2f1994&language=en; Amnesty International, "Amnesty International Annual Report 1987," 19.

[120] Christina G. Hioureas, "Behind the Scenes of Protocol No. 14: Politics in Reforming the European Court of Human Rights," *Berkeley Journal of International Law* 24, no. 2 (2006): 37.

[121] This refers to the meetings of the Committee of Ministers of the CofE.

[122] Amnesty International et al., "Recommendations Regarding the Draft Declaration for Interlaken Ministerial Conference of 11 December 2009"; Amnesty International et al., "Recommendations to Strengthen the Draft Declaration for Interlaken Ministerial Conference."

[123] Council of Europe Committee of Ministers, "Interlaken Declaration," February 19, 2010, https://wcd.coe.int/ViewDoc.jsp?id=1591969.

[124] Council of Europe Committee of Ministers, "Izmir Declaration," April 27, 2011, https://wcd.coe.int/ViewDoc.jsp?Ref=IzmirDeclaration&Language=lanEnglish&Ver=original&Site=COE&BackColorInternet=DBDCF2&BackColorIntranet=FDC864&BackColorLogged=FDC864.

or Eastern Europe, as well as not providing civil society with updated draft declarations.[125] The joint NGO comments on the draft declaration stressed three points: not limiting the access of the ECtHR, not amending the Convention to include legal tools of subsidiarity and margin of appreciation, and placing future reforms on hold.[126] Again, the Brighton declaration only partially conformed to NGO recommendations. Many of the proposals to limit access were not included, but the declaration did propose to change the timeframe to file a petition from six months to four months. The declaration did not remove discussion of amending the Convention with regard to subsidiarity and the margin of appreciation, but stated they should be moved to the preamble. Lastly, the declaration proposed drafting Protocols 15 and 16, not heeding NGO advice to place a hold on future reforms.[127]

NGOs vary on how much they think their involvement impacts the ECtHR reform process. A staff member of Amnesty International believes that NGOs have impact and that governments pay attention to what they say and share many of the concerns that Amnesty raises.[128] A staff member of Liberty – a member of the coalition of NGOs that coordinates with Amnesty on reform issues – believes that NGO presence is more symbolic and is important because it represents an alternative voice to that of states.[129] A staff member of a London-based human rights organization takes a more pessimistic standpoint and believes that NGO work on court reform is important but may not be very impactful: "We meet them and do formal submissions about changes to the Court. I think that it has been important. It does seem to be a difficult process. It is an intergovernmental body – states run it and decide what changes to make. Can civil society get a look in and be influential? I have my doubts."[130]

Even with the expansion of NGO participatory roles at the European System, states still view themselves, not human rights NGOs, as the foremost protectors and proponents of human rights in Europe. In an interview, an official of the CofE mirrored the founders of the European Convention and spoke of the "usual suspects" – Russia and Eastern European countries – that undermined the human rights agenda of the CofE. This official believed that the role of the ECtHR should

[125] James Goldston, "European Court Reform: Civil Society Excluded from Debate | Open Society Foundations," April 11, 2012, www.opensocietyfoundations.org/voices/european-court-reform-civil-society-excluded-debate.

[126] Amnesty International et al., "Joint NGO Input to the Ongoing Negotiations on the Draft Brighton Declaration on the Future of the European Court of Human Rights."

[127] Council of Europe Committee of Ministers, "Brighton Declaration," April 20, 2012, https://wcd.coe.int/ViewDoc.jsp?Ref=BrightonDeclaration&Language=lanEnglish&Ver=original&Site=COE&BackColorInternet=DBDCF2&BackColorIntranet=FDC864&BackColorLogged=FDC864.

[128] Author interview with a staff member of Amnesty International, September 24, 2010.

[129] Author interview with a staff member of Liberty, September 15, 2010.

[130] Author interview with a staff member of a UK-based human rights organization, September 3, 2010.

be to protect individuals from grievous and large-scale human rights abuses that were occurring in Russia and Eastern Europe, not the length of trial proceedings and lesser issues that were being brought against Western European countries. In terms of the role of NGOs, the official stated NGOs were important in gathering on-the-ground information and sharing it with the states, particularly about the crimes committed by the "usual suspects," but that their role was supplemental to the role of states in ensuring and protecting human rights in Europe.[131]

In addition to consultations with the Committee of Ministers, NGOs have a formal channel to consult with the ECtHR through attending a biennial meeting with the senior registrars of the Court.[132] A wide swath of NGOs that represent petitioners and submit third-party observations attend these meetings – attendance is not restricted to select NGOs.[133] However, these meetings do not represent a great participatory point of access for NGOs to influence the ECtHR. According to an ECtHR official, the Court maintains a dialogue with NGOs but that the dialogue is not particularly fruitful in terms of NGOs shaping Court procedures. Prior to these meetings, NGOs put forward issues for the meeting agenda, which almost always includes why the ECtHR does not give more explanatory reasons for its judgments. An ECtHR official says this repeated NGO request makes NGOs appear unrealistic and out of touch with the overwhelming caseload of the Court.[134] NGOs also feel that many of these meetings are routine and unproductive. A staff member of a UK-based human rights organization describes these meetings as follows: "They [the Court] do have consultation meetings ... there is an NGO consultation meeting in Strasbourg in October. I have my doubts about how useful they are actually. There will be a discussion ... and there will be people from the Court there to answer questions that you raise. But, I think some of it is ritualistic ... we have to consult with NGOs. This is our day of consultation."[135] On occasion, NGOs have additional opportunities to share their opinions and recommendations with the ECtHR. For

[131] Author interview with an official from the CofE, September 30, 2010.
[132] NGO staff members also have informal, personal relationships with lawyers at the ECtHR registry. These relationships formed through continual contact with one another over cases in which NGOs represented petitioners. In interviews, several NGOs mentioned these informal relationships, but none described them as avenues to influence Court procedure or outcomes. An ECtHR official confirmed that these relationships exist, but emphasized that these relationships were personal, not institutional, and felt that they would be problematic if they were institutional. Author interviews with: a Court official, September 21, 2010; a staff member of the AIRE Centre, September 3, 2010; a staff member of a UK-based human rights organization, September 3, 2010; and Catronia Vine, Legal Director of the KHRP, September 9, 2010.
[133] European Court of Human Rights, "Séminaire Organisé à l'occasion Du 10è Anniversaire de l'entrée En Vigueur Du Protocole N° 11 à La Convention Européenne Des Droits de l'homme: Liste Des ONGs," 2008, www.echr.coe.int/NR/rdonlyres/AF0368E7-DF14-4D5B-921D-C342C44E4C44/0/2008__Liste_des_ONG_13_10_2008.pdf.
[134] Author interview with a Court official, September 27, 2010.
[135] Author interview with a staff member of a UK-based human rights organization, September 3, 2010.

example, in 2010 the Registry invited submissions on the development of the rules on the Pilot Judgment Procedure, one of the ECtHR reforms. In response, Amnesty International, EHRAC, and the AIRE Centre submitted joint recommendations directly to the Court Registrar.[136]

Aiding the Execution of Judgments

The Committee of Ministers of the CofE supervises the execution of judgments made by the ECtHR. As part of the reforms to decrease the growing backlog of the Court and the delays in execution of judgments, Protocol 14 revised Article 46 of the Convention and gave the Committee of Ministers new authorities and procedures regarding the execution of judgments. To implement these reform procedures, the Committee of Minsters drafted new rules regarding the execution of judgments. One of these new rules – a small portion of the larger reforms – grants NGOs the right to submit information to the Committee of Ministers on state compliance with measures dictated in the judgment (this can include structural reforms or monetary damages).[137] This rule was adopted in 2006, but did not come into force until June 1, 2010, when Protocol 14 entered into force.

This new point of NGO participatory access appears to be the result of NGO input and lobbying as observers at the CDDH of the Committee of Ministers. In May 2005, the AIRE Centre, Amnesty International, and EHRAC, submitted to the CDDH a jointly drafted six-page document of recommendations "to facilitate inclusion of civil society in ensuring the implementation of judgments of the European Court of Human Rights and debates on the future of the Court."[138] A portion of this document responded to the draft Rules of the Committee of Ministers on the execution of judgments written by the CDDH. Based upon this NGO document, the 2005 draft Rules did not include a rule that allowed NGO communications.[139] The NGO document advocated for the inclusion of such a rule based on symbolic claims that civil society represents petitioners and advocates for

---

[136] Amnesty International, European Human Rights Advocacy Centre, and The AIRE Centre, "Submission Regarding Rules of the European Court of Human Rights on the Pilot Judgment Procedure," June 30, 2010, TIGO IOR 61/2010.009.

[137] Rule 9.2 of the Rules of the Committee of Ministers for the supervision of the execution of judgments states: "The Committee of Ministers shall be entitled to consider any communication from non-governmental organisations, as well as national institutions for the promotion and protection of human rights, with regard to the execution of judgments under Article 46, paragraph 2, of the Convention."

[138] AIRE Centre, Amnesty International, and European Human Rights Advocacy Centre, "Recommendations to the Council of Europe on Implementing Judgments," May 20, 2005, www.londonmet.ac.uk/research-units/hrsj/affiliated_centres/ehrac/advocacy/recommenda tions-to-the-council-of-europe-on-implementing-judgments/home.cfm.

[139] It is not possible to corroborate this with the actual 2005 draft, as all drafts of the Rules of the Committee of Ministers written by the CDDH are confidential and not publicly accessible.

the public interest.[140] These claims translated to success and the subsequent May 2006 final version of the rules adopted by the Ministers' Deputies included Rule 9.2, which allows NGO submissions about state enforcement of judgments.[141] As the CDDH meeting minutes are not publicly available, it is not possible to know why member states allowed NGOs to take on this new participatory role. It is likely that NGOs were afforded this new role because it fits with the principle of civil society representation and inclusion in the reform process. This principle of civil society inclusion and representation is espoused in almost all of the reform documents.[142]

Since June 1, 2010, NGOs have submitted over 300 communications to the Committee of Ministers regarding the execution of judgments in 28 different countries.[143] Some of the NGOs that submitted these communications also participate in other ways, such as representing petitioners, filing third-party interventions, or acting as observers to the ECtHR reform process. NGOs who have submitted communications include: Human Rights Watch, Amnesty International, Open Society Justice Initiative, the European Roma Rights Centre, EHRAC, the Helsinki Foundation, and the AIRE Centre. Although hundreds of communications may seem like a substantial contribution, when viewed within the larger caseload of the Court, it is very small. To understand the extent of the Court's caseload – in particular completed cases that are waiting for states to execute the judgments – in 2014, the Committee of Ministers closed 1,502 cases and had 10,904 pending cases that were awaiting execution of judgment.[144] Granted, many of the NGO communications

---

[140] AIRE Centre, Amnesty International, and European Human Rights Advocacy Centre, "Recommendations to the Council of Europe on Implementing Judgments."

[141] Council of Europe Committee of Ministers, "Rules of the Committee of Ministers for the Supervision of the Execution of Judgments and of the Terms of Friendly Settlements (Article 46, Paragraphs 2 to 5, and Article 39, Paragraph 4, of the European Convention on Human Rights)," May 10, 2006, https://wcd.coe.int/ViewDoc.jsp?Ref=CM/Del/Dec%282006%29964/4.4&Language=lanEnglish&Ver=app4&Site=COE&BackColorInternet=9999CC&BackColorIntranet=FFBB55&BackColorLogged=FFAC75.
    Interestingly, Rule 9 (which includes the provision allowing for NGO communications) was at first not approved by the Ministers' Deputies. Only after a compromise was the Rule adopted. Because the draft version of the Rules as well as proposed versions by the Ministers' Deputies are confidential and are not publicly accessible, it is not possible to know whether Rule 9.2 was part of the objection, or not. Ministers' Deputies of the Council of Europe, "Notes on the Agenda, 964 Meeting, 10 May 2006," May 10, 2006, CM/Notes/964/4.4 5 May 2006.

[142] Council of Europe Committee of Ministers, "Interlaken Declaration"; Council of Europe Committee of Ministers, "Izmir Declaration"; Council of Europe Committee of Ministers, "Brighton Declaration"; Council of Europe, "Protocol 14: The Reform of the European Court of Human Rights."

[143] These data are current as of December 2015. See: www.coe.int/t/cm/System/WCDsearch.asp?ShowRes=yes&FilingPlan=fplCM-Supervision9_2&Language=lanEnglish&ShowBreak=yes&SortBy=Geo&Sector=secCM&ShowFullTextSearch=yes&ResultTitle=Information%20from%20NGOs%20and%20National%20human%20rights%20institutions#.

[144] Committee of Ministers of the Council of Europe, "Supervision of the Execution of Judgments and Decisions of the European Court of Human Rights," 2014: 27, www.coe.int/t/dghl/monitoring/execution/Source/Publications/CM_annreport2014_en.pdf.

relate to controversial and important cases, such as those that involve prisoner voting rights and police investigations. However, in cases that one might expect NGO monitoring, such as abortion and trafficking, no NGOs have submitted communications.[145]

It is uncertain whether NGO communications have any impact on the execution of judgments. The Committee of Ministers needs current information on the status of the execution of judgments in order to supervise their completion.[146] Through submitting communications, NGOs may help provide this necessary information. Nevertheless, the information NGOs provide must be helpful and reliable and the Committee of Ministers must be willing to pay attention to such information. A handbook for NGOs now provides information on how to best monitor the execution of judgments and provide quality information to the Committee of Ministers.[147] Assuming that the NGO-provided information is helpful and reliable, it is questionable whether the Committee of Ministers would utilize the information. The system has operated without NGOs for so long that state representatives may not take the time to consider NGO contributions.[148]

Alternatively, NGO communications may work to foster compliance through domestic channels.[149] If NGOs have informal channels of communication with officials in their home governments, the same report submitted to the Committee of Ministers could be shared with government officials. The French NGO, ANAFE, who has a strong reputation as an expert on migration, shares communications with

---

[145] Lucja Miara and Victoria Prais, "The Role of Civil Society in the Execution of Judgments of the European Court of Human Rights," *European Human Rights Law Review* 5 (2012): 528–37.
   The aforementioned cases with NGO communications include: *Hirst v. the United Kingdom* and *McKerr v. the United Kingdom*. The cases without NGO communications include: *A v. Ireland* and *Rantsev v. Cyprus*.

[146] E. Lambert-Abdelgawad, *The Execution of Judgments of the European Court of Human Rights* (Council of Europe, 2008): 497.

[147] Basak Cali and Nicola Bruch, *Monitoring the Implementation of Judgments of the European Court of Human Rights: A Handbook for Non-Governmental Organisations*, 2011, https//ecthr project.files.wordpress.com/2011/07/monitoringhandbook_calibruch1.pdf.

[148] Author interview with an academic that studies the implementation of judgments at the ECtHR, October 1, 2010.

[149] While not included in this analysis, NGOs may indirectly contribute to compliance of ECtHR judgments by fostering general public support for human rights principles. See: Sebastian Müller and Christoph Gusy, "The Interrelationship between Domestic Judicial Mechanisms and the Strasbourg Court Rulings in Germany," in *European Court of Human Rights: Implementing Strasbourg's Judgments on Domestic Policy*, ed. Dia Anagnostou (Edinburgh University Press, 2013): 40; Kerstin Buchinger, Barbara Liegl, and Astrid Steinkellner, "European Human Rights Case Law and the Rights of Homosexuals, Foreigners and Immigrants in Austria," in *European Court of Human Rights: Implementing Strasbourg's Judgments on Domestic Policy*, ed. Dia Anagnostou (Edinburgh University Press, 2013): 113.

the French government and works with it on policy reforms.[150] NGO communications could also be used to name and shame states to domestic constituents or other governments, who would then pressure the government to execute the judgment and change human rights practices.[151] For example, NGOs who litigated before the ECtHR regarding disappearances in the North Caucuses worked with the CofE Parliamentary Assembly Committee on Legal Affairs and Human Rights on a report about Russian non-execution of judgments.[152] Nevertheless, lack of information is only one impediment to the successful execution of judgments. Political, budgetary, and logistical problems also contribute to the substantial lag in implemented judgments.[153]

CONCLUSION

At the European System of Human Rights, restricted NGO participatory roles and modest impact of these roles largely result from two compounding factors: historical exclusion and strong state support and adequate resources. As there were few openings for NGOs to request new participatory channels based on the functionalist needs of the ECtHR, motivated NGOs sought alternate routes to new forms of participation including taking advantage of rule changes and making claims to civil society and victims' representation. These alternate routes opened new channels of access, but did not yield robust NGO participatory roles in number or impact. Skepticism towards NGOs by member states and the judicial institutions remained and largely relegated NGO engagement to symbolic participants rather than actors with the ability to prominently shape the functioning, governance or judicial outcomes of the system. Yet in a few situations – such as representing petitioners from conflict or post-conflict zones or providing the Court with comparative law or specialized expertise as third parties – NGOs do provide much needed information or services. It is also in these situations that NGO participation is most substantive and influential. It remains to be seen whether NGOs sharing information on the execution of judgments will become a similar service utilized and relied upon by member states.

---

[150] Shai Dothan, "A Virtual Wall of Shame: The New Way of Imposing Reputational Sanctions on Defiant States," SSRN Scholarly Paper (Rochester, NY: Social Science Research Network, May 3, 2016): 40, http://papers.ssrn.com/abstract=2774040.

[151] Hillebrecht, *Domestic Politics and International Human Rights Tribunals*, 24; Emilie M. Hafner-Burton, "Sticks and Stones: Naming and Shaming the Human Rights Enforcement Problem," *International Organization* 62, no. 4 (2008): 689–716, https://doi.org/10.1017/S0020818308080247.

[152] Lisa McIntosh Sundstrom, "Advocacy Beyond Litigation: Examining Russian NGO Efforts on Implementation of European Court of Human Rights Judgments," *Communist and Post-Communist Studies*, Disintegration of the Soviet Union. Twenty Years Later. Assessment. Quo Vadis?, 45, no. 3–4 (September 2012): 263, https://doi.org/10.1016/j.postcomstud.2012.06.003.

[153] Lambert-Abdelgawad, *The Execution of Judgments of the European Court of Human Rights*.

In the future, it is likely that NGOs will continue to engage in strategic litigation and seek to bring innovative cases to the Court that challenge existing jurisprudence. According to a ECtHR official, the AIRE Centre, an NGO based in the United Kingdom, is "chasing ambulances" on the age of consent laws in the United Kingdom.[154] NGOs I spoke with also had specific issues – such as discrimination and human trafficking – that they would like to take before the ECtHR and were seeking out strategic cases that would allow them to do so.[155] NGO requests to file third-party observations will likely also increase. NGOs highlight the fact that filing third-party observations is a cost-effective way to participate in more cases than representing petitioners.[156] This desire to file more third-party observations is coupled with the fact that the ECtHR has improved its case database, which makes NGOs better able to monitor cases that would be of interest to them. It is unclear whether NGOs' third-party observations will become more influential. NGOs did not discuss any plans to alter the content of their observations, and one NGO noted that they do not consider whether their third-party observations change the judges' minds or whether judges already think that way.[157]

Future expanded NGO participatory access does not look promising. Even the crushing caseload of the past decade did not prompt the ECtHR or member states to seek out or rely more heavily upon services, resources, information, or expertise that NGOs could provide.[158] If expanded NGO access does occur in the future, it will likely center on a select few NGOs. Among court officials and member state diplomats, some NGOs have developed sterling reputations, while others are viewed with reproach. For example, the NGO, KHRP, has repeatedly represented PKK fighters, which has put the ECtHR in the politically tenuous position of paying legal aid to Kurdish guerilla fighters that "are on the wrong side of criminal law." In order to not directly give funds to the PKK, the ECtHR used an intermediary in the United Kingdom, who then transferred the funds to the petitioners.[159] Conversely, other NGOs are known to regularly provide meticulous and comprehensive comparative data to the ECtHR. This reputational variation among NGOs may discourage general openings for new participatory roles for NGOs in favor of increased participation or closer relationships with select NGOs with well-regarded

---

[154] Author interview with a Court official, September 27, 2010.

[155] Author interviews with Catriona Vine of the KHRP, September 9, 2010, and with a staff member of the AIRE Centre, September 3, 2010.

[156] Author interviews with a staff member of a UK-based human rights organization, September 3, 2010 and a staff member of the AIRE Centre, September 3, 2010.

[157] Author interviews with a staff member of the AIRE Centre, September 3, 2010; a staff member of Liberty, September 15, 2010; and a staff member of Amnesty International, September 24, 2010.

[158] In 2012, the Court has 150,000 pending applications. See: European Law Institute, "Statement on CASE-OVERLOAD AT THE EUROPEAN COURT OF HUMAN RIGHTS," July 6, 2012: 12, www.europeanlawinstitute.eu/home/. (Current as of January 31, 2012.)

[159] Author interview with a Court official, September 27, 2010.

reputations. To some extent, this has already occurred with the select three NGOs – Amnesty International, the ICJ, and FIDH – receiving observer status at the CDDH meetings. While this does not represent as pronounced a situation of NGO gate-keeping as occurs at the ICC, it does restrict some NGO voices and amplify others.

It is also possible that the heretofore stable motivations underlying NGO participation may shift and NGOs could scale back engagement vis-à-vis the ECtHR. Historically, NGOs have sought greater access at the European System because it was a court of last resort with no comparable alternative. But, as countries like the United Kingdom have incorporated the European Convention into domestic law through the Human Rights Act, NGOs may focus their attention on domestic advocacy and litigation as opposed to focusing on the Court in Strasbourg. This is already beginning to occur in select situations. The UK-based NGO, Liberty, currently favors strategic litigation in domestic courts under the Human Rights Act over litigating at the ECtHR.[160]

---

[160] Author interview with a staff member of Liberty, September 15, 2010.

3

Revitalizing the Inter-American Human Rights System

In 1975, WOLA was looking for allies. Human rights was a voice crying in the wilderness. WOLA approached Charlie Moyer, who was eager to cooperate ... WOLA had hundreds of case dossiers from Argentina, we physically carried them to Charlie, set them on his desk and said: 'Do something'.[1]

INTRODUCTION

On December 15, 2010, the Organization of American States (OAS) held a celebration in honor of Human Rights Day. In the stately OAS building a few blocks from the White House, three prominent officials delivered speeches on the progress and pitfalls of human rights in the Americas. Their words and professional positions wove a prescient story of budgetary challenges, inconsistent state support, and civil society triumphs. To a salon of diplomats and policy experts, the Secretary General of the OAS, José Miguel Insulza, delivered unvarnished introductory remarks stating that the Inter-American Human Rights System (IAS) was precarious, incomplete, and plagued by yearly financial problems.[2] The challenges of the System were also prominent in the speech by Santiago Canton, the Executive Secretary of the Inter-American Commission. His comments on the budget appeared almost like a public reprimand and shaming of the OAS officials in the audience as he successively announced that neither the Court or Commission have the budget to complete their mandate and urged member states to contribute financially – he then thanked the United States, Spain, France, and Mexico for providing funding to allow the institutions to operate. Canton not only attempted to shame OAS member states from underfunding the human rights system, but also subtly addressed the English-speaking countries of the

---

[1] Author interview with Joseph Eldridge, co-founder of WOLA, December 9, 2010. WOLA is the Washington Office on Latin America.

[2] All references to the speeches of the OAS Human Rights Day are derived from notes taken by the author at the event.

Americas, including the United States, by highlighting the need for all states to ratify the Convention. This comment was particularly audacious as the previous speaker was a US official, Maria Otero, who did not mention the American Convention in her remarks – a Convention to which the United States is not a party.

Another thematic thread heard in the speeches was the pronounced role of civil society in the IAS. Canton referred to civil society as one of the key pillars of the IAS and stated, "If not for civil society, the system would be an empty shell with no contents." Canton acclaimed the IAS for securing the human right to freedom of expression, collective land ownership for indigenous people, domestic violence protection, and for overturning amnesty laws. All of the landmark cases mentioned by Canton were litigated at the Court by a single NGO: the Center for Justice and International Law (CEJIL).[3] The contributions of civil society – and NGOs in particular – in building and strengthening the human rights mechanisms of the IAS also featured prominently in the remarks of the final speaker, Juan Méndez. Méndez's personal history epitomizes the outsized role of NGOs in jumpstarting and sustaining the human rights advancements of the IAS. Méndez – whose activism for political prisoners under the Argentine military dictatorship prompted his own arrest and torture – launched the Americas Division of Human Rights Watch. Americas Watch helped forge the relationship between NGOs and the Commission in the 1970s and early 1980s and founded CEJIL in 1991. Méndez later served as the Executive Director of the IIHR, the Court-created NGO, and the President of the Inter-American Commission.

As reflected in the Human Rights Day speeches, NGOs are highly involved and influential actors in the IAS. According to current and former Commission and Court officials, NGO participation is of such paramount importance to the IAS that "the IAS is driven by NGOs" and "the Commission and Court could not work without them."[4] NGOs significantly shape the jurisprudence of the Court by representing nearly half of the cases heard as well as providing critical information as amicus brief filers. NGOs have also been instrumental in augmenting the functionality of the Commission and Court through providing or advocating for critical funding, sharing information, facilitating in-country fact finding, and servings as consultants to the Commission before the Court (see Table 3.1).

NGOs have not always occupied such a pre-eminent place within the IAS. In fact, when the Commission was established in 1959, NGOs were not afforded any access to the Commission, similar to the European System of Human Rights. Sustained NGO interaction with the Commission did not arise until the mid 1970s, during the midst of repressive and abusive military dictatorships across much of Latin America. The human rights crisis – characterized by rampant state sponsored political

---

[3] These cases include: *Maria da Penha v. Brazil IACHR* 2000; *Barrios Altos v. Peru*, IACtHR 2001; and *Yakye Axa Indigenous Community v. Paraguay*, IACtHR 2005.

[4] Author interviews with: a former official of the Inter-American Commission and Court of Human Rights, November 25, 2010 and an official of the Inter-American Commission on Human Rights, December 8, 2010.

TABLE 3.1: *NGO Participatory Roles, Frequency, and Impact at the Inter-American Human Rights System*

Types of NGO Participation	Roles	NGO Participatory Frequency*	NGO Participatory Impact*
Formal roles in litigation/trials	• Representing petitioners/ Providing information on execution of judgments[5]	High	High
	• Filing amicus curiae briefs	High	High
State-directed advocacy/ consultative roles	• Advocating for funding and treaty ratification	Low	Medium
	• Consultants and advocates at the OAS	Medium	Medium
Information sharing/ operational support	• Sharing information on human rights abuses	Medium	High
	• Aiding Commission in investigations and cases	High	High
	• Providing funding for special sessions	Low	High

*Note: For frequency, low means infrequent participation, medium means some participation, and high means sustained and intense participation. For impact, low means mostly symbolic effect, medium means general substantive effect, and high means essential for functionality. For the specific measures and data of each participatory role, see Appendix C.

repression, torture, and murder – catalyzed the emergence of NGO participation by galvanizing NGOs to utilize and support the Commission even though it was weak and lacked significant authority and capacity. NGOs were motivated to aid and use this weak institution because it was state-based, and therefore could provide legitimacy to the accounts of human rights abuses occurring throughout the region.[6] Conversely, the commissioners and their staff accepted various forms of NGO assistance because they were mission-oriented and wanted to address the ongoing human rights, but lacked the capacity and functionality to do so.[7] NGO participation

---

[5] At the Inter-American Human Rights System, the NGO participatory role of "providing information about the execution of judgments" is categorized under formal roles in trials instead of sharing information, as is the case at the ECtHR. The same role is categorized differently because the role is qualitatively different at the two institutions. At the ECtHR, a political body, the Committee of Ministers of the CofE, supervises the execution of judgments and the submission of information. Any NGO can provide such information. At the Inter-American System, the Court supervises the execution of judgments and the submission of information. Usually, only the NGO that represented the petitioner can submit information about the execution of judgment. See Lambert-Abdelgawad, *The Execution of Judgments and the European Court of Human Rights*.

[6] Author interview with Joseph Eldridge, December 9, 2010.

[7] Author interview with Joseph Eldridge, December 9, 2010.

was a means for the Commission to expand its functionality and the Commission subsequently depended on NGO information, advocacy, and on-the-ground investigative services.

NGO engagement with the Court followed on the heels of expanded functionality at the Commission. In 1979, when the Court was established, NGOs already had strong participatory relationships with the Commission and were increasingly prominent actors in the struggle for human rights in Latin America.[8] At its inception, court officials recognized the potential of NGO relationships to supplement institutional deficiencies, as occurred with the Commission. The Court also struggled with limited resources and state support, which prompted it to allow NGOs formal participation in trials as well as take the unprecedented step of establishing its own NGO – the IIHR – to provide financial support and political cover from the OAS. Through these roles, NGOs provided funding and information essential for the fledgling Court to operate.

ORIGINS AND STRUCTURE OF THE INTER-AMERICAN HUMAN RIGHTS SYSTEM

The Inter-American Human Rights System is an institution of the OAS. The OAS is an intergovernmental organization founded in 1948 with the goal to legally establish the principle of non-interference in the domestic affairs of other states in the region.[9] The OAS is the governance body of the Inter-American Commission and Court and is responsible for electing judges and commissioners, providing the Commission and Court's budget, responding to the Commission's country reports, and reforming the Commission and Court. The main decision-making body of the OAS is the General Assembly, which is comprised of foreign ministers from each member state, and meets annually.

As opposed to the European System of Human Rights, the IAS is based on two human rights instruments: The American Declaration of the Rights and Duties of Man and the American Convention on Human Rights. In 1948, concurrent to the signing of the OAS charter that articulated the principle of non-interference in domestic affairs, the OAS member states also signed the first international human rights declaration: The American Declaration of the Rights and Duties of Man (see Figure 3.1). The American Declaration preceded the Universal Declaration of

---

[8] Brysk, "From Above and Below: Social Movements, the International System, and Human Rights in Argentina"; Edward L. Cleary, *Mobilizing for Human Rights in Latin America* (Sterling, VA: Kumarian Press, 2007); Kathryn Sikkink, "Human Rights, Principled Issue-Networks, and Sovereignty in Latin America," *International Organization* 47, no. 3 (1993): 411–41.

[9] Robert Goldman, "History and Action: The Inter-American Human Rights System and the Role of The Inter-American Commission on Human Rights," *Human Rights Quarterly* 31 (2009): 856–87.

1948	American Declaration of the Rights and Duties of Man adopted by the OAS
1959	Inter-American Commission on Human Rights created by political resolution
1965	Inter-American Commission on Human Rights granted authority to receive individual petitions
1969	American Convention on Human Rights adopted
1978	American Convention on Human Rights enters into force
1979	Inter-American Commission reformed and Inter-American Court of Human Rights established
1988–1989	Inter-American Court issues first decision in contentious case
1990s	Inter-American Commission shifts from country reports to hearing cases
2001	Inter-American Commission rule change that automatically refers cases to the Court in situations of non-compliance

FIGURE 3.1 Historical Timeline of the Inter-American Human Rights System

Human Rights by seven months. The American Declaration enumerates both civil and political and economic and social rights but is not a binding convention – it is merely a declaration without any enforcement mechanisms. In 1959, in reaction to the Cuban Revolution and the dictatorship of Rafael Trujillo in the Dominican Republic, the OAS established the Commission on Human Rights by political resolution, not through a treaty.[10] The Commission was not charged with hearing human rights cases, but was meant to be a research and educational institution. The only powers given to the Commission were to undertake studies and organize meetings on human rights, without discussing the human rights situations in specific countries. This changed in the mid 1960s when reforms allowed the Commission to hear specific cases of human rights abuses. In 1969, the OAS adopted the second human rights instrument of the IAS: The American Convention on Human Rights. As opposed to the non-binding declaration, the Convention is a legally binding treaty, which requires state signature and ratification. It also provided for enforcement mechanisms, including the restructuring of the Commission and the establishment of an Inter-American Court of Human Rights. Nine years passed before the Convention entered into force in 1978 and the Court was established in Figure 3.1.

Even though the Inter-American Human Rights System was modeled on the European System, there are differences in the functions of the Commission and Court. The Inter-American Commission, while allowed to hear petitions and refer cases to the Court, primarily focused on writing country reports from 1960 to 1990.[11] Because of the systematic and grievous nature of the human rights violations in Latin America during this time, the Commission utilized its authority to hold on-the-ground meetings whereby the commissioners would visit countries and investigate and report on the human rights situations. In this way, the Commission

---

[10] Felipe González, "Experience of the Inter-American Human Rights System," *Victoria University of Wellington Law Review* 40 (2009–2010): 103–26.

[11] González, "Experience of the Inter-American Human Rights System."

paralleled the work of the United Nations Commission on Human Rights by documenting and publicizing widespread, systematic human rights violations, such as executions, disappearances, and torture.[12] It was not until the end of the Cold War that the Commission shifted from writing country reports on right to life cases committed by military regimes to the less grievous cases of civilian governments.[13] In the 1990s, the Commission also established thematic rapporteurships on specific areas of human rights. The Court also differs from the ECtHR in that it can hear advisory cases, or cases in which the ruling is non-binding, in which a state can request the Court's interpretation of an issue relating to the American Convention. The Court can also hear contentious cases, or cases in which the ruling is binding, but only if the state has signed an additional declaration granting jurisdiction to the Court and the case has been referred by either the Commission or a member state. The Court did not hear a contentious case for almost a decade after its establishment. The Commission first referred a case to the Court in 1986 and the Court issued its first decision in a contentious case in 1989.[14] Lastly, both the Inter-American Commission and Court are part-time institutions and meet only a few times each year.[15]

While the membership of the OAS is expansive and covers all 35 independent states of the Americas, state parties to the American Convention and the optional declaration submitting to the Court's jurisdiction are much smaller. Currently, 24 countries are parties to the American Convention and 21 countries have accepted the contentious jurisdiction of the Court, meaning that the Court can hear cases in which the ruling is binding.[16] The majority of the English-speaking countries of the Americas – including the United States, Canada, and many Caribbean nations – are not signatories to the American Convention, and therefore cannot be taken before the Commission or Court under the Convention.[17]

---

[12] David Harris, "Regional Protection of Human Rights: The Inter-American Achievement," in *The Inter-American Human Rights System*, ed. David Harris and Stephen Livingstone (Oxford: Clarendon Press, 1998): 1–30.

[13] González, "Experience of the Inter-American Human Rights System," 113.

[14] These cases are collectively referred to as the *Honduran Disappearance Cases*.

[15] The Commission holds two three-week regular meetings per year with the occasional extraordinary meeting. The Court holds four two-week regular meetings per year along with occasional special sessions.

[16] The state parties to the Convention are: Argentina, Barbados, Bolivia, Brazil, Chile, Colombia, Costa Rica, Dominica, Dominican Republic, Ecuador, El Salvador, Grenada, Guatemala, Haiti, Honduras, Jamaica, Mexico, Nicaragua, Panama, Paraguay, Peru, Suriname, and Uruguay. The states that have voluntarily submitted to the Court's jurisdiction are: Argentina, Barbados, Bolivia, Brazil, Chile, Colombia, Costa Rica, Dominican Republic, Ecuador, El Salvador, Guatemala, Haiti, Honduras, Mexico, Nicaragua, Panama, Paraguay, Peru, Suriname, and Uruguay. Trinidad and Tobago and Venezuela have both renounced the American Convention in May 1998 and September 2012, respectively.

[17] States that have signed the American Declaration of the Rights and Duties of Man but are not parties to the American Convention, can be taken to the Commission and held to the standards of the Declaration.

TABLE 3.2: *Theoretical Factors that Shape NGO Participatory Roles, Frequency, and Impact at the Inter-American Human Rights System*

Roles (Access)	• Varied history of NGO inclusion among Commission, Court, and the OAS
	• Pronounced deficiencies of Commission and Court resources and legitimacy
	• Motivated and resourced NGOs seeking new participatory roles, particularly in response to human rights crisis
Frequency	• Motivated and resourced international NGOs
Impact	• Roles that mitigated Commission or Court deficiencies resulted in substantive impact

In essence, the Inter-American Human Rights System is a Latin American institution, as almost all Latin American countries are signatories to the Convention and allow contentious jurisdiction at the Court.

NGOS AND THE INTER-AMERICAN HUMAN RIGHTS SYSTEM

At the IAS, NGOs enjoy broad participatory access, strong and long-standing engagement, and are crucial and influential actors. International human rights NGOs – WOLA, Americas Watch, and Amnesty International – were instrumental in reviving and building the capacity of the stagnant Commission in the 1970s through sharing critical information, arranging country visits, and advocating for greater resources. Following the successful relationship between NGOs and the Commission, the Court strategically allowed for NGOs to file amicus briefs and even established an affiliated NGO, the IIHR, to provide the Court with financial and political support. The early relationships between NGOs and the Commission also morphed into NGOs becoming predominant players in taking cases before the Court. CEJIL litigates over half of the cases at the Court. The significant partnerships between NGOs and the Commission and Court are a consequence of the judicial institutions being underfunded, understaffed, and oftentimes met with threats, hostility, or neglect by member states. These deficiencies were amplified during the grave human rights situation in Latin America during the 1970s and spurred the Commission to cooperate with NGOs in unprecedented ways. The human rights crisis also galvanized NGOs – many of them headquartered in Washington, DC with prominent reputations and relatively deep pockets – to support and utilize the judicial institutions because of the unique leverage of these bodies to publicize, legitimize, and provide redress for human rights abuses and their future legacies.

Revitalizing the Inter-American Commission

The Inter-American Commission and Court were established 20 years apart – in 1959 and 1979, respectively. In 1959, when the Commission was instituted, there were few human rights NGOs, and the Commission rules did not afford them any participatory access.[18] Similarly to the European System of Human Rights, the Commission likely did not see NGOs as potential or appropriate participatory partners. The mid 1970s represents the inflection point at which human rights NGOs gained global prominence and first sought to utilize the Commission.[19] At this time, NGOs and civil society members in Latin America searched for a means to bring public attention to halt, and obtain justice for, victims of severe and systematic human rights abuses occurring throughout the region.[20] As domestic courts ignored the abuses and other states abided by the norm of non-interference in domestic affairs, NGO attention turned to the Commission. One particular NGO, WOLA, which is based in Washington, DC where the Commission is headquartered, first started participating at the Commission. WOLA's participation at the Commission was motivated by the belief that "a tap on the wrist by the Commission – since it was administered by peer governments – would have a greater impact than ten reports by NGOs, which they would try to discredit."[21]

NGOs turned to the Commission even though the Commission in the 1970s was "moribund."[22] The Commission was a part-time, seriously understaffed, institution with a budget of a few hundred thousand dollars to address the human rights situations in all of Latin America and parts of the Caribbean.[23] The majority of Latin America was under harsh military rule, yet the Commission did not have the formal powers to investigate human rights situations on the ground in OAS countries. The Commission could receive complaints of human rights violations by individual petitioners (for those countries that were parties to the American Convention), but many of the complaints that the Commission did receive were handwritten notes saying someone had disappeared. These notes "hardly contained any facts" and because of the lack of facts, the Commission could not act on the allegations.[24] The inability of the Commission to address the grave human rights violations occurring across the region highlighted the insufficient resources of the Commission and shifted the incentive structure of the Commission to allow NGO participation when NGOs approached the Commission with information and services. These early Commissioners and their staff were generally "mission-driven"

---

[18] Cecilia Medina Quiroga, *The Battle of Human Rights: Gross, Systematic Violations and the Inter-American System* (Leiden: Martinus Nijhoff Publishers, 1988): 67.

[19] Cleary, *Mobilizing for Human Rights in Latin America*; Sikkink, "Human Rights, Principled Issue-Networks, and Sovereignty in Latin America."

[20] Brysk, "From Above and Below: Social Movements, the International System, and Human Rights in Argentina"; Cleary, *Mobilizing for Human Rights in Latin America*.

[21] Author interview with Joseph Eldridge, December 9, 2010.

[22] Author interview with a former official of the Inter-American Commission and Court of Human Rights, November 25, 2010.

[23] This constituted less than 1 percent of the OAS budget. See: Tom J. Farer, ed., *The Future of the Inter-American System* (Westport, CT: Praeger, 1979): 125.

[24] Author interview with a former official of the Inter-American Commission and Court of Human Rights, November 25, 2010.

and took their positions as a "serious charge," and therefore were willing to form participatory relationships with NGOs that could help the Commission.[25]

WOLA was one of the organizations that first connected with the Commission through providing documentation of abuses in Argentina from local people and organizations seeking external help. According to Joseph Eldridge, the co-founder of WOLA:

> In 1975, WOLA was looking for allies. Human rights was a voice crying in the wilderness. WOLA approached Charlie Moyer, who was eager to cooperate. At that time, the process for filing cases before the Commission was daunting. WOLA assisted organizations and individuals to put together complaints. WOLA had hundreds of case dossiers from Argentina ... we physically carried them to Charlie, set them on his desk and said: "Do something."[26]

The Commission had no profile in the region, so WOLA channeled the information assembled by groups on the ground to the Commission, which along with WOLA is based in Washington, DC.[27] This information proved incredibly useful to the Commission. As opposed to the handwritten notes the Commission had formerly received, the case dossiers were "professionalized and manageable" and allowed the Commission to either move forward with complaints or use them in country reports.[28] During the 1970s and 1980s, Amnesty International also forged a "cooperative" relationship with the Commission and shared information – often repeatedly – on human rights situations in Argentina, Bolivia, Chile, Colombia, Ecuador, El Salvador, Guatemala, Haiti, Honduras, Nicaragua, Paraguay, Peru, Suriname, the United States, and Uruguay.[29] According to a former official of the Inter-American Commission and Court, "the Commission allowed their [NGO] help because of the help that they could provide."[30]

NGO help to the Commission did not end with the sharing of information gathered from in-country sources. NGOs shortly discovered that additional services would be needed for the Commission to be able to have a marked impact on human rights in the region. According to Joseph Eldridge, the co-founder of WOLA, "until

[25] Author interview with Joseph Eldridge, December 9, 2010.
[26] Author interview with Joseph Eldridge, December 9, 2010.
[27] Author interview with Joseph Eldridge, December 9, 2010.
[28] Author interview with a former official of the Inter-American Commission and Court of Human Rights, November 25, 2010.
[29] Amnesty International, "Amnesty International Annual Report 1975–1976," June 1, 1976,: 45, www.amnesty.org/en/documents/document/?indexNumber=pol10%2f0001%2f1976&language=en; Amnesty International, "Amnesty International Annual Report 1984," 10; Amnesty International, "Amnesty International Annual Report 1983," 12; Amnesty International, "Amnesty International Report 1985," 14; Amnesty International, "Amnesty International Annual Report 1986," 16; Amnesty International, "Amnesty International Annual Report 1987," 19.
    In the 1980s, Americas Watch also became a major player in documenting and sharing abuses with the Commission.
[30] Author interview with a former official of the Inter-American Commission and Court of Human Rights, November 25, 2010.

1978–9, the Commission was a weak ally."[31] Before this time, the reports of the Commission were taken note of by the OAS, but nothing was formally adopted in response to the reports.[32] To bolster the Commission, NGOs augmented the Commission's functionality through securing additional sources of funding for the Commission and aiding the Commission with on-the-ground investigations.

In 1975, the Commission's budget was $303,100, which was meant to cover the costs of permanent staff, administration, and country visits to states hostile to the work of the Commission.[33] The same year, WOLA worked with US Senator Edward Kennedy and his aide, Mark Schneider, to engineer an earmark that would grant the Commission funding through the United States Agency for International Development (USAID).[34] This earmark doubled the budget of the Commission for two years and specified that the money could not be absorbed by the OAS but had to go directly to the Commission.[35] According to Joseph Eldridge, the co-founder of WOLA, this money was meant to "give the Commission institutional capacity to follow-up as it became more vital and alive."[36] Senator Kennedy's support of the Commission continued, and in the late 1970s, when the OAS threatened to cut the budget of the Commission, Senator Kennedy said that the United States would fund whatever the OAS cut.[37] During the Carter administration (1977–1981), NGOs also worked with Congress, particularly Congressman Donald Fraser, on organizing hearings on human rights. According to a former official of the Commission, "NGOs would help the staff member prepare ... often times they would design the whole hearing ... would bring so and so from x country ... [it was a] very successful strategy."[38]

NGOs also provided vital assistance to the Commission through connecting victims and local human rights groups to commissioners when they travelled to OAS countries. The Commission did not have formal authority to investigate human rights abuses, but could conduct on-the-ground meetings and write country reports based on information acquired during these meetings and the case information submitted to the Commission. According to Juan Méndez, a former

---

[31] Author interview with Joseph Eldridge, December 9, 2010.
[32] Quiroga, *The Battle of Human Rights.*
[33] Farer, *The Future of the Inter-American System,* 125; Quiroga, *The Battle of Human Rights.*
[34] Author interview with Joseph Eldridge, December 9, 2010.
[35] Public Law 94–161 (89 Stat.849) enacted on December 10, 1975 added the following provision to Sec. 302 (a)(2) of Public Law 87–195: "The Congress reaffirms its support for the work of the Inter-American Commission on Human Rights. To permit such Commission to better fulfill its function of insuring observance and respect for human rights within this hemisphere, not less than $357,000 of the amount appropriated for fiscal year 1976 and $358,000 of the amount appropriated for fiscal year 1977, for contributions to the Organization of American States, shall be used only for budgetary support for the Inter-American Commission on Human Rights."
[36] Author interview with Joseph Eldridge, December 9, 2010.
[37] Author interview with a former official of the Inter-American Commission and Court of Human Rights, November 25, 2010.
[38] Author interview with a former official of the Inter-American Commission and Court of Human Rights, November 25, 2010.

member of the Inter-American Commission on Human Rights and founder of the HRW Americas Program, NGOs often persuaded the Commission to have on-site visits. The Commission would arrange the visit but would contact NGOs to get specific information – such as the latest information on prisoners – or to meet with victims.[39] During the Commission's 1979 visit to Argentina, communications between an on-the-ground "contact" and a member of the Commission's staff facilitated the Commission's discovery and documentation of secretly held prisoners who were hidden behind the walls in a prison in Córdoba.[40] In this situation, it is not known whether this "contact" was an individual affiliated with an NGO, or whether an NGO connected the member of the Commission's staff to this person. But based on interviews with current and former Commission officials, NGOs have linked and continue to link the Commission to victims and individuals or groups with specialized information during Commission visits.[41]

Sharing information, aiding the Commission with case investigations, and linking the Commission with victims during country visits helped awaken the Commission and spur it to address the systematic and widespread human rights violations occurring throughout Latin America. Following the onset of NGO participation in the mid 1970s, the Commission produced two country reports, with regard to Nicaragua and Argentina, that began to generate attention about the dire human rights situations in these countries and are reported to have contributed to the cessation of forced disappearances in Argentina and to Somoza's subsequent defeat in Nicaragua.[42] According to a staff member of CEJIL, "NGOs are crucial . . . all the reports that the Commission has issued, the visits, many of them have been pushed by NGOs . . . Have to visit this country, have to make this statement, have to do this, have to do that."[43] In the 1990s, NGOs also expanded their information sharing roles and pressured the Commission to look into and hold hearings on cross-country thematic human rights issues, such as migration or women's rights. The Commission was usually open to these recommendations and often created a long-term project or rapporteurship on the issue.[44] According to an official of the Inter-American Commission, when the Commission did hold hearings on these cross-country human rights themes, "almost the entire thematic hearings are local NGOs presenting information."[45]

In the 1980s and 1990s, when the Commission shifted strategies from primarily writing country reports to hearing cases, NGO aid shifted in tandem. According to a

[39] Author interview with Juan Méndez, December 14, 2010.
[40] Thomas Buergenthal, Robert E. Norris, and Dinah Shelton, *Protecting Human Rights in the Americas: Selected Problems* (Kehl, Strasbourg, and Arlington, VA: N.P. Engel, 1990): 299–301.
[41] Author interviews with: Juan Méndez, December 14, 2010 and an official of the Inter-American Commission of Human Rights, December 8, 2010.
[42] González, "Experience of the Inter-American Human Rights System," 109.
[43] Author interview with a staff member of CEJIL, November 29, 2010.
[44] Author interview with Juan Méndez, December 14, 2010.
[45] Author interview with an official of the Inter-American Commission of Human Rights, December 8, 2010.

former official of the Commission and Court, NGOs, particularly Americas Watch and CEJIL, often did the Commission's investigative legwork:

> Oftentimes the Commission would assign someone from a NGO on the team that was responsible for a particular case... Americas Watch pretty much ran the case ... [this was] especially necessary if the Commissioner/investigator was a dud and didn't know what they were doing or anything about the case. NGOs would often work on the whole case ... doing fact-finding and presentation before the Court.[46]

NGOs consistently aided the Commission in preparing and presenting cases before the Court during this period. In the 24 cases with court judgments between 1988 and 2000, at least one representative of either Americas Watch or CEJIL was appointed as an official advisor or assistant to the Commission in 19 cases.[47] According to a former official of the Commission and Court, NGOs were so involved because the Commission was an understaffed part-time institution that did not have the time to present and prepare for cases before the Court.[48]

Targeting the OAS

Although the Commission, and later the Court, came to regard NGOs as potential aids in fulfilling their missions, OAS member states were much more reticent about NGO engagement as NGOs threatened the tenet of non-interference. Even the establishment of the Commission in 1959 represented an expression of the region-wide principle of non-interference in the domestic affairs of other states. While this may seem counterintuitive as the Commission is an institution of a regional human rights regime, member states did not intend the Commission to monitor and enforce governmental treatment of its citizens.[49] The primary reason the member states created the Commission was in reaction to the Cuban Revolution and the dictatorship of Trujillo in the Dominican Republic, and therefore the Commission was not given many powers.[50] When the Commission, aided by NGOs, began to assert and stretch its limited authority through writing country reports on human rights situations, many states either ignored the reports or accused the Commission of political bias and threatened to pull out of the American Convention.[51] Some of the later threats to the Commission and Court were not merely rhetorical. Trinidad and

---

[46] Author interview with a former official of the Inter-American Commission and Court of Human Rights, November 25, 2010.

[47] Information was gathered by examining each case during this period from the Court database.

[48] Author interview with a former official of the Inter-American Commission and Court of Human Rights, November 25, 2010.

[49] Quiroga, *The Battle of Human Rights*.

[50] González, "Experience of the Inter-American Human Rights System."

[51] Christina M Cerna, "Inter-American System for the Protection of Human Rights," *Florida Journal of International Law* 16 (2004): 195; Quiroga, *The Battle of Human Rights*.

Tobago formally denounced the Convention in 1998 over the issue of the death penalty, Peru attempted to withdraw from the contentious jurisdiction of the Court in 1999 (the Court ruled this was not allowed under the Convention), and Venezuela denounced the Convention in 2012. In 2011, Brazil broke off relations with the Commission over its request that Brazil suspend the Belo Monte hydro-electric dam project until it met environmental standards and implemented measures to protect indigenous communities.[52]

In the late 1970s, WOLA targeted the OAS. WOLA requested observer status at the OAS General Assembly, the first request of any group. According to Joseph Eldridge, the co-founder of WOLA, "the General Assembly staff was startled when we requested it ... but it was within the rules ... we pushed, prodded, and cajoled to get the status. WOLA opened the door and helped get democratic access to the decision-making body of the OAS."[53] WOLA was not allowed inside General Assembly meetings, but would wait outside the door and approach diplomats as they arrived and left. The main campaign by WOLA at the OAS was to pressure the General Assembly meetings to "embrace, claim, and adopt" the country reports written by the Commission.[54] Following WOLA's pressure for NGO access, Amnesty International was sometimes allowed to attend the General Assembly as a "special guest."[55]

WOLA lobbying for access as observers to the OAS General Assembly opened the way for NGO advocacy in multiple capacities and on various issues at the OAS. Currently, NGOs advocate around the annual OAS General Assembly meetings, meet with the Permanent Council of the OAS, and submit information to OAS special working groups on reform.[56] The issues NGOs raise in these venues include elections of judges and commissioners, reforms to the Commission and Court, state compliance with Commission and Court decisions, the creation of a legal aid fund,

---

[52] Mari Hayman, "Brazil Breaks Relations With Human Rights Commission Over Belo Monte Dam," *Latin America News Dispatch*, May 3, 2011, http://latindispatch.com/2011/05/03/brazil-breaks-relations-with-human-rights-commission-over-belo-monte-dam/.

[53] Author interview with Joseph Eldridge, December 9, 2010.

[54] Author interview with Joseph Eldridge, December 9, 2010.

[55] Amnesty International, "Amnesty International Annual Report 1986," 16; Amnesty International, "Amnesty International Annual Report 1987," 18.

[56] In 1989, prior to the General Assembly meeting, Amnesty International sent letters to member states urging them to adopt the draft optional protocol to the American Convention on Human Rights to abolish the death penalty. See: Amnesty International, "Amnesty International Annual Report 1990," January 1, 1990: 22, www.amnesty.org/en/documents/document/?index Number=pol10%2f0003%2f1990&language=en. At OAS General Assembly meetings, NGOs also meet with Court and Commission officials although these meetings "are not deemed important." This is according to an interview with Juan Méndez, December 14, 2010.

See also: Carlos Quesada, *Using the Inter-American System for Human Rights: A Practical Guide for NGOs* (London: Global Rights, 2004); Lisa Reinsberg, "The Future of Human Rights in the Americas: Update on the Inter-American Reform Process," *IntLawGrrls* (blog), December 10, 2012, www.intlawgrrls.com/2012/12/the-future-of-human-rights-in-americas.html.

Author interview with a staff member of CEJIL, December 17, 2010.

and attention to specific human rights situations.[57] Recently, CEJIL helped organize a coalition of local and international NGOs – the International Coalition of NGOs for the Inter-American System – that advocates positions as a collective through drafting joint positions and statements. When the Coalition has funding, they meet prior to Commission hearings and OAS General Assembly meetings to coordinate their advocacy efforts.[58]

NGOs also engage in direct advocacy and consultation with states over joining or remaining party to the American Convention on Human Rights and its protocols. In 2002, Amnesty International and CEJIL participated in a review by the Canadian government on the potential impact of ratification of the American Convention.[59] In 2008, CEJIL co-sponsored a conference in New York on the United States and its relationship to the Inter-American Human Rights System.[60] Additionally, CEJIL consults with member states on possible reservations to Article 4 to the American Convention, the right to life, as well as encouraging the adoption of the San Salvador protocols that enumerate social and economic rights.[61] Human Rights Watch, CEJIL, and Amnesty International also publically decried the withdrawals of Trinidad and Tobago and Venezuela from the American Convention on Human Rights.[62]

The impact of NGO advocacy on OAS member states is mixed. One area in which NGOs have had impact is on the elections of commissioners and judges. NGOs monitor the nomination of candidates and mobilize against candidates that they deem are not qualified or are politically motivated.[63] A staff member of CEJIL

[57] International Coalition of Human Rights Organizations in the Americas, "Request for Action to Protect the Autonomy, Independence and Impartiality, of the Inter-American Human Rights System," November 8, 2007; International Coalition of Human Rights Organizations in the Americas, "Pronunciamiento de La Coalicion de Organizaciones Por Los Derechos Humanos En Las Americas: Coalicion Condena Hostigamientos a Organizaciones y Defensores/as de Derechos Humanos En Venezuela," August 12, 2010; Reinsberg, "The Future of Human Rights in the Americas: Update on the Inter-American Reform Process."
Author interviews with staff members of CEJIL, November 29, 2010 and December 17, 2010.
[58] Author interviews with staff members of CEJIL, November 29, 2010 and December 17, 2010.
[59] Report of the Standing Senate Committee on Human Rights, "Enhancing Canada's Role in the OAS: Canadian Adherence to the American Convention on Human Rights," May 2003, https://sencanada.ca/content/sen/committee/372/huma/rep/repo4mayo3part1-e.htm.
[60] Elizabeth A.H. Abi-Mershed, "The United States and the Inter-American Court of Human Rights," in *The Sword and the Scales: The United States and International Courts and Tribunals*, ed. Cesare P. R. Romano (Cambridge University Press, 2009): 190.
[61] Author interview with a staff member of CEJIL, November 29, 2010.
[62] Amnesty International, "Venezuela's Withdrawal from Regional Human Rights Instrument Is a Serious Setback," September 2, 2013, www.amnesty.org/en/latest/news/2013/09/venezuela-s-withdrawal-regional-human-rights-instrument-serious-setback/; Human Rights Watch, "HRW and CEJIL Call on Trinidad and Tobago to Reconsider Withdrawal from the American Convention on Human Rights," Human Rights Watch, June 1, 1998, www.hrw.org/news/1998/06/01/hrw-and-cejil-call-trinidad-and-tobago-reconsider-withdrawal-american-convention.
[63] Verónica Gómez, "The Interaction between the Political Actors of the OAS, the Commission and the Court," in *The Inter-American System of Human Rights*, ed. David Harris and Stephen Livingstone (Oxford: Clarendon Press, 1998): 173–212; J. Schönsteiner, "Alternative

states: "We [CEJIL] will not issue a statement for people [specific candidates] but if we know that one person is really horrible and that some state is proposing him/her because it would weaken the Commission. In those cases, we will say something as a Coalition."[64] NGO mobilization prompted Argentina's withdrawal of a specific candidate that NGOs deemed unfit due to a controversial political background.[65] NGOs have also contributed to the rule changes that force the Commission to send cases to the Court if states do not comply with the Commission's decisions and proposed the establishment of a legal aid program.[66] Even though the legal aid program was established, states have not allocated sufficient funds in order for it to operate.[67]

OAS member states have pushed back against the increasing advocacy presence of NGOs. In the late 1990s, states attempted to curb the rights and presence of NGOs at the OAS through a proposal to regulate civil society access to OAS deliberations.[68] In the current reform process, NGO access is limited. Civil society representatives were granted their first meeting with the OAS Permanent Council on reform issues 18 months after the reform process was initiated.[69]

Manufacturing NGO Aid

NGO engagement with the Court arose because of the tremendous needs of the institution but was first initiated by the Court rather than NGOs. At the time of the Court's establishment in 1979, there were only a handful of democracies in Latin American and member states of the OAS did not want to support a new institution that could adjudicate claims of human rights violations in the region. The OAS initially did not give the fledgling Court any money for its budget or help it arrange for headquarters.[70] In parallel, NGOs were gaining global prominence for their

Appointment Procedures for the Commissioners and Judges in the Inter-American System of Human Rights," *Revista IIDH*, 2007: 195–215.

[64] Author interview with a staff member of CEJIL, November 29, 2010.

[65] "The Interaction between the Political Actors of the OAS, the Commission and the Court," 209.

[66] Author interview with an official of the Inter-American Commission of Human Rights, December 8, 2010. Rule 44 is part of the new Rules of Procedure of the Commission, which entered into force in 2001.
The legal aid program was proposed exclusively by CEJIL, not the larger Coalition of NGOs.

[67] OAS, "Legal Assistance Fund Enters into Force," March 1, 2011, www.oas.org/en/iachr/media_center/PReleases/2011/017.asp.

[68] Felipe González, "El Control Internacional de Las Organizaciones No Gubernamentales," *Revista IIDH* 25 (1997); author interview with Joseph Eldridge, December 9, 2010.

[69] Reinsberg, "The Future of Human Rights in the Americas: Update on the Inter-American Reform Process."

[70] Thomas Buergenthal, "Remembering the Early Years of the Inter-American Court of Human Rights," *New York University Journal of International Law and Politics* 37 (2004–2005): 259–80.

human rights reporting and advocacy.[71] Several prominent, international NGOs – including Amnesty International, WOLA, and Americas Watch – were actively aiding the Commission in an effort to combat human rights violations in Latin America.[72] Newly established court officials saw the benefits that NGO partnerships provided the Commission, and thus strategically choose to engage with NGOs from its inception. This was done in two ways. First, the Court created its own NGO to help financially support and insulate it from the politics of the OAS. Second, the Court allowed NGOs to file third-party amicus briefs. If the Court had been established concurrent to the Commission, it would be unimaginable that it would view NGOs in such an instrumental way and directly position itself to benefit from NGO participation.

When the Court was established in 1979, the OAS did not provide it any funding so the judges had to write the Court's rules, hire staff, purchase judicial robes, and arrange a headquarters agreement on their own.[73] Only with financial assistance from Costa Rica and a special provision of the OAS was the Court able to come into fruition as a part-time body.[74] The financial strain on the judicial institution continued through the 1980s as the OAS experienced a severe financial crisis due to a region-wide foreign debt crisis and mandated a 10 percent cut to its budget.[75] The Court's budget in 1982 was already incredibly small at $30,000.[76] Former judge Thomas Buergenthal described these cuts as having "a paralyzing effect on the Court and its ability to properly discharge its obligations."[77] In terms of funding and staff, the IAS pales in comparison to the European System of Human Rights. In 2014, the budget of the ECtHR was over $70 million greater than that of the IAS (see Figure 3.2).[78] The ECtHR has 47 full-time judges, while the Court has only seven part-time judges. This combination of restricted time in session, chronic underfunding, and few staff limits the capacity of the Inter-American Commission and Court. Former judge Sonia Picado attributed the limited reach of the Court to capacity problems:

> The Court has very little money, and one of these cases is very expensive. We meet only twice a year, which prevents the Court from being very active ... If we want the Court to really play a role in Latin America, we have to have a permanent court,

---

[71] Cleary, *Mobilizing for Human Rights in Latin America*; Sikkink, "Human Rights, Principled Issue-Networks, and Sovereignty in Latin America."

[72] Author interview with a former official of the Inter-American Commission and Court of Human Rights, November 25, 2010.

[73] Buergenthal, "Remembering the Early Years of the Inter-American Court of Human Rights."

[74] Buergenthal, "Remembering the Early Years of the Inter-American Court of Human Rights."

[75] Thomas Buergenthal, "The Inter-American Court, Human Rights, and the OAS," *Human Rights Law Journal* 7 (1986): 157–64.

[76] Inter-American Court of Human Rights, "Inter-American Court of Human Rights Annual Report," 1982.

[77] Buergenthal, "The Inter-American Court, Human Rights, and the OAS," 163.

[78] It is important to note that the comparative funding is not adjusted for jurisdiction or caseload, which limits the value of this comparison. Nevertheless, the substantial resource division is still profound, especially as the IAS was modeled on the European System.

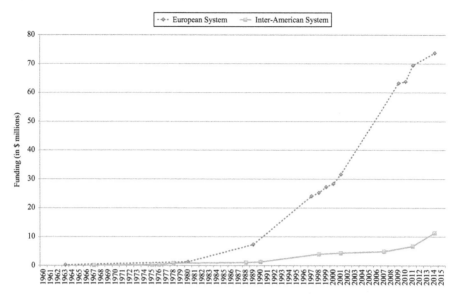

FIGURE 3.2: Comparative Funding of the European and Inter-American Systems of Human Rights (1960–2014)
Note: The statistics on funding are not adjusted for jurisdiction and caseload.
Sources: Annual reports of the ECtHR and the CofE and the annual budget reports from the OAS. Funding figures for European system were converted from Euro to US dollars at the exchange rate of 1 EUR= 1.09 USD.

or at least a court that will meet for a few months [each year]. The budgetary situation of the Court is very bad; bringing [members of the Court] to Costa Rica is very expensive. The Court will keep getting more cases, but they come in and it is not until one year later that there is an audience on those cases. That is very frustrating. But of course, the staff of the Court is very small; there is a secretary and an undersecretary and three or four other persons. It really makes it very inefficient.[79]

The lack of funding, staff, and state support hamstrung the fledgling Court and made it seek out assistance from a variety of actors, including states and non-state actors. The Commission and Court sought external funding from non-OAS donors, which resulted in the European Union being their principal financial supporter.[80] The Court also sought to utilize NGOs to enhance its functionality through the

[79] Lynda E. Frost, "The Evolution of the Inter-American Court of Human Rights: Reflections of Present and Former Judges," *Human Rights Quarterly* 14, no. 2 (May 1992): 177, 189.
[80] González, "Experience of the Inter-American Human Rights System"; Andrew Solomon, "International Tribunal Spotlight: The Inter-American Court of Human Rights (IACHR)," *International Judicial Monitor* 2, no. 3 (2007).

unprecedented creation of its own NGO. Two years after its establishment, the Court created the Inter-American Institute of Human Rights (IIHR/IIDH) to promote and aid the Court. While the IIHR is an academic and educational institute and therefore does not take claims before the Commission or Court, it nonetheless was of crucial assistance to the Court. Because the Court was so resource-poor and its budget was at the whim of the OAS, the IIHR became an external support mechanism that could provide supplemental financing to the Court.[81] In the Court's early years, the IIHR would arrange academic conferences that coincided with court special sessions. The IIHR would then pay for the transportation and lodging of the judges and the Court would hold session in tandem with the academic conference.[82] The IIHR was strategically made autonomous, and was funded by international donors, not the OAS, to shield it from OAS political influence.[83]

The second way that the Court sought to strategically utilize NGOs was by allowing amicus briefs by NGOs and other non-state actors both in advisory and contentious cases.[84] Amicus curiae briefs are submissions by third parties – actors that are not a party to the case – that consist of legal arguments and information relevant to the issues of a case. The allowance of amicus briefs by the Court is unexpected, as the American Convention makes no mention of amicus briefs and the predominantly civil law systems of Latin America have no history of utilizing amicus briefs. The Court allowed amicus briefs – from its first advisory case – because the first judges thought that amicus briefs could be helpful to a fledgling and resource-poor court. One of the first judges, Thomas Buergenthal, had knowledge and experience with amicus briefs in the United States and suggested that they could be helpful to the Court. According to a former judge:

> It [allowing amicus briefs] wasn't in the statute but we felt it was very important for us to get amicus briefs. So, the best thing for us to do was leave it vague – if an amicus brief came, we would just exercise our authority to accept it or reject it. That's how it happened. Basically, it was a decision by the seven judges to have the benefit of amicus briefs without giving states an opportunity to challenge them.[85]

---

[81] The IIHR also supported the Court by facilitating communication and cooperation between the Commission and Court, which experienced some organizational tensions over referral of cases. In 1991, the Institute organized a seminar on cooperation and how to better facilitate the Commission sending cases to the Court. See: Frost, "The Evolution of the Inter-American Court of Human Rights," 177.

[82] Buergenthal, "Remembering the Early Years of the Inter-American Court of Human Rights."

[83] Early donors included USAID, Norway, Sweden, Denmark, The Netherlands, as well as international foundations. Author interview with consultant for the IIHR, November 17, 2010.

[84] Article 34(1) of the original Rules of Procedure of the Court was interpreted as allowing for consideration of amicus briefs by a wide variety of actors, including NGOs, political groups, and corporations. See: Charles Moyer, "The Role of Amicus Curiae in the Inter-American Court of Human Rights," in *La Corte Inter-Americana de Derechos Humanos: Estudios y Documentos* (San José: IIDH, 1986): 103–14, www.bibliojuridica.org/libros/4/1996/8.pdf.

[85] Phone interview with a former judge of the Commission and Court, December 17, 2010.

The decision by judges to allow amicus briefs had nothing to do with democratic representation or public interest, but was viewed as a means to receive quality legal analysis by a resource-starved court.[86]

NGOs have taken advantage of this participatory opening and participate as third parties with high frequency. Prominent international NGOs, such as the International Human Rights Law Group, the Lawyers Committee for International Human Rights, WOLA, and CEJIL, have participated as amici curiae in nearly all of the advisory proceedings.[87] In contentious cases, NGOs have submitted at least one amicus brief in approximately 43 percent of all cases.[88] In comparative terms, human rights NGOs have submitted 58 percent of the approximately 500 amicus briefs received by the court in its first 35 years.[89] While the impact of amicus briefs written by NGOs on judicial decisions varies depending on the reputation of the NGO and the quality of the information and argument, many international NGOs have had significant impact on the judicial decisions and jurisprudence of the Court. Through amicus briefs, NGOs are not just engaging in advocacy, but are providing "very deliberate legal work."[90] In the early years of the Court, these briefs were instrumental to the resource-starved Court. According to a former Secretary of the Court: "There is no doubt that the amicus brief has been a valuable aid to the Court during its early years when it has been served by a very small staff and has not had access to a first-rate legal library."[91] In the experience of a former official of the Commission and Court, NGO briefs are often very well-researched and written by talented legal scholars and practitioners. Some of the briefs have been so thorough that large portions could be copied into judicial decisions.[92] Another Court official praised NGO briefs for bringing forth new legal issues and arguments but said that NGO influence can be difficult to trace, as sometimes judges use something from an NGO brief, but do not attribute it to the NGO in the decision.[93] Similar to the

---

[86] Author interview with a former official of the Court, November 25, 2010.

[87] Mónica Pinto, "NGOs and the Inter-American Court of Human Rights," in *Civil Society, International Courts and Compliance Bodies,* ed. Tullio Treves et al. (The Hague: T.M.C. Asser Press, 2005): 53.

[88] As of February 2013, 76 of 157 contentious cases had third parties submit amicus briefs. In 67 of these cases, NGOs submitted at least one amicus brief. This statistic was calculated by searching the judicial judgments of each contentious case at the Court (via the database on the Court's website) for mention of amicus briefs. This is a reasonable way to measure the frequency of amicus brief submission, as the standard judicial decision format includes a listing of the parties that submitted briefs.

[89] Francisco Rivera Juaristi, "The Amicus Curiae in the Inter-American Court of Human Rights (1982–2013)," SSRN Scholarly Paper (Rochester, NY: Social Science Research Network, August 1, 2014): 4, https://papers.ssrn.com/abstract=2488073.

[90] Author interview with a faculty member of American University Washington College of Law, December 15, 2010.

[91] Moyer, "The Role of Amicus Curiae in the Inter-American Court of Human Rights," 113.

[92] Author interview with a former official of the Inter-American Commission and Court of Human Rights, November 25, 2010.

[93] Author interview with an official of the Court, November 22, 2010.

ECtHR, NGO briefs can also serve a symbolic function by signaling pluralistic viewpoints on a specific issue. For example, in the 2012 *Artavia Murillo* case on in vitro fertilization, the Court received 46 amicus briefs from various NGOs, individuals, biomedical labs, and universities. According to a Court official, amicus briefs serve as expressions of deliberative democracy, which is important for a court that has very few public hearings.[94]

From Country Reports to Cases

In the late 1980s and early 1990s, NGOs began utilizing the case mechanism of the Commission and Court by representing petitioners and filing petitions. NGOs did not use this mechanism earlier because the Commission was focused on writing country reports, not hearing individual petitions, as country reports fit better with publicizing the systematic bodily harm violations of the 1970s and 1980s. By the late 1980s, a wave of democratization in Latin America shifted the nature of human rights violations away from systematic bodily harm to civil and political rights, which are more amenable to individual case petitions. In addition, in 1988–1989, the Court issued its first decision in the *Velasquez Rodriguez* case, which garnered significant public attention. These factors increased the attention of both international and domestic NGOs to the Court. International NGOs, such as the International Human Rights Law Group (IHRG, later renamed and restructured as Global Rights) started utilizing the IAS after the first cases went to the Court.[95] Local human rights organizations also wanted their cases heard at the Court after becoming stymied by domestic laws and judicial institutions that were holdovers from the time of the dictatorships.[96] According to Juan Méndez:

> After this case [the *Velasquez Rodriguez* case] Human Rights Watch, who had relationships with local NGOs, was "flooded" with cases within a few months. They [Human Rights Watch] had 50 cases before the Commission ... it was impossible to maintain. Human Rights Watch started looking for funding for these cases. Human Rights Watch and the Americas Division had other needs. Donors were more inclined to help if the organization was not part of Human Rights Watch and was purely Latin America focused. Human Rights Watch seemed like an already wealthy organization.[97]

---

[94] Author interview with an official of the Court, November 22, 2010.
[95] Author interview with faculty member of American University Washington College of Law, December 15, 2010.
[96] Author interview with Juan Méndez, December 14, 2010.
[97] Author interview with Juan Méndez, December 14, 2010.

In 1991, to obtain funding for the many cases before the Commission, Human Rights Watch created an adjunct NGO, named the Center for Justice in International Law (CEJIL), which would exclusively focus on litigation before the Inter-American Commission and Court. CEJIL partners with local NGOs or victims to provide pro bono legal services to litigate cases before the Commission and Court. In this way, CEJIL is a Latin American version of the strategic litigation NGOs based in the UK, such as Interights and the AIRE Centre.

The frequency with which CEJIL participates as legal counsel in the IAS is unparalleled. CEJIL represents petitioners in about 6 percent of the cases before the Commission and 50–60 percent of the cases before the Court.[98] When viewed within the context of Central America, CEJIL's involvement is even greater. CEJIL has litigated approximately 60–65 percent of all cases at the Court from the Central American/Mexico region, including all of the cases against El Salvador and Panama, the majority of the cases against Honduras, and half of the cases against Guatemala and Mexico.[99] CEJIL not only litigates with high frequency, but CEJIL has litigated many of the Court's landmark cases. Most notably, CEJIL has litigated cases that have overturned the amnesty laws enacted during the military regimes or during the transition to democracy. CEJIL litigated the 2001 *Barrios Altos* case in Peru, which found that amnesty laws across the region violated the American Convention, and the 2012 *Gelman* case in Uruguay, which ordered Uruguay to publically recognize its responsibility for forced disappearances. These cases have contributed to the repeal or annulment of all of the amnesty laws in Latin America. CEJIL also represented the petitioners in the *Maria da Penha* case about domestic violence in Brazil, and several prominent cases in Paraguay about indigenous peoples' right to reclaim ancestral land.[100]

CEJIL's motivation to continually take cases before the Court is essentially the same reason that prompted WOLA and Amnesty International to build the capacity of the Commission in the 1970s and 1980s: the intergovernmental nature of the institution provides legitimacy and enforcement that cannot be achieved through traditional NGO advocacy. With the advent of optional protocols in the 1990s that allow individual petition and give jurisdiction to the Court, state punishments are even more severe and have a higher likelihood of enforcement.[101] CEJIL became

---

[98] Author interview with a staff member of CEJIL, December 17, 2010. These approximate statistics were confirmed by an interview with an official of the Inter-American Commission on Human Rights, December 8, 2010. According to CEJIL's 20 year Activities Report, CEJIL litigated 65 cases at the Court from 1991 to 2001, which comes out to approximately 50 percent of all of the Court's cases CEJIL, "CEJIL Activities Report - 20 Years," 24.

[99] Author interview with a staff member of CEJIL, November 29, 2010.

[100] These cases are: *Yakye Axa Indigenous Community* v. *Paraguay*, IACtHR 2005; *Sawhoyamaxa Indigenous Community* v. *Paraguay*, IACtHR 2006; and *Xámok Kásek Indigenous Community* v. *Paraguay*, IACtHR 2010.

[101] Author interview with a staff member of CEJIL, November 29, 2010.

such a major player in pushing forward the jurisprudence of the Court because CEJIL had both the funds and expertise to compensate for the resource scarcity at the Commission and Court. Whereas the European System of Human Rights has had a functioning legal aid program since 1962, which allows individuals to utilize local lawyers to submit petitions, the IAS only established a legal assistance fund in 2008.[102] Because the fund has only been operational since 2011, with limited financing, victims of human rights violations typically either self-finance legal counsel or partner with a NGO, such as CEJIL, that will provide pro bono legal services.[103] CEJIL, while not a large organization, does have stable international funding, experienced lawyers, and offices in Washington, DC and throughout Latin America.[104] CEJIL has the resources to finance litigation, bring expert witnesses to Washington, DC or San José, and to follow the jurisprudence of the Court. In comparative terms, the Ford and MacArthur Foundations have historically allocated more funds to NGO projects relating to the IAS than the ECtHR, even though the caseload is a fraction of that of the European Court (see Figure 3.3). According to Juan Méndez, "this [NGO involvement] makes opinions sharper and with more sophisticated arguments . . . this comes from the quality of the representation. CEJIL is an essential actor."[105] CEJIL also has extensive experience litigating before the Commission and Court and this expertise often exceeds that of the lawyers representing the governments.[106] This high level of expertise and experience persuades petitioners whose case was referred to the Court to allow CEJIL to become involved, even if CEJIL was not involved with the case at the Commission stage.[107]

NGO involvement with litigation does not end with the Court judgment, but continues into the period of state compliance and implementation of judgments. CEJIL, and other NGOs, are actively involved in the implementation process, which is supervised by the Court.[108]

---

[102] The Legal Assistance Fund is supported by voluntary contributions and has separate accounts relating to cases before the Commission and Court. For the rules of operation, see: www.oas.org/en/iachr/mandate/basics/fund.asp and www.corteidh.org.cr/index.php/en/jurisprudence/12-anuncios/218-legal-assistance-fund-for-victims.

[103] Since the 1990s, the Commission held that NGOs must be representatives of the victims, not of larger societal interests. Previously, as seen in the *Baby Boy* case, NGOs could submit petitions to the Commission without acting as legal representatives to the victims.

[104] Some of CEJIL's donors include: Ford Foundation, The John D. and Catherine T. MacArthur Foundation, National Endowment for Democracy, the Oak Foundation, and Swedish NGO Foundation for Human Rights; CEJIL, "CEJIL Activities Report - 20 Years," 8.

[105] Author interview with Juan Méndez, December 14, 2010.

[106] Author interview with a former official of the Inter-American Commission and Court of Human Rights, November 25, 2010.

[107] Author interview with an official of the Inter-American Commission on Human Rights, December 8, 2010.

[108] Since 2007, the Court has held hearings on the enforcement of judgments.

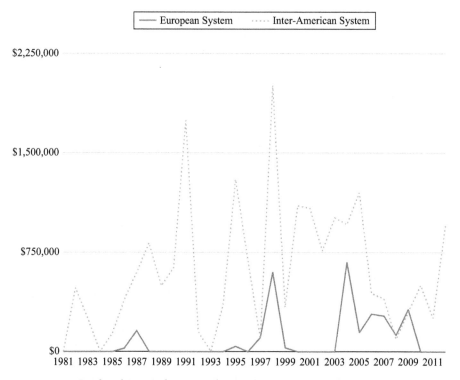

FIGURE 3.3 Ford and MacArthur Foundation NGO Grant Funding Comparison between the European and Inter-American Systems of Human Rights (1981–2011)
Source: Data are triangulated from two sources: (1) from searches of grant descriptions from Internal Revenue Service (IRS) filings compiled in the Foundation Search database. The search criteria used include: strategic litigation, European Court, Inter-American. All search results were then examined to make sure that the project description did pertain to an international judicial mechanism; (2) from Ford and MacArthur Foundation annual reports from 1981 to 2012.

NGOs monitor compliance with judgments, submit information to the Court, demand hearings on compliance, and participate in said hearings before the Commission and Court. According to a staff member of CEJIL:

> One of our main worries is compliance of the Court and Commission's resolutions. We have invested a lot of resources regarding implementation. I think that it is my main worry for the years to come ... We litigate the cases so that they can have a major impact beyond the victims that we represent and are committed to. Now we have to focus on bona fide fulfillment of resolutions. This is part of the challenge right now of our organization.[109]

CEJIL also invests resources into implementation through education, awareness, and advocacy. CEJIL has published manuals on best practices of implementation,

---

[109] Author interview with a staff member of CEJIL, November 29, 2010.

advocates directly with public institutions about compliance, and organizes events, meetings, and workshops on compliance.[110]

Additionally, in the 1990s, NGOs began focusing on outreach and education. CEJIL sponsors multiple trainings per year with public institutions on due diligence and with NGOs and victims on how to use the IAS.[111] CEJIL also conducts research and has published books, including volumes on the comparative law on violence against women and due diligence.[112]

CONCLUSION

NGO participation at the IAS is expansive, frequent, and influential. Participatory relations with NGOs first emerged in response to the rampant and grave human rights abuses occurring in Latin America during the 1970s. At this time, NGOs provided the Commission important information and services that bolstered its ability to publicize and shame states for their egregious human rights records. The Commission was receptive to NGO aid because such help was necessary for the beleaguered and resource-poor Commission to fulfill its mission. Similarly, the Court also saw relationships with NGOs as a potential source of financial and expert-based resources. At its inception, the Court manufactured NGO assistance by establishing its own NGO that would provide funding for the Court to run special sessions and leaving open the possibility for NGOs to provide needed legal research and information as amicus brief filers. Even today, NGOs are instrumental to the functioning of the Commission and Court and through providing the judicial institutions with necessary information, resources, and services, NGOs constitute the "heart of the IAS."[113]

NGOs will likely remain critical participants at the Inter-American Commission and Court. The IAS still struggles with funding, state support, and compliance and therefore still depends on NGOs to share information on human rights abuses, provide sophisticated and comparative legal arguments, and bring landmark cases to the Commission and the Court. Currently, several reform issues are paramount to the IAS, including making the judicial institutions full-time and incorporating English-speaking countries into the Convention.[114] While NGOs do consult on reform issues at the OAS, NGO influence vis-à-vis states is circumscribed and therefore NGO ability to shape the future jurisdiction and functionality of the IAS through state reform is unclear.

[110] Author interviews with staff members of CEJIL, November 29, 2010 and December 17, 2010.
[111] Author interview with a staff member of CEJIL, December 17, 2010.
[112] Author interview with a staff member of CEJIL, November 29, 2010.
[113] Author interview with a faculty member of American University Washington College of Law, December 15, 2010.
[114] Paolo Carozza, "Anglo–Latin Divide and the Future of the Inter-American System of Human Rights," *Notre Dame Journal of International and Comparative Law* 5 (2015): 153.

Another element of uncertainty with regard to the future of NGO engagement vis-à-vis the IAS is continued NGO motivation to play such paramount roles. The instigation for NGO attention to the IAS is to utilize and build the capacity of judicial institutions because of their unique character. No other judicial institution exists that can provide comparable and enforceable judgments for human rights violations. This calculus could change as other international and domestic mechanisms gain strength and teeth, including national human rights institutions and the UN human rights treaty commissions. CEJIL is the most prominent player at the Commission and Court, and its mission is to specifically engage in strategic litigation using the IAS. Nonetheless, even with CEJIL's great influence and success utilizing the IAS, it is expanding its strategies and looking to utilize other enforcement institutions, such as the UN mechanisms, which could provide supplemental or alternative avenues for redress.[115]

---

[115] Author interview with a staff member of CEJIL, November 29, 2010.

4

Rearing the Fledgling International Criminal Court Part I

We have a civil society that defends the Rome Statute as if they were defending dolphins, whales.[1]

INTRODUCTION

Mathieu Ngudjolo Chui and Germain Katanga sat stone-faced at the far side of the courtroom as the trial proceedings slowly unfolded. Judge Diarra of Mali napped as the presiding Judge of the International Criminal Court (ICC) discussed the terms of bringing in the witnesses. The shade separating the public viewing gallery from the courtroom continually went up and down and the audio from the headphones shut off as the proceedings hiccupped between public and private every few minutes. The prosecution sought to introduce 17 short video clips taken by a protected witness during the violence in Ituri in the DRC in 2002–2003.[2] The public was told that the videos would be graphic and depict bodies. At the end of four hours, only four videos were shown – none seemingly incriminating or graphic – and the prosecution was only able to definitively establish that Mr. Ngudjolo Chui attended a public meeting about the pacification in Ituri, one that human rights NGOs also attended. The sluggish pace of the trial resulted from myriad logistical and procedural problems. The protected witness spoke in a dialect of Swahili, which caused significant delays as court interpreters simultaneously translated it into English and French. The prosecution's questions continually jumped from public to confidential, which forced the Court to institute protectionary measures (shutting the shade, turning off the cameras and audio) every few minutes. The video clips were of poor quality and the audio was so

---

[1]   Author interview with Deborah Ruiz Verduzco, Senior Programme Officer, Parliamentarians for Global Action (PGA), September 8, 2010.
[2]   Author witnessed the trial in August 2010. At this time, the *Katanga* and *Ngudjolo Chui* cases were combined on the basis that they allegedly shared responsibility for the attack on Bogoro.

garbled that the interpreters could not translate most of them. The President did not allow the prosecution's written transcript of the videos because it was not performed by court interpreters or previously presented to the defense.

The case of *The Prosecutor* v. *Germain Katanga and Mathieu Ngudjolo Chui* is illustrative of some of the functional challenges facing the ICC, specifically the Office of the Prosecutor. In November 2012, the judges separated the two cases – after over four years of combined trial proceedings – in order to re-characterize the charges against, and essentially retry, Germain Katanga.[3] In December 2012, Mathieu Ngudjolo Chui, the alleged former leader of the National Integrationist Front (FNI), was acquitted of all charges relating to the FNI attack on Bogoro in which over 200 people were murdered and raped. In the verdict, the ruling judges stated that finding an accused not guilty does not mean he is innocent, but that it demonstrates that the evidence presented by the prosecution did not meet the threshold of beyond reasonable doubt.[4] The *Ngudjolo Chui* case was the second completed case at the ICC.[5] More than a year following the re-characterization of charges against Germain Katanga, he was found guilty as an accessory for a crime against humanity and war crimes in March 2014. Judge van den Wyngaert wrote a scathing dissent that essentially accused her fellow judges of re-characterizing and retrying Germain Katanga to avoid another acquittal similar to the *Ngudjolo Chui* trial. She argued that re-characterization to a lesser charge was motivated by the demands of justice by victims at the expense of procedural fairness and the rights of the accused.[6]

Prosecutorial shortcomings are not limited to the *Katanga* and *Ngudjolo Chui* cases. The *Lubanga* case was nearly derailed by allegations of prosecutorial miscon-duct and due process issues related to the use of intermediaries. Multiple cases – including Bahar Idris Abu Garda, Callixte Mbarushimana, Major General Mohammed Hussein Ali, Henry Kiprono Kosgey, and Francis Kirimi Mutharura – were either withdrawn or have not made it past the confirmation stages, mostly due to lack of evidence.[7] In addition to the legal specifics of the cases themselves, critics fault the ICC for bias in the selection of cases. Some African countries and the AU

---

3   Similar to Ngudjolo, Katanga was originally charged as an "indirect co-perpetrator." Using Regulation 55, the charges were re-characterized to the lesser mode of "common purpose liability" based on Katanga's testimony.

4   ICC, *Prosecutor* v. *Mathieu Ngudjolo*, ICC-01/04–02/12, Judgment Pursuant to Article 74 of the Statute (December 18, 2012), www.icc-cpi.int/EN_Menus/icc/situations%20and%20cases/situ ations/situation%20icc%200104/related%20cases/icc-01-04-02-12/court-records/chambers/trial% 20chamber%20ii/pages/3.aspx.

5   On March 14, 2012, Thomas Lubanga Dyilo (the *Lubanga* case) was found guilty of the war crimes of conscripting and enlisting children under the age of 15 and using them to actively participate in military hostilities during the conflict in Ituri, Democratic Republic of the Congo (DRC).

6   ICC, *The Prosecutor* v. *Germain Katanga*, ICC-01/04–01/07, Minority Opinion of Judge Christine Van den Wyngaert (March 7, 2014), www.icc-cpi.int/iccdocs/doc/doc1744372.pdf.

7   ICC, "Situations and Cases," www.icc-cpi.int/en_menus/icc/situations%20and%20cases/Pages/ situations%20and%20cases.aspx [accessed May 6, 2015].

have sharply critiqued the ICC for an Africa bias, as all situation countries prior to 2016 were African.[8] Human rights and civil society groups have also critiqued the ICC for within-case selection bias, or in the case of state referrals, the Court not targeting and investigating government officials who also likely orchestrated abuses.[9]

The ICC also faces the perennial problem of state cooperation. According to multiple ICC officials, state cooperation is the single greatest challenge to the Court.[10] The Court is dependent on states to function: it requires funding, assistance with investigations, enforcement of arrest warrants, and domestic implementation of the Rome Statute. Funding for the ICC has stagnated when viewed in proportion to the number of situation countries. Over one hundred states are party to the Rome Statute, yet only two of the five permanent members of the United Nations Security Council (UNSC) are member states of the Court.[11] The prosecution's suspension of the case against Sudanese President Omar al-Bashir highlights the unwillingness of many states, even member states, to enforce an arrest warrant for a sitting head of state.

These challenges translate to the consistent refrain heard in the media, and among academics and human rights groups: the ICC is in crisis, at risk, or beleaguered.[12] Some question whether the Court will continue to exist and, if so, whether its future influence will be purely symbolic.[13] These questions are particularly salient because the ICC is so

---

[8] BBC News, "African Union Accuses ICC of 'hunting' Africans," accessed May 7, 2015, www .bbc.com/news/world-africa-22681894; Richard Lough, "African Union Accuses ICC Prosecutor of Bias," *Reuters*, January 30, 2011, www.reuters.com/article/2011/01/30/ozatp-africa-icc-idAF JOE70T01R20110130; Michael Birnbaum, "African Leaders Complain of Bias at ICC as Kenya Trials Get Underway," *The Washington Post*, December 5, 2013, www.washingtonpost.com/ world/europe/african-leaders-complain-of-bias-at-icc-as-kenya-trials-are-underway/2013/12/05/ 0c52fc7a-56cb-11e3-bdbf-097ab2a3dc2b_story.html.
   In January 2016, the ICC Prosecutor was authorized to open a *proprio motu* investigation into the 2008 conflict in Georgia.
[9] Human Rights Watch, "Unfinished Business."
[10] Author interviews with ICC officials, August 12, 13, and 17, 2010.
[11] France and the United Kingdom are member state parties; China, Russia, and the United States are not.
[12] David Bosco, "How to Destroy the International Criminal Court From Within," *Foreign Policy*, October 10, 2014, http://foreignpolicy.com/2014/10/10/how-to-destroy-the-international-criminal-court-from-within/; Mark Kersten, "Yes, the ICC Is in Crisis. It Always Has Been," *Justice in Conflict* (blog), February 24, 2015, http://justiceinconflict.org/2015/02/24/yes-the-icc-is-in-crisis-it-always-has-been/; Washington Post Editorial Board, "The International Criminal Court on Shaky Ground," *The Washington Post*, December 28, 2014, www.washingtonpost .com/opinions/the-international-criminal-court-on-shaky-ground/2014/12/28/8d11a3d6-815c-11e4-81fd-8c4814dfa9d7_story.html; Joshua Meservey, "International Criminal Court Hurts Its Own Credibility in Africa - US News," *US News & World Report*, January 2, 2015, www.usnews.com/ opinion/blogs/world-report/2015/01/02/international-criminal-court-hurts-its-own-credibility-in-africa; Elizabeth M. Evenson and Jonathan O'Donohue, "The International Criminal Court at Risk," *Open Democracy*, April 30, 2015, www.opendemocracy.net/openglobalrights/elizabeth-evenson-jonathan-o%E2%80%99donohue/international-criminal-court-at-risk.
[13] Chandra Lekha Sriram and Stephen Brown, "Kenya in the Shadow of the ICC: Complementarity, Gravity and Impact," *International Criminal Law Review* 12, no. 2 (2012): 219–44; Kenneth Roth, "Africa Attacks the International Criminal Court," *The New York Review of*

TABLE 4.1 *NGO Participatory Roles, Frequency, and Impact at the International Criminal Court*

Types of NGO Participation	Roles	NGO Participatory Frequency*	NGO Participatory Impact*
Formal roles in trials	• Filing amicus curiae or "friend of the court" briefs	Medium	Medium
Court-directed advocacy/ consultative roles	• Formal meetings with each organ of Court and ASP Secretariat	High	Low
	• Informal meetings with Court organs	High	Medium
State-directed advocacy/consult- ative roles	• Ratification of Rome Statute	High	High
	• Lobbying the ASP	High	Medium
	• Enforcement of decisions/warrants	High	Low
Information sharing/ operational support roles	• Article 15 communications to the ICC Prosecutor	High	Medium
	• Intermediaries and sharing information	High	High
	• Communications and outreach	High	High
	• Legal counsel for victims and defense	Medium	Medium

*Note: For frequency, low means infrequent participation, medium means some participation, and high means sustained and intense participation. For impact, low means mostly symbolic effect, medium means general substantive effect, and high means essential for functionality. For the specific measures and data of each participatory role, see Appendix D.

young without a firmly established record. Nevertheless, the ICC has not faced the challenges of state cooperation, functionality, and prosecutorial failings alone. International and domestic NGOs, while also critics and monitors, aid the Court in countless ways: from pressuring the Assembly of States Parties (ASP) for a larger budget, helping draft the prosecutorial strategy, facilitating investigations and state cooperation, to performing communications and outreach functions in coordination with the Court (see Table 4.1). NGOs engage in these roles to buffer the challenges facing the Court and help actualize their vision of it. In 2005, William Pace, the convener of the NGO, the Coalition for the International Criminal Court (CICC), stated: "the great majority of the work on the ICC is being done by NGOs: I estimate that more than 200 CICC members have full- or part-time staff focusing on the ICC on a daily basis; there are likely another 400 to 500 organisations that have staff, volunteers or interns work on ICC issues on a regular basis; and thousands of others that promote the Court throughout the year."[14]

Books, February 6, 2014, www.nybooks.com/articles/archives/2014/feb/06/africa-attacks-inter national-criminal-court/.

[14] William R. Pace, "1995–2005: Coalition Celebrates Ten Years," *Insight on the ICC*, no. Tenth Anniversary Special Edition (2005): 1.

NGO support was not limited to when the ICC first became operational. According to ICC officials, NGOs currently play a paramount and critical role at the Court and that the ICC affords NGOs the most wide-ranging roles, access, and influence of any international court.[15]

Many NGOs – such as the CICC, the Women's Initiatives for Gender Justice (WIGJ), FIDH, and Human Rights Watch – became stakeholders at the Court because of their prominent roles in advocating for the creation of the Court.[16] Their previous work afforded these NGOs pre-established relationships, legitimacy from known expertise, and "name recognition" with key court officials and government representatives as they sought to expand their participation at the operational court. NGOs sought new participatory roles because they felt bound to the principles of the Rome Statute and wanted the Court to succeed and actualize the principles for which they so fervently fought. Expansion was further facilitated by ample grant money from foundations that prioritized NGO grants related to the ICC during its early years. The fledgling Court with a huge mandate accepted NGO participation because NGOs could aid the Court in its existential struggle for state cooperation. The Court's need for money, enforcement, strategies, procedures, and outreach not only galvanized NGOs to seek new participatory roles but also convinced court officials to allow NGOs to become critical players at the Court.

ORIGINS AND STRUCTURE OF THE INTERNATIONAL CRIMINAL COURT

The ICC is the first permanent, treaty-based, international criminal court. International criminal courts hold individuals criminally responsible for violations of international criminal law, such as genocide, crimes against humanity, and war crimes. While the idea of a permanent international criminal court dates back to 1872, the genesis of the ICC occurred in 1989 when the Prime Minister of Trinidad and Tobago proposed at the UN General Assembly the establishment of an international criminal court to cover crimes including, but not limited to, drug trafficking.[17] Following this proposal, the UN General Assembly referred the matter to the International Law Commission (ILC), which spent the next four years drafting a statute for the court.[18] In 1994, in response to the ILC's draft statute, the UN General

[15] Author interviews with ICC officials, August 12 and 17, 2010.
[16] Bruce Broomhall, *International Justice and the International Criminal Court* (Oxford University Press, 2003); Benjamin N. Schiff, *Building the International Criminal Court* (Cambridge University Press, 2008); Struett, *The Politics of Constructing the International Criminal Court*.
[17] Gustave Moynier, one of the founders and President of the International Committee of the Red Cross (ICRC), made the first proposal for a permanent criminal court at a meeting of the ICRC on January 3, 1872. See: Christopher Keith Hall, "The First Proposal for a Permanent International Criminal Court," *International Review of the Red Cross* (1961–1997) 38, no. 322 (March 1998): 57–74, https://doi.org/10.1017/S0020860400090768; Glasius, *The International Criminal Court*.
[18] The ILC is a commission of legal experts that meets annually to promote the codification of international public law. The UN General Assembly established it in 1948.

Assembly established a committee to prepare for the final negotiations of a draft statute in Rome in 1998. At the 1998 Rome Conference, the joint coordination of a coalition of civil society organizations and a group of like-minded states resulted in the last-minute approval of the Rome Statute, the treaty that lays out the parameters of the ICC.[19] With the United States and other major states opposed to the proposed structure of the Court and actively seeking to undermine the proposal, the fact that the majority of states approved the Rome Statute was hailed as a victory of justice over power politics. Jubilation followed the final voting and some delegates cried with joy.[20] Philippe Kirsch, the Chairman of the Rome Conference, stated that the strong emotions of the delegates reflected their commitment to "an instrument that they hoped would mark the beginning of a new era in which humanitarian values and protection of victims might finally become center stage, and not the usual side show to the protection of sovereignty or even the exercise of raw power."[21]

As opposed to past international criminal courts and tribunals – which were established by war victors or UNSC resolution – states must sign, ratify, or accede to the Rome Statute to become member states. Sixty states needed to do so in order for the Rome Statute to take effect, which occurred in 2002 (see Figure 4.1). The Rome Statute has jurisdiction to try individuals for war crimes, crimes against humanity, genocide, and aggression and can obtain jurisdiction in three ways: (1) the crimes are committed within the territory of a state party to the Rome Statute or a state which is not a party to the Rome Statute accepts jurisdiction, (2) the alleged perpetrator is a national of a state party to the Rome Statute or a state which is not a party to the Rome Statute but accepts jurisdiction, or (3) the UN Security Council refers a specific situation within a country to the prosecutor for investigation. [22] Apart from the UNSC referral, investigations can be triggered either by a state referral (self-referral or otherwise) or by the prosecutor, upon receiving information from an NGO or other actor. The ICC does not investigate or try all cases – it targets only those individuals most responsible for alleged crimes and operates under the principle of complementarity.[23] Complementarity means that the Court is a last resort and only exercises jurisdiction when domestic, national courts are either unable or unwilling to prosecute.

---

[19] Nicole Deitelhoff, "The Discursive Process of Legalization: Charting Islands of Persuasion in the ICC Case," *International Organization* 63, no. 1 (2009): 33–65, https://doi.org/10.1017/S002081830909002X.

[20] Bosco, *Rough Justice*, 50; Glasius, *The International Criminal Court*.

[21] Philippe Kirsch and John T. Holmes, "The Birth of the International Criminal Court: The 1998 Rome Conference," *Canadian Yearbook of International Law* 36 (1998): 37.

[22] In December 2017, following 30 state ratifications of the amendments to the Rome Statute, the ASP adopted a resolution to activate the jurisdiction of the ICC to the crime of aggression in July 2018.

[23] For more information on the principle and practice of responsibility at the ICC, see: Susana SaCouto and Katherine Cleary, "The Gravity Threshold of the International Criminal Court," *American University Law Review* 23, no. 5 (2007): 807–54.

1989	The Prime Minister of Trinidad and Tobago proposes to the UN General Assembly the establishment of an international criminal court
1989–1993	At the request of the UN General Assembly, the International Law Commission (ILC) explores the possibility of a court and prepares a draft ICC statute
1994	The UN General Assembly considers the draft, establishes a preparatory committee for a final conference negotiation in Rome in 1998
1998	Rome Conference
2002	On July 1, the ICC is established with the 60 state ratifications of the Rome Statute
2003	On March 11, the ICC is inaugurated
2004	In June, the OTP opens its first investigation into crimes committed in the Democratic Republic of the Congo
2009	In January, the first trial begins (*Prosecutor* v. *Thomas Lubanga Dyilo*)
2010	Review conference of the Rome Statute in Kampala, Uganda
2012	In March, the first trial is completed (*Prosecutor* v. *Thomas Lubanga Dyilo*)

FIGURE 4.1: Historical Timeline of the International Criminal Court

The Court consists of four organs – the Registry, the Office of the Prosecutor, the Presidency, and the Judicial Divisions (Chambers). The Registry is responsible for the non-judicial aspects of the Court and assembles the budget, organizes and implements the Court's communications, outreach and work with victims, as well as coordinates the semi-autonomous Office of Public Council for Victims, the Office of Public Council for Defense, and the Trust Fund for Victims. The Office of the Prosecutor (OTP) receives referrals, examines and investigates crimes, and conducts trial prosecutions. The Presidency is responsible for the overall administration of the Court – except for the Office of the Prosecutor – and consists of three judges, a President, a First Vice-President, and a Second Vice-President. The Presidency is actively involved in the campaign for ratification and implementation of the Rome Statute. The Judicial Divisions consist of 18 judges that make up the Pre-Trial Division, the Trial Division, and the Appeals Division.[24] In addition to the four organs of the Court, there is also the ASP. The ASP comprises diplomatic representatives from each state party to the Rome Statute. It has a Secretariat, Working Groups, the Oversight Committee for the Permanent Premises, the Committee on Budget and Finance, a Board of Directors of the Trust Fund for Victims, and a Bureau that consists of a President, two Vice-Presidents, and 18 members elected for three years. The ASP is the management oversight and legislative body of the Court and adopts the rules and procedures of the Court, elects judges and the prosecutor, approves the budget of the Court, and provides general governance functions to the Court.[25]

[24] International Criminal Court, "Structure of the Court," accessed April 25, 2013, www.icc-cpi .int/en_menus/icc/structure%20of%20the%20court/Pages/structure%20of%20the%20court.aspx.
[25] International Criminal Court, "ICC-Assembly of States Parties," accessed April 25, 2013, www .icc-cpi.int/en_menus/asp/assembly/Pages/assembly.aspx.

The initial expectations placed on the ICC were immense and lofty. The overview of the Rome Statute declares the Court is necessary to: "achieve justice for all," "end impunity," "help end conflicts," "remedy the deficiencies of the ad hoc tribunals," "take over when national criminal justice institutions are unwilling or unable to act," and to "deter future war criminals."[26] In 1998, William Pace, the coordinator of the NGO CICC, further asserted the deterrent effect of the Court: "[The ICC] will save millions of humans from suffering unspeakably horrible and inhumane death in the coming decades."[27] Diplomats and academics claim that the ICC will strengthen the common bonds of humanity and help cultivate democracy through the establishment of new democracy-promoting domestic institutions.[28] The ICC is also touted as a triumph of legalism over politics – even though it is governed by states and requires their cooperation and buy-in in order to operate as intended.[29]

NGOS AND THE INTERNATIONAL CRIMINAL COURT

Prominent human rights NGOs, such as Human Rights Watch, FIDH, the CICC Secretariat, and Redress – both individually and through the coordination of the CICC – play a multiplicity of roles at the Court, many of which are critical to its functioning. The close relationships between NGOs and the ICC are a result of three factors (see Table 4.2). First, NGOs were instrumental in the drafting of the Rome Statute and the subsequent establishment of the ICC. This prior advocacy work conferred on NGOs legitimacy and name recognition as well as facilitated relationships with stakeholders that eased formal and informal participatory access at the Court and the ASP and made it more likely that subsequent NGO participatory advocacy or services would be valued and utilized. Second, many of the NGOs that advocated for the establishment of the ICC have a continuous and unwavering commitment to the success of the judicial project for which they fought. Buoyed by high donor interest in the early years of the Court, NGOs had the capacity to vertically and horizontally scale up participatory engagement in order to better support and monitor the Court. Lastly, the ICC is a young court with a substantial mandate that has constantly struggled with adequate resources and state support.

---

[26] Rome Statute of the International Criminal Court, "Overview, Rome Statute of the International Criminal Court," accessed May 11, 2015, www.un.org/law/icc/index.html.

[27] "United Nations Diplomatic Conference of Plenipotentiaries on the Establishment of an International Criminal Court, 1998 - Volume II," 1998: 129, http://legal.un.org/diplomaticconferences/icc-1998/vol_II_e.html.

[28] Statement by Mr. Minoves Triquell of Andorra. See: "United Nations Diplomatic Conference of Plenipotentiaries on the Establishment of an International Criminal Court, 1998 – Volume II," 129; Jamie Mayerfeld, "The Democratic Legacy of the International Criminal Court," *Fletcher Forum of World Affairs* 28 (2004): 147.

[29] Kirsten Ainley, "The International Criminal Court on Trial," *Cambridge Review of International Affairs* 24, no. 3 (2011): 309–33; Bosco, *Rough Justice*, 4.

TABLE 4.2: *Theoretical Factors that Shape NGO Participatory Roles, Frequency, and Impact at the International Criminal Court*

Roles (Access)	• Prior advocacy work afforded NGOs pre-established relationships, legitimacy, and brand recognition with the Court and member states
	• Pronounced deficiencies of state cooperation and funding
	• Motivated and resourced NGOs continually seeking new roles to fill gaps of the fledgling Court
Frequency	• Highly motivated and resourced NGOs beholden to the Rome Statute
Impact	• Pre-established relationships, legitimacy, and brand recognition coupled with roles filling Court deficiencies led to many roles with significant impact

Court officials recognize the cooperation and budgetary challenges of their institution and have allowed NGO participation because NGOs help it fulfill its mandate through information sharing, expertise, investigative and operational assistance.

NGO BRAND RECOGNITION AND GOODWILL

NGOs were an integral part of the ICC's establishment and were major stakeholders at the time of its creation. NGO involvement dates back to the inception of the Court when the Prime Minister of Trinidad and Tobago proposed the idea of an international criminal court to the UN General Assembly in 1989. Prime Minister Arthur Robinson was a member of the NGO, Parliamentarians for Global Action (PGA), as well as the executive director of an NGO called the Foundation for the Establishment of the International Criminal Court.[30] Human rights NGOs, including Amnesty International, were also involved in the drafting of the Court's statute. In 1990, a NGO Committee of Experts chaired by M. Cherif Bassiouni met in Siracusa, Italy and prepared a draft statute on an international criminal court as well as submitted comments on the ILC's version of the statute.[31]

Sustained and organized NGO involvement in the establishment of the ICC began in 1995 with the formation of the CICC. The CICC was formed by William Pace, the Executive Director of the World Federalist Movement (WFM), and Christopher Hall, the legal advisor of Amnesty International, to facilitate NGO cooperation and advocacy for the establishment of a permanent international court.

[30] According to William Pace, the Convener of the CICC, NGO involvement began even earlier in 1987 with the World Federalist Movement (WFM) leading a small group of NGOs who supported the establishment of an international criminal court; Pace, "1995–2005: Coalition Celebrates Ten Years."

[31] Amnesty International, "Memorandum to the International Law Commission: Establishing a Just, Fair and Effective Permanent International Criminal Tribunal," July 11, 1994, www .amnesty.org/en/library/info/IOR40/007/1994/en; M. Cherif Bassiouni, "Historical Survey 1919–1998," in *ICC Ratification and National Implementing Legislation* (Saint-Agne, France: Association Internationale de Droit Penal, 1999): 21.

This coalition was formed with the stated mission of advocating for the establishment of an international criminal court and later incrementally expanded its mission to include the capacity building functions taken on after Rome Conference and the establishment of the Court.[32]

In 1995, there were 25 NGO members of the Coalition, which included the CICC Steering Committee members: Amnesty International, Human Rights Watch, ICJ, Lawyers Committee for Human Rights (YUCOM), Parliamentarians for Global Action (PGA), and the WFM.[33] In the period leading up to the 1998 Rome Conference, the CICC exploded in growth to include over 800 member NGOs and became intimately involved in the conference preparations and negotiations surrounding the drafting of the Rome Statute. The CICC lobbied governments to support the ICC, organized regional meetings, and produced informational materials, newsletters, and position papers.[34] At the Rome Conference, the CICC played a pivotal role in the successful drafting of the Rome Statute and contributed to the inclusion of gender-specific crimes and the *proprio motu* prosecutorial authority.[35] With over 236 NGO members in attendance, the CICC organized into regional and thematic groups and sought to facilitate and shape all aspects of the negotiations. To this end, the CICC served on state delegations, conducted advocacy and liaised with state delegates, and produced a newsletter, daily updates on states' positions, and position papers.[36] Following the Rome Conference, the CICC's efforts to construct the court continued. As 60 state ratifications were necessary for the court's establishment, it launched a worldwide ratification campaign. Two years later, in 2000, when 60 state ratifications appeared imminent, it also began working on the operational and logistical structure of the ICC at the Preparatory Commission on the Establishment of the International Criminal Court (PrepCom), including drafting the Rules of Procedure and Evidence and Elements of Crimes and generating headquarters agreements, financial rules, the initial court budget, and the rules of procedure of the ASP.[37]

NGOs were highly lauded for their instrumental role in the establishment of the ICC. The CICC has been nominated for the Nobel Peace Prize four times and in September 2003, the ASP adopted a resolution recognizing the contributions of the

[32] Haddad, "After the Norm Cascade."
[33] CICC, "Steering Committee," *The MONITOR*, no. 1 (1996); CICC, "Our History," accessed May 19, 2012, www.iccnow.org/?mod=cicchistory.
[34] Schiff, *Building the International Criminal Court*.
[35] Broomhall, *International Justice and the International Criminal Court*; Schiff, *Building the International Criminal Court*; Struett, *The Politics of Constructing the International Criminal Court*; Marlies Glasius, "Expertise in the Cause of Justice: Global Civil Society Influence on the Statute for an International Criminal Court," in *Global Civil Society Yearbook 2002*, ed. Marlies Glasius, Mary Kaldor, and Anheier Helmut (Oxford University Press, 2002): 137–68; Deitelhoff, "The Discursive Process of Legalization."
[36] Schiff, *Building the International Criminal Court*; Glasius, *The International Criminal Court*; Struett, *The Politics of Constructing the International Criminal Court*.
[37] Schiff, *Building the International Criminal Court*; Haddad, "After the Norm Cascade."

CICC to the establishment of the ICC.[38] The work of NGOs on the Court's establishment not only resulted in gratitude and respect by diplomats and court officials, but increased the likelihood that future NGO participation would be allowed by court officials and member states because of pre-established relationships, legitimacy, and name recognition.

The CICC, and many of its steering committee NGOs, have substantial levels of access and influence at the ICC as formal and informal consultants to the Court organs and to the ASP. This tremendous role of the CICC and its affiliates as consultants directly grew out of the relationships and roles that NGOs played in the Rome Conference and afterwards at PrepCom. Because NGO personnel knew member state diplomats and the first court officials from their previous advocacy and consultative work, NGOs had both pre-established relationships and legitimacy that facilitated continued consultative roles after the Court was established. A CICC staff member articulates how the combination of name recognition, personal relationships, and gratitude towards the CICC enabled NGOs to have substantial access and influence at the Court and the ASP:

> I think the fact that we are there [the ASP meetings] is a testament to the fact that these individuals were around in 1995. Because you had these grand ol' dinosaurs, that they would say themselves, of the international criminal justice world within civil society. Because of their presence, because they pushed for the creation of the Court, that there has been an acknowledgment of some sort of the role that they have played in the establishment of the Court ... Our [the CICC's] Convener William Pace, who is based out of New York, has a very good relationship with President Wenaweser of the ASP. So, over time there is a great deal of goodwill that has been established with, not just court organs, but with the ASP Secretariat, with the Assembly of States Parties as a whole. There is a lot of brand recognition with the Coalition ... going back to 1995, it is something that has grown since then.[39]

The CICC's "brand recognition" is evident at the ICC. The CICC's cachet and broad base of members has made the organization the official and unofficial civil society liaison to the Court. The CICC has been formally designated to coordinate civil society representation at the annual NGO meeting with the Court organs, the ASP annual meetings, and the "People's Space" at the Review Conference in Kampala in 2010.[40] Many member state diplomats also coordinate civil society

---

[38] CICC, "1999," *Insight on the ICC*, no. Tenth Anniversary Special Edition (2005): 4.
  At the ASP fourth meeting on September 11, 2003, the ASP adopted resolution ICC-ASP/2/Res.8 on the recognition of the coordinating and facilitating role of the NGO Coalition for the ICC.

[39] Author interview with a CICC staff member, August 20, 2010.

[40] Author interview with an ICC official, August 12, 2010; Rome Statute of the International Criminal Court, "NGO Participation in the Assembly of States Parties," accessed May 12, 2015, http://legal.un.org/icc/asp/2ndsession/ngoinasp.2nd.htm; International Criminal Court, "ICC Review Conference," accessed May 13, 2015, www.icc-cpi.int/en_menus/asp/reviewconference/Pages/review%20conference.aspx#general.

participation at The Hague Working Group meetings through the CICC.[41] This is not a new role for the CICC: the UN granted the CICC the authority to accredit NGOs at the Rome Conference.[42]

In many ways, the CICC *is* civil society at the ICC and serves as a facilitator and gatekeeper of most civil society access to the Court and court governance. According to a state diplomat, the CICC resists viewing itself as a NGO "superstructure" but that it is perceived to represent and be able to reach all of civil society.[43] Utilizing the CICC as a superstructure – delegating it the role to coordinate civil society engagement – also benefits the Court and diplomats, who worry that inviting some NGOs, and excluding others, could create unwanted disruptions.[44]

DEFENDING THE ROME STATUTE

The prior advocacy work of the CICC and its steering committee members facilitated relationships, goodwill, and recognition on which to build new participatory roles, but it did not ensure continued participation once the Court was established. NGOs could have decided that they did not want to pursue a relationship with the Court after its establishment or court officials could have soured on the relationship and denied further NGO access. An ICC official recounts how after the Court's establishment the relationship between NGOs was uncertain:

> They [NGOs] played a huge role ... maybe the first time NGOs played such a huge role in a treaty negotiation ... Then there was an evolution. Because in the very first NGO meetings, some NGOs also got up and said: "this is all well and good but we will also be opposing you at some point. If you want to do x during the prosecution, and we want to do y in terms of expanding the scope or whatever, then we may be on opposite sides"... Some people from the Court said: "the love affair has ended." That was an extreme statement; it had not ended as such but it became much more nuanced after the Rome Conference and after we started working.[45]

The relationship between NGOs and the ICC did not sour and NGO participatory roles actually grew and flourished as the Court evolved. This resulted not only because of the critical roles that the NGOs came to play at the ICC, but that NGOs amongst themselves and with the Court were able to negotiate expectations and criticism. Some within the Court feel that NGO expectations are unattainable and

---

[41] Author interview with a state diplomat that attends ASP meetings, August 25, 2010.12/14/17 3:25:00 PM.

[42] William R. Pace, "The Relationship Between the International Criminal Court and Non-Governmental Organizations," in *Reflections on the International Criminal Court*, ed. Herman A.M. von Hebel, Johan G. Lammers, and Jolien Schukking (The Hague: T.M.C. Asser Press, 1999): 209.

[43] Author interview with a state diplomat that attends ASP meetings, August 25, 2010.

[44] Author interview with a state diplomat that attends ASP meetings, August 25, 2010.

[45] Author interview with an ICC official, August 12, 2010.

will never be met, that NGOs often push too far into the internal affairs of the Court, or that NGOs want to micromanage the Court's operations. Yet, there is a general consensus that the relationships with NGOs are positive and that most of the critiques are done in a constructive way.[46] Tensions exist among NGOs – particularly among the CICC member NGOs – about what issues warrant attention and whether critiques should be public or private.[47] But because the CICC has substantial access with court officials to provide constructive criticism in confidence, its public statements tend to be more subdued and less critical. Member NGOs of the CICC, in their individual capacity, have more freedom to forcefully and publically critique the Court.[48]

The missions and goals of NGOs morphed from the establishment of an international criminal court to continued participatory roles at an operational court because of NGOs' normative commitment to an idealized vision of the Court. NGOs did not and do not feel beholden to the Court as an organization but to the *principles* of the Rome Statute that underlie the Court. These were the principles that guided and motivated their advocacy efforts to establish the Court and continue to guide their quest to actualize those principles. In the opinion of a CICC staff member, the CICC should not be named the Coalition for the International Criminal Court but the Coalition for the Rome Statute.[49] According to a staff member of PGA: "We have a civil society that defends the Rome Statute as if they were defending dolphins, whales ... We support the Court, our support is unconditional, but it is not a blind support ... we can be effective in the extent that the Court works in a proper way. We are very concerned not in protecting the Court but in protecting the integrity of the Rome Statute. That is what we are protecting: the Rome Statute ... We have a very clear vision of what the Rome Statute is supposed to be achieving."[50]

As previously mentioned, this adherence to the Rome Statute does not mean that NGOs will not be critical of the Court. Conversely, because there will always be a gap between how the ICC actually operates and the aspirational goals of the Rome Statute, NGOs see a perpetual and unconditional role for themselves in monitoring that gap and suggesting ways to better actualize the principles of the Rome Statute. This monitoring role locates the guiding moral compass outside of the Court and member states and places it within a subset of civil society and their vision of the how the Court should operate, grow, and react to difficult political or legal questions. This monitoring role – particularly because some of the NGOs were involved

---

[46] Author interviews with ICC officials, August 12 and 17, 2010.
[47] Author interview with a CICC staff member, July 6, 2010; Author interview with the WIGJ staff members, August 23, 2010.
[48] Author interview with the WIGJ staff members, August 23, 2010.
[49] Author interview with a CICC staff member, August 20, 2010.
[50] Author interview with Deborah Ruiz Verduzco, Senior Programme Officer, PGA, September 8, 2010.

in the establishment of the Court – can seem somewhat paternalistic, where NGOs steer and support the Court, much as a parent would for a child.[51]

Principles are by their very nature abstract. Therefore, NGOs had to translate their commitment to the principles found in the Rome Statute into organizational functions and campaigns that dealt with the operational court. How NGOs did this varied across NGOs, depending on their identities, missions, capacity, and expertise. Some NGOs, such as the ICJ, largely stopped doing work related to the ICC following the Rome Conference and have taken up other advocacy projects, such as the establishment of a permanent human rights court.[52] Because it is comprised of diplomats, PGA focused on the ratification campaign and garnering state support for ongoing situations, such as Kenya.[53] For the CICC – whose raison d'être was the establishment of the ICC – its adherence to the Rome Statute translated into providing nearly any support or expertise that it deemed necessary to the Court. A CICC staff member describes this continual expansion of its role with relation to the Court:

> The Rome Statute required 60 ratifications. To achieve that, there was a global campaign launched for early entry into force as part of ratification and of course, implementation too. Then once the court launched, a whole new area came up . . . it's not that we stopped working on an area, we just added new ones: establishment issues of the court, which were elections, rules, regulations . . . who, not in terms of the person, but what kinds of qualifications a judge should have, the prosecutor and all of that.[54]

NGOs not only had the motivation to continually shape the Court, but NGOs also had the expertise, institutional knowledge, and financial resources to pay for the proliferation of services to the Court.

Many of the prominent NGOs involved in the drafting of the Rome Statute – including the CICC, Human Rights Watch, Amnesty International, the WIGJ, FIDH, and Redress – comprise esteemed experts with substantial experience

---

[51] This echoes the Convener of the CICC, William Pace's, take on the role of NGOs with regard to the ICC: "Just as with a child, the birth and youth of a new international organization are crucial, especially formative, extremely vulnerable periods. It will take years, probably one or two decades, for the ICC to reach maturity – and it will need all that parents, family and community must give to survive and thrive." William Pace, "Civil Society Presentation in the International Criminal Court: NGOs Advocacy for a Fair, Independent and Effective ICC from Rome to Today," speech delivered at the HURIDOCS conference, "Human Rights Council and International Criminal Court: The New Challenges for Human Rights Communications," Geneva, February 2009.

[52] Author interview with Ian Seiderman, the Legal and Policy Director of the ICJ, August 20, 2014.

[53] Author interview with Deborah Ruiz Verduzco, Senior Programme Officer, PGA, September 8, 2010.

[54] Author interview with a CICC staff member, July 6, 2010.

relating to international criminal justice.[55] At the Court, this expertise is recognized and respected and officials laud the organizations for their high levels of expertise and professionalism.[56] In addition, because the ICC is a young court with substantial turnover in its personnel, some NGO staff with long-standing experience on the Court have more institutional memory than court officials.[57] Many NGOs are both experts and advocates. Expertise allows NGOs to provide legal and administrative guidance in various matters of the Court, including prosecutorial strategy, budget, and rules and procedures. Advocacy informs their legal and technical opinions but also allows NGOs to be more political and frame issues to member states in ways that the Court cannot. NGOs can advocate to non-member states to sign and ratify the Rome Statute and can frame budgetary issues in terms of responsibilities to victims and their communities.[58]

Participatory engagement with the ICC also requires monetary resources to pay for staff, programming, travel, and headquarters. While securing financing is a perennial struggle for nearly all international and domestic NGOs, funding for ICC-related grants was plentiful during the time of the Rome Conference and the early years of the Court. During this period, Ford and MacArthur Foundation funding for NGO projects relating to the ICC generally outpaced grants for projects relating to other international courts or tribunals (see Figure 4.2). Donor spikes in funding to NGO grants even coincided with landmark events of the ICC: the 1998 Rome Conference, the establishment of the Court in 2002, and the first indictments in 2005. The majority of grant monies given during these spikes were not to new NGOs or NGOs with peripheral missions seeking to capitalize on the grant emphasis on the ICC. 75 percent of grant monies relating to the ICC between 1999 and 2006 were given to human rights NGOs that attended the 1998 Rome Conference – many of which were steering committee members of the CICC – planning to scale up or add new participatory roles with regard to the Court.

The CICC was the largest recipient of Ford and MacArthur Foundation grants relating to the ICC. Between 1996 and 2011, the CICC received approximately $13 million for general operations and special projects relating to the ICC.[59] This money went exclusively to the CICC Secretariat – the organizing structure of the coalition – and does not include additional grants made to the steering committee

---

[55] Nouwen terms the CICC Secretariat and NGOs within the coalition, along with like-minded court officials and state diplomats, "the international criminal-justice movement." See: Sarah M. H. Nouwen, *Complementarity in the Line of Fire: The Catalysing Effect of the International Criminal Court in Uganda and Sudan* (Cambridge University Press, 2013): 23.

[56] Author interviews with ICC officials, August 12, 13, and 17, 2010.

[57] Author interview with Deborah Ruiz Verduzco, Senior Programme Officer, PGA, September 8, 2010.

[58] Author interview with an ICC official, August 17, 2010.

[59] Data are triangulated from two sources: (1) from searches of grant descriptions from IRS filings compiled in the Foundation Search database and (2) from Ford and MacArthur Foundation annual reports from 1981 to 2012.

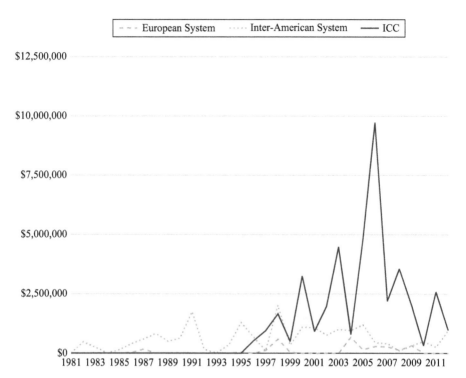

FIGURE 4.2: Combined Ford and MacArthur Foundation Funding by Court (1981–2012)
Note: The "European System" refers to the European Court (and now retired Commission) of Human Rights. The "Inter-American System" refers to the Inter-American Commission and Court of Human Rights. The "ICC" refers to the International Criminal Court. Data are triangulated from two sources: (1) from searches of grant descriptions from IRS filings compiled in the Foundation Search database. The search criteria used include: ICC, ECtHR, and Inter-American. All search results were then examined to make sure that the project description did pertain to the respective international judicial mechanism; (2) from Ford and MacArthur Foundation annual reports from 1981 to 2012.

members, such as Human Rights Watch, FIDH, and the WIGJ, who also engage with the ICC through their individual programs.[60] Financial support to the CICC is not limited to the Ford and MacArthur Foundations. The Open Society Institute, the Sigrid Rausing Trust, the European Union, and many European countries are also long-standing donors who provided additional support to the CICC.[61]

[60] Previously the Women's Caucus for Gender Justice.
[61] CICC, "About the Coalition for the International Criminal Court," accessed May 19, 2015, www.google.com/url?sa=t&rct=j&q=&esrc=s&source=web&cd=2&ved=0CCcQFjAB&url= https%3A%2F%2Fwww.iccnow.org%2Fdocuments%2FCoalition_Factsheet.pdf&ei= wWNbVYfqKYTeoAT4voHYBw&usg=AFQjCNG9_1tlGrD6a5sfP8FJ3AZReOGMog&bvm= bv.93756505,bs.1,d.cGU.

CONCLUSION

The paramount role NGOs played in the establishment of the ICC facilitated court officials and member states in viewing NGOs as legitimate participatory partners. Commitment to the principles espoused in the Rome Statute motivated many prominent NGOs to remain engaged following the Rome Conference. Donors, including private philanthropic foundations and states, were receptive to continued NGO activities vis-à-vis the ICC. Once the Court was initiated in 2003, and began to investigate situations, and later build and try cases, deficiencies in resources, legitimacy, and state buy-in created substantial opportunities for the proliferation of NGO participatory roles. As detailed in Chapter 5, NGOs took on roles typical of human rights advocacy NGOs, such as pushing for universal ratification of the Rome Statute, naming and shaming recalcitrant states, and sharing information about on-the-ground human rights situations. Due to the immense needs of the Court, NGOs also took on unexpected service provision roles such as aiding the Court with investigations, consulting on prosecutorial strategy, conducting outreach in situation countries, and helping the Court assemble its budget and communicate budgetary priorities to member states. Taken together, NGOs have propped up and shaped nearly all aspects of the Court's functioning.

5

Rearing the Fledgling International Criminal Court Part II

You know the role that civil society has played in getting this court established. You know the role that civil society continues to play . . . we are partners and we respect each other's mandate but we also understand each other's mandate.[1]

INTRODUCTION

A former judge of the ICTY, Antonio Cassese, likened the tribunal to a giant without arms and legs that depended on the artificial limbs of state authorities to function.[2] The International Criminal Court (ICC) suffers the same structural dependence. Because of its global jurisdiction and permanent nature, the ICC needs the sustained assistance of an even larger number of states than the ICTY. States must ratify or accede to the Rome Statute and adopt domestic implementing legislation for the Court to have jurisdiction and for cooperation with the Court to become a part of domestic law.[3] States also govern the Court, provide its financing, refer cases, aid investigations, and enforce arrest warrants. For the Court "to breathe, it needs states" yet the single greatest challenge of the operational ICC is state cooperation.[4] Inadequate state cooperation stymies the functionality of the Court in multiple ways. If states do not provide the Court with a sufficient budget, the Court

---

[1] FIDH, *Fatou Bensouda, ICC Prosecutor, Visits FIDH*, 2015, www.fidh.org/International-Feder ation-for-Human-Rights/international-justice/international-criminal-court-icc/fatou-bensouda-icc-prosecutor-visits-fidh.

[2] Antonio Cassese, "On the Current Trends towards Criminal Prosecution and Punishment of Breaches of International Humanitarian Law," *European Journal of International Law* 9, no. 1 (1998): 13. For analysis on the "virtual trials" of the ad hoc tribunals to secure state cooperation see: Peskin, *International Justice in Rwanda and the Balkans.*

[3] The ICC can also obtain jurisdiction of a situation in a non-member state through a UNSC Resolution.

[4] Author interviews with ICC officials, August 12, 13, and 17, 2010.

cannot sustain general operations, outreach, investigations, and trial costs across all of its caseload.[5] Without states providing logistical support, the Court may not have access to crucial on-the-ground information or obtain custody of indicted war criminals. Lastly, state non-cooperation threatens the Court's legitimacy by limiting the reach of its jurisdiction, which lends the appearance that justice is not universally applied.

Even sympathetic and cooperative member states place financial pressures on the young Court to operate efficiently and deliver expeditious trials. These pressures force the Court to acknowledge that it needs help.[6] To supplement the Assembly of States Parties' (ASP) budget, the Court may ask states directly for resources to conduct investigations, such as providing a plane to get to the country under investigation as well as paying for the plane's gas.[7] Another strategy is allowing expanded or new NGO participatory roles. According to an ICC official, "We [the Court] are very aware how weak we are. We are very aware how limited state cooperation is. As a result, there is significant effort to keep NGOs in the fold ... There is definite wooing."[8]

NGOS AND THE OPERATIONAL ICC

A coordinated group of mostly international, well-funded NGOs, with pre-established relationships to court officials recognized and responded to the fledgling Court's deficiencies.[9] This was a court that was a product of their advocacy and that they wanted to become efficacious, fair, and impactful. Therefore, as the ICC struggled to establish procedures, conduct investigations, obtain custody of those indicted, and receive funding commensurate to its ever-growing caseload, various NGOs took on participatory roles that facilitated state cooperation or mitigated the effects of lack of state cooperation. The Court, and sometimes member states, allowed them to do so. This resulted in NGOs performing a multiplicity of participatory roles, many of them substantive, some essential to the Court's viability. NGOs run the campaign for universal state ratification of the Rome Statute and its respective implementing legislation, which increases the jurisdiction of the Court and obligates more states to cooperate with ICC investigations. NGOs pressure the ASP to increase the Court's budget. NGOs "name and shame" member states that do not execute arrest warrants or non-member states that act in ways hostile to the

---

[5] For trials, the Court must pay to keep the accused in custody, transport victims and witnesses to and from The Hague, and provide legal aid for counsel for victims and the accused. Trials generally take several years and on average, an accused person spends 2.3 years in custody awaiting trial at the ICC. See: Heidi L. Hansberry, "Too Much of a Good Thing in Lubanga and Haradinaj: The Danger of Expediency in International Criminal Trials," *Northwestern Journal of International Human Rights* 9, no. 3 (2011): 357–401.

[6] Author interview with an ICC official, August 17, 2010.

[7] Author interview with an ICC official, August 17, 2010.

[8] Author interview with an ICC official, August 12, 2010.

[9] Author interview with a CICC staff member, August 20, 2010.

Court. NGOs aid investigations by acting as intermediaries who share information of crimes and link victims to the Court. NGOs conduct on-the-ground outreach in coordination with the Court that seeks to bridge the disconnect between The Hague and local communities in situation countries. NGOs have close formal and informal relationships with most of the Court organs and submit pertinent information or legal analysis in amicus briefs during trials.

Universal Ratification of the Rome Statute

As the ICC is a treaty-based institution, states must ratify or accede to the Rome Statute in order to become parties to the treaty. Member states automatically submit to the Court's jurisdiction and have governance privileges through the ASP. Following the Rome Conference in 1998, 60 state ratifications of the Rome Statute were necessary to prompt the establishment of the ICC. Additional states parties strengthen the Court, not only through the increased legitimacy of a larger member base, but because it expands the Court's jurisdiction. Even though nearly two-thirds of all states are parties to the Rome Statute, the Court is very aware of the omissions. Much of Asia and the Middle East are not member states, which leaves the ongoing human rights situations in Syria, Iraq, and North Korea, at the discretion of the UN Security Council (UNSC). The Court also very acutely feels the absence of the United States, Russia, and China as member states – the non-member states that are Permanent Members of the UNSC.[10] According to an ICC official, "the Court pays a high price in efficiency and effectiveness not having them."[11] The absence of the UNSC members weakens the Court as UNSC resolutions can expand the jurisdiction of the Court to states that have not ratified or acceded to the Rome Statute and can sanction non-compliance with Court decisions, such as execution of arrest warrants. The UNSC did refer the Darfur and Libya situations to the ICC, but those referrals did not include any additional funds for the investigations and contained immunity provisions for non-citizens.[12] The historical relationship between the Court and the United States is also quite adversarial as the United States "unsigned" the Rome Statute, created bilateral immunity agreements with countries not to turn over US citizens to the ICC contingent on foreign aid, and passed the 2002 American Servicemembers' Protection Act that restricted the United States from providing any support to the Court.[13]

---

[10] Britain and France are the P5 members that are state parties.

[11] Public presentation made by Gilbert Bitti, Senior Legal Adviser to the Pre-Trial Division, August 16, 2010.

[12] See UNSC Resolution 1593 (March 31, 2005) and UNSC Resolution 1970 (February 26, 2011).

[13] The legal basis of these agreements is in Article 98 of the Rome Statute (sometimes they are called Article 98 agreements), which prevents the ICC from requesting states to surrender individuals if it would require the state to "act inconsistently with its obligations under international agreements."

Following ratification or accession, states are required by the Rome Statute to enact implementing legislation. Implementing legislation, or domestic legislation that incorporates the ICC rules and brings domestic laws into conformity with international obligations under the Rome Statute, also bolsters the Court's legitimacy and ability to operate. Implementing legislation creates both domestic legal obligations to cooperate with the Court as well as providing for the principle of complementarity, where domestic courts, if willing and able, can hold criminal trials in lieu of the ICC. According to former Prosecutor Luis Moreno Ocampo: "Implementing legislation strengthens the interaction between States and the ICC, and contributes to ending the culture of impunity by condemning these crimes with a louder, more unified voice."[14] As of early 2014, only 65 states had enacted domestic implementing legislation that contained either cooperation or complementarity provisions.[15] In particular, only four of the 30 member states in Africa – the location of nearly all of the current situation countries – have incorporated both complementarity and cooperation legislation domestically.[16] This means that the reach of the Court into domestic law, both to serve as a deterrent to future crimes through domestic criminalization and to force cooperation with the Court, is quite limited.

NGO advocacy campaigns for states to sign and ratify the Rome Statute and incorporate implementing legislation into domestic law – both in the initial stages to reach the required 60 ratifications and the subsequent goal of universality – constitute some of the most impactful work NGOs do to support the Court.

The Obama Administration's stance on the Court was much more neutral yet the Court was seemingly leery of taking cases that encroached on the United States' geopolitical interests. Bosco coins the ICC's deference toward major powers the strategy of "mutual accommodation." David Bosco, *Rough Justice: The International Criminal Court in a World of Power Politics*, 1st edition (Oxford and New York, NY: Oxford University Press, 2014). See also: David Kaye, "America's Honeymoon with the ICC," *Foreign Affairs*, April 16, 2013, www.foreign affairs.com/articles/2013-04-16/americas-honeymoon-icc.

The American Servicemembers' Protection Act (22. U.S.C. 7424), which prohibits US support of the Court, created uncertainty when the Obama Administration wanted to work with the Court, such as when rebels handed over the Lord's Resistance army (LRA) senior commander Dominic Ongwen to US forces or when Bosco Ntaganda turned himself in to the US Embassy in Rwanda. Craig Whitlock, "Detention of African Warlord Raises Legal Questions for Pentagon," *The Washington Post*, January 13, 2015, www.washingtonpost.com/world/national-security/detention-of-warlord-raises-legal-questions-for-pentagon/2015/01/13/3839c43e-9b4b-11e4-96cc-e858eba91ced_story.html; Max Fisher, "Why Did Infamous War Criminal Bosco Ntaganda Just Surrender at a U.S. Embassy?," *The Washington Post*, March 18, 2013, www.washingtonpost.com/blogs/worldviews/wp/2013/03/18/why-did-infamous-war-criminal-bosco-ntaganda-just-surrender-at-a-u-s-embassy/.

[14] Luis Moreno-Ocampo, "The International Criminal Court: Seeking Global Justice," *Case Western Reserve Journal of International Law* 40 (August 2007): 217.

[15] CICC, "Implementation of the Rome Statute," accessed May 18, 2015, www.iccnow.org/?mod=romeimplementation.

[16] The countries with both complementarity and cooperation legislation are: Kenya, Senegal, South Africa, and Uganda.

According to an ICC official, NGO work on universality is "crucial" to the Court.[17] A Coalition for the International Criminal Court (CICC) staff member also credits NGOs with the quick succession of 60 state ratifications by 2002 and the ensuing growth of member states parties: "the CICC's fingerprints are all over them."[18] NGOs are particularly suited towards ratification efforts. NGOs – such as the CICC – that figured prominently in the Rome negotiations already had close coordination and personal relationships with diplomats from like-minded states. These relationships and shared values translated to channels for advocacy and providing technical assistance regarding ratification and implementing legislation. The CICC also had member NGOs across the globe and set up regional offices that utilized local expertise to advance ratification efforts.[19] Even after the Court was established, it did not adopt a dynamic or holistic practice of promoting universal ratification that would compete with the universality campaign of NGOs. One part of the ICC President's commission is to promote ratification; the President frequently travels and meets with non-member states to encourage them to sign and ratify the Rome Statute. Nevertheless, as a figurehead of the Court, the President also cannot appear to threaten wary non-member states or embroil the Court in global politics. Therefore, most of the rhetoric is limited to urging states to join. Former Prosecutor Moreno Campo felt that "campaigning" for ratification was not an appropriate role for his office: it was the job of advocates external to the Court.[20]

Two major NGO players campaign for universality: the CICC and Parliamentarians for Global Action (PGA).[21] The CICC's involvement with the campaign for universality grew from their prior advocacy efforts to achieve 60 state ratifications of the Rome Statute. Following the 1998 Rome Conference, NGOs initiated a campaign for the 60 state ratifications necessary for the Court's

---

[17] Author interview with an ICC official, August 17, 2010.

[18] Author interview with a CICC staff member, July 6, 2010.

[19] NGO involvement in ratification efforts does not mean that NGO advocacy is *solely* responsible for state ratification. Scholars have attributed treaty ratification to state incentives to credibly commit to accountability measures to reduce future violence as well as state conformity with international legal culture. NGO advocacy could represent a positive contributing factor in both arguments. NGO campaigns – which have strong domestic civil society components – may generate domestic accountability costs, similar to those that bind the country after ratification, to state non-ratification. NGO campaigns may also help socialize states about international norms and expectations regarding human rights accountability.

For credible commitment and international culture arguments, see: Simmons and Danner, "Credible Commitments and the International Criminal Court"; J. W. Meyer et al., "World Society and the Nation-State," *The National Journal of Sociology* 103, no. 1 (1997): 144–81.

[20] Human Rights Watch, "Unfinished Business," 2011; Human Rights Watch, *Courting History* (New York, NY: Human Rights Watch, 2008).

[21] PGA is a founding member of the CICC and is also a steering committee member. Human Rights Watch and Amnesty International have also campaigned for universal ratification of the Rome Statute. See: www.amnestyusa.org/our-work/issues/international-justice/international-criminal-court.

establishment. In late 1999 and early 2000, when the necessary 60 ratifications seemed imminent, the CICC expanded its campaign to universal ratification because it strengthened the Court's jurisdiction and level of state cooperation.[22]

The CICC's work on universality involves both the CICC Secretariat targeting and working with states directly as well as mobilizing domestic NGOs within the targeted state. One strategy of the CICC Secretariat, which began in 2005, is to focus advocacy efforts on one specific state, or a few states, each month. During that month, the CICC, in coordination with local groups, provides educational information about ratification, works with governments on constitutional or legislative obstacles to ratification, and organizes a letter-writing campaign to key officials in the government pressuring ratification.[23] The CICC seeks to "create momentum with those territories" and raise awareness among local groups to approach parliamentarians and government officials and press for ratification.[24] Sometimes the ICC President will coordinate with the campaign and meet with national leaders during the advocacy push.[25] The hallmark success of the CICC's ratification campaign was the quick ratification of 60 states that led to the establishment of the Court. The subsequent universality campaign has been fruitful, particularly in the early years, but has since run up against the regional recalcitrance of the Middle East, North Africa, and Asia.[26] Since 2005, 17 of the 22 states that ratified or acceded to the Rome Statute were targets of the CICC's monthly advocacy campaigns. Of those 17 states, 11 states ratified or acceded within one year of the campaign and four ratified or acceded within two months or less (see Table 5.1).[27] Because the campaign also pressures states to implement domestic legislation, and provides technical assistance to do so, the campaign is still quite active and impactful even if fewer states ratify the Rome Statute.

PGA also engages in substantial advocacy on ratification and universality. Because PGA comprises parliamentarians campaigning in their personal capacity,

[22] CICC, "Our History"; author interview with a CICC staff member, July 6, 2010.
[23] CICC, "Ratification and Implementation," accessed May 19, 2012, www.iccnow.org/?mod=ratimp.
[24] Author interview with a CICC staff member, August 20, 2010.
[25] Author interview with a CICC staff member, July 6, 2010.
[26] The linked map shows the geographic underrepresentation of state parties in the Asian and MENA regions: www.pgaction.org/campaigns/icc/.
[27] There is no accessible information on the criteria or reasoning behind the selection of each country that NGOs target; therefore, the claim could be made that NGOs choose states that would ratify the Rome Statute without NGO advocacy. This appears unlikely for several reasons. First, this strategy would be antithetical to NGOs' stated goals of expanding the jurisdiction of the ICC and number of states that must cooperate with it. Second, NGOs actively target countries in the Middle East, a region with only a few countries that have ratified, and NGOs target countries multiple times. For example, the CICC has targeted Turkey eight times from 2005 to 2012, without Turkey ratifying the Rome Statute, which would suggest that at least some of the states NGOs target are states unlikely to ratify the statute apart from NGO advocacy; CICC, "Universal Ratification Campaign," accessed May 5, 2013, www.iccnow.org/?mod=urc.

TABLE 5.1 *CICC and PGA Advocacy and State Ratification of the Rome Statute*
(2005–2015)

State	Time Lapse from CICC Campaign to Ratification/Accession *(in months)*	Date of Ratification/ Accession (a)
Grenada	1	May 19, 2011
Bangladesh*	2	March 23, 2010
St. Kitts and Nevis	2	August 22, 2006
Kenya	2	March 15, 2005
Maldives*	4	September 21, 2011
Moldova	7	October 12, 2010
Saint Lucia*	8	August 18, 2010
The Czech Republic	10	July 21, 2009
Cape Verde*	11	October 10, 2011
Côte d'Ivoire*	11	February 15, 2013
Chad*	12	November 1, 2006
Palestine	16	January 2, 2015
Philippines*	23	August 30, 2011
Suriname*	25	July 15, 2008
Chile*	27	June 29, 2009
Madagascar*	30	March 14, 2008
Guatemala*	44	April 2, 2012

Note: The list above comprises all states that ratified or acceded to the Rome Statute from 2005 to Summer 2015 which the CICC targeted in a monthly ratification campaign. The five states that ratified/ acceded to the Rome Statute that were not targeted with a CICC advocacy campaign are: Comoros,* Cook Islands,* Dominican Republic,* Japan,* Mexico,* Montenegro,* Seychelles,* Tunisia,* and Vanuatu.* Data are from the websites of the CICC, PGA, and the ICC.
* These are states in which PGA claims to have contributed to ratification/accession.

the activities of PGA members differ from those of the CICC Secretariat. PGA engages in parliamentary meetings, provides technical assistance on implementing legislation, and sponsors workshops, roundtables and conferences on implementation and ratification. PGA claims that it has directly contributed to 76 state ratifications/accessions to the Rome Statute and to the adoption of implementing legislation in more than 25 countries.[28] As seen in Table 5.1, the ratification efforts of PGA and the CICC often overlapped as many states that ratified the Rome Statute were pressured by both organizations.

Recently, both the CICC and PGA expanded the scope of their advocacy efforts. The CICC Secretariat began advocating for states to adopt the Agreement on

---

[28] PGA, "PGA ICC Campaign for the Effectiveness and Universality of the Rome Statute – International Law and Human Rights – Parliamentarians for Global Action (PGA)," accessed June 4, 2015, www.pgaction.org/programmes/ilhr/icc-campaign-map.html.

Privileges and Immunities (APIC) that protects ICC officials performing their duties and PGA began pushing for ratification and implementation of the amendments to the Rome Statute adopted by the Review Conference in Kampala regarding the crime of aggression and prohibited weapons as war crimes.[29]

Expanding the Court's Budget

A major cornerstone of state cooperation is the ASP providing adequate financial resources to the Court. The budget for the ICC covers all administrative and judicial costs, investigations, outreach, as well as the ASP administration. International criminal trials are extremely expensive – ten years of trials at the ICTY and ICTR totaled approximately $2 billion. This averages between $10–15 million per accused.[30] The Court's budget is a continual source of friction between the Court and member states. Member states are reluctant to continuously approve budgetary increases without measures of anticipated accomplishments or completed trials.[31] Prior to the first judgment in the *Lubanga* case in 2012, both ICC officials and diplomatic observers pressed for a judgment in a case; it did not matter whether it was an acquittal or conviction, just that the Court complete an entire case.[32] Additionally, in the early years of the ICC, the Court continually sought greater budgets, even though it did not use its entire allocated budget due to administrative inefficiencies or delays in investigations and trials.[33] The ASP's reticence about increasing the Court's budget is reflected in the yearly budgetary allocations made by the ASP. Every year the ASP has approved a budget less than the Court's proposed budget (see Figure 5.1). Nearly every year since the financial collapse in 2009, some of the highest-contributing member states – including Japan, Germany,

[29] CICC, "Ratification and Implementation"; PGA, "Programme Overview – International Law and Human Rights – Parliamentarians for Global Action (PGA)," accessed May 19, 2012, www.pgaction.org/programmes/ilhr/overview.html.
[30] Rupert Skilbeck, "Funding Justice: The Price of War Crimes Tribunals," *Human Rights Brief* 15, no. 3 (2008): 6–10.
[31] In 2004, the ASP approved the Committee on Budget and Finance's recommendation that the Court "prepare a set of overarching objectives and expected accomplishments for the Court as a whole, reflecting the collective plans for advancing the aims of the Rome Statute," Assembly of States Parties Committee on Budget and Finance, "Report of the Committee on Budget and Finance," 2004, ICC-ASP/3/18, www.icc-cpi.int/Menus/ASP/Sessions/Documentation/3rd+Session/Third+session+of+the+Assembly+of+States+Parties.htm. This resulted in two planning processes known as the "Strategic Plan" and the "Court Capacity Model."
[32] Author interview with a journalist that covers the ICC, August 7, 2010.
[33] Prior to 2007, the Court's budgetary implementation rate was below 90 percent. In 2004, 2005, and 2006, the respective rates were 81.4 percent, 83.4 percent, and 79.7 percent. Since 2007, the implementation rates have all been above 90 percent. Data gathered from the annual "Reports of the Committee on Budget and Finance" of the annual ASP sessions. See: http://www.icc-cpi.int/Menus/ASP/Sessions/Official+Records/.

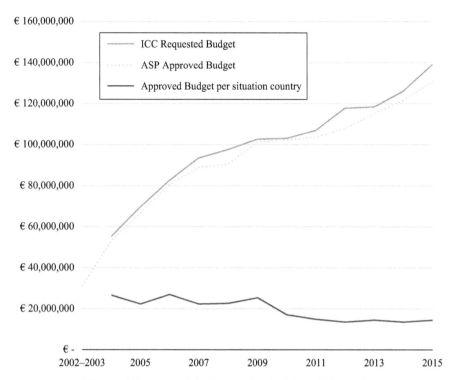

FIGURE 5.1: Historical Funding of the International Criminal Court (2002–2015)
Note: Data gathered from the "Proposed Programme Budget" and "Programme Budget"
documents of the annual ASP Sessions. See: www.icc-cpi.int/en_menus/asp/sessions/
official%20records/Pages/official%20records.aspx. "Situation countries" are the countries
currently under investigation or with active cases at the ICC.

the United Kingdom, France, Italy, and Canada – have called for zero budgetary
growth.[34] Member states have also pushed the Court to improve its efficiency and do
more with less by requesting court-wide efficiency measures established by a special
ASP study group.[35]

Even though the 2015 budget topped €139 million, the Court is continuously in
need of greater resources, especially as the number of countries in which the Court
is conducting investigations increases and more trials are underway. Due to budget

[34] Robbie Corey-Boulet, "Concern over ICC Funding," *IPS Inter Press Service*, September 28,
2011, www.ips.org/africa/2011/09/concern-over-icc-funding/; Evenson and O'Donohue, "The
International Criminal Court at Risk."

[35] In 2008, the Court initiated a court-wide exercise to improve efficiency in all of its processes;
Assembly of States Parties, "Status Report on the Court's Investigations into Efficiency Meas-
ures for 2010*," 2009, ICC-ASP/8/6. At the 2010 review conference, the ASP established a
"Study Group" to enhance the efficiency and effectiveness of the Court Assembly of States
Parties, "Part III Resolutions Adopted by the Assembly of States Parties," 2010, ICC-ASP/9/
Res.2.

constraints, the OTP has had to stagger investigations and focus on specific individual allegations in succession rather than a comprehensive investigation of a situation.[36] Following the landmark decision in the *Lubanga* case – the first completed trial – the local ICC communications team in Ituri claimed that it did not have sufficient funds to broadcast the ruling to the local public.[37] The two referrals of Sudan (Darfur) and Libya by the UNSC exacerbated the Court's lack of resources. The UNSC resolutions did not include any provision that provided additional funding for the investigations – the Court and the ASP were expected to shoulder the additional costs.[38] After the referral of the situation in Libya, the ICC's Investigative Division was only able to hire 12 additional personnel to assist in the investigation on a provisional 12-month basis that required yearly approval by the ASP.[39]

Working on the court budget is not an area that one would imagine significant NGO involvement because of its bureaucratic and administrative nature. However, because withholding adequate resources for the Court to perform its key functions is a powerful indirect mechanism for states to undermine the work of the Court, NGOs became involved in the process.[40] Currently, NGOs assist in nearly all stages of the budget process – from working with the Court Registry on assembling the budget, liaising with the ASP's Committee on Budget and Finance, and lobbying the ASP to approve the budget.

NGO activities related to the Court's budget is one of the longest-standing NGO participatory roles. The CICC's NGO Team on Budget and Finance was created in 1998 following the sixth and final session of the Preparatory Committee on the Establishment of the International Criminal Court (PrepCom).[41] Initially, the NGO Team on Budget and Finance had limited access and influence regarding the Court's budget.[42] The ASP's Financial Rules and Regulations that covered the budget process did not afford NGOs any consultative or observer status and NGO requests for documents and consultations regarding the budget to both the Court

---

[36] Elena A. Baylis, "Outsourcing Investigations," *UCLA Journal of International Law and Foreign Affairs* 14 (2009); Human Rights Watch, *Courting History* (Human Rights Watch, 2008).

[37] Mark Kersten, "Lubanga and the Trouble with ICC Deterrence," *Opinio Juris* (blog), March 19, 2012, http://opiniojuris.org/2012/03/19/lubanga-decision-roundtable-lubanga-and-the-trouble-with-icc-deterrence/.

[38] See UNSC Resolution 1583 at www.un.org/News/Press/docs/2005/sc8351.doc.htm and UNSC Resolution 1970 at www.un.org/News/Press/docs/2011/sc10187.doc.htm.

[39] Assembly of States Parties, "Proposed Programme Budget for 2012 of the International Criminal Court," July 21, 2011, 42, ICC-ASP/10/10.

[40] CICC, "Budget and Finance Background," accessed June 6, 2012, www.iccnow.org/?mod=budgetbackground.

[41] CICC, "Budget and Finance," accessed June 6, 2012, www.iccnow.org/?mod=budget.

[42] The NGO Team on Budget and Finance was led by Jonathan O'Donohue of Amnesty International and worked closely with the Victims' Rights Working Group facilitated by REDRESS. Human Rights Watch also lobbies the ASP on budget issues separately from the CICC's NGO Team.

Registry and the ASP's Committee on Budget and Finance were rebuffed.[43] By 2005, the CICC was granted more access and influence regarding the budget as the Court struggled with conducting sufficient outreach and preliminary investigations.[44] In 2006, NGO advocacy to member states was important in enlarging the Court's budget for outreach and victims' participation and reparations.[45] A CICC staff member describes the importance of the Court's budget to the Coalition's work:

> Budget is a huge part. It's a significant part of our mandate … it's also another example of the credence given to the Coalition. Right now, we are in the budget cycle for next year. And next week, the Committee on Budget and Finance [CBF], which is the ASP subsidiary mechanism, that provides recommendations to the ASP on the budget, will be meeting. We have been invited year in and year out pretty much since the budget process started to present to the CBF on civil societies' concerns and views of the budget: has the Court asked for enough? Should they be supported in this particular area?…The Registry… has a significant role in putting the budget together. So, we'll work with the Registry and the other court organs on things like budgetary issues as well.[46]

NGO influence on the Court's budget not only stems from NGO expertise on outreach and victims' issues but also because NGOs can lobby and frame the situation to states, who approve the budget, in ways that the Court cannot. According to an ICC official, NGOs can say to the ASP "please help the Court from a different angle." Because there are limits to what the Court can say due to its need to appear impartial, NGOs can "talk about the victims and accused in a way

---

[43] CICC's Budget and Finance Team, "The 2004 Programme Budget of the International Criminal Court and the Report of the Committee on Budget and Finance," 2003, www.iccnow.org/documents/Budget_ASP_Paper_2003.FINAL.pdf; CICC's Budget and Finance Team, "The Report of the Committee on Budget and Finance Third Session, The Hague, 6–10 September 2004," 2004, www.google.com/url?sa=t&rct=j&q=&esrc=s&source=web&cd=1&ved=0CDoQFjAA&url=http%3A%2F%2Fwww.iccnow.org%2Fdocuments%2FCICCBudgetTeam_CommentsCBFreport26Aug04.pdf&ei=asrPT9nuN8qO2wWCy9GgDw&usg=AFQjCNHqZuiAGBfXNAGXbPOipo8a4ROBHA&sig2=vZujK9MdfQQflQI7NcVr4g.

[44] CICC's Budget and Finance Team, "Commentary on the Report of the Committee on Budget and Finance on the Work of Its Fifth Session (10 to 14 October 2005)," 2005, www.iccnow.org/.../CICC_CommentaryOnCBFReport_Nov05.pdf; Human Rights Watch, *Courting History*; Jonathan O'Donohue, "The 2005 Budget of the International Criminal Court: Contingency, Insufficient Funding in Key Areas and the Recurring Question of the Independence of the Prosecutor," *Leiden Journal of International Law* 18, no. 3 (2005): 591–603.

[45] CICC's Budget and Finance Team, "Comments on the Proposed Programme Budget for 2006 of the International Criminal Court," 2005, www.google.com/url?sa=t&rct=j&q=&esrc=s&source=web&cd=1&ved=0CE8QFjAA&url=http%3A%2F%2Fwww.iccnow.org%2Fdocuments%2FBFteam_CommentaryProgrammeBudget_23Sept05_en.pdf&ei=_8zPT8-xMMPi2QXPpsW8DA&usg=AFQjCNG82w2fG3piAhWEiJgPzyizOhFmqg&sig2=Y4mNGUwAZrGkvBqBD8REdA; Jonathan O'Donohue, "The Proposed 2006 Budget for the ICC: What Impact for Victims?," *Victims Rights Working Group Bulletin*, October 2005, 4th edition: 2.

[46] Author interview with a CICC staff member, August 20, 2010.

that the Court cannot," or frame outreach and victims' issues in ways that resonate with governments.[47] For example, at the 2014 ASP annual meeting, Human Rights Watch claimed that inadequate resources related to investigations and communications "has an impact in ensuring that justice is not only done, but seen to be done," which resonated with the current critiques that the Court is disconnected from local African communities in situation countries.[48]

NGOs also advocate to ASP member states against zero growth policies or across-the-board cuts, which were proposed following the financial crisis, and for increased funding for investigations, outreach, and victims' participation and reparations.[49] The CICC – a major player with regard to the budget – regularly encourages the Court to ask for more money. NGOs feel somewhat frustrated that the Court has taken a practical approach and not asked for everything it needs.[50] Prosecutor Moreno Ocampo championed this approach and underplayed the resources the Court needed, while simultaneously promoting efficiency.[51] Because underplaying needs can hamstring the functionality of the Court, the CICC is seeking a more pronounced role in budget setting at the Court to influence what the Court initially asks for.[52]

Monitoring Elections and Consulting at the Assembly of States Parties

Although a major element of NGO work regarding the ASP relates to the budget, NGOs also draft papers, arrange informal briefings with diplomats prior to the annual meetings, and attend and participate at the annual ASP meetings. At the ASP annual meetings, NGOs organize side events that state delegates can attend such as regional meetings on universality, experiences from the field on victims' participation, and the launch of the Women's Initiatives for Gender Justice (WIGJ) gender report card.[53] NGO access to the ASP is explicitly written into the ASP's rules, yet only specific NGOs are pre-authorized to attend and receive copies of official documents.

---

[47] Author interview with an ICC official, August 17, 2010.
[48] Elizabeth M. Evenson, "Human Rights Watch Memorandum for the Thirteenth Session of the International Criminal Court Assembly of States Parties," accessed May 22, 2015, www.hrw.org/news/2014/11/25/human-rights-watch-memorandum-thirteenth-session-international-criminal-court-assemb.
[49] CICC, "ASP Reaches Controversial Compromise on ICC Budget," December 21, 2011, www.google.com/url?sa=t&rct=j&q=&esrc=s&source=web&cd=1&ved=0CE8QFjAA&url=http%3A%2F%2Fwww.iccnow.org%2Fdocuments%2FCICC_PR_ASP10__BUDGET_ADOPTION_FINAL_211211.pdf&ei=nDbqT4qAGKrhoQHvrKnTAQ&usg=AFQjCNETwWZj9J4pp_e-YrgIzM3M5AAZDQ&sig2=oUOO376d7V86jzAF7PgVNw.
[50] Author interview with a CICC staff member, June 1, 2015.
[51] Author interview with Jennifer Schense, International Cooperation Adviser in the Jurisdiction, Complementarity and Cooperation Division of the Office of the Prosecutor, ICC, June 3, 2015.
[52] Author interview with a CICC staff member, June 1, 2015.
[53] CICC, "Report on the Eighth Session of the Assembly of States Parties to the Rome Statute," January 2010, www.iccnow.org/documents/CICC_-_ASP_8_Report.pdf.

According to Rule 93 of the Rules of Procedure of the ASP, NGOs must be invited by the ASP unless the NGO was invited to the Rome Conference, registered at PrepCom, or has consultative status with the Economic and Social Council of the United Nations (ECOSOC) and engages in activities related to the Court. Additionally, NGOs must be invited in order to make any oral statements at the opening or closing of the meetings.[54] These rules essentially pre-approve participation by NGOs – such as the CICC and its steering committee members – that played significant roles at the Rome Conference and PrepCom or notable, international NGOs with consultative status at ECOSOC. Because of this, the CICC plays a particularly strong role at the ASP sessions. At nearly every ASP annual session, the CICC has made statements during the general debate and is mentioned in the official records of the proceedings, which is the greatest representation of any NGO.[55]

The CICC also utilizes the ASP annual meetings as a platform to monitor judicial and prosecutorial elections. In 2003, the CICC called for the ASP to establish an Advisory Board on Nominations and since 2006 has sent out an extensive questionnaire to all nominated judicial candidates. The questionnaire enquires about the candidates' qualifications, legal and linguistic competence, judicial and human rights experience, and viewpoints on judicial independence. The results are distributed to member states prior to the election.[56] The CICC's efforts are not to lobby for specific candidates, but to provide information to states that facilitates the election of qualified and non-politicized judges. According to a Court official, the information is helpful but only produces a marginal impact on the election outcomes.[57]

In addition to the questionnaire, the CICC lobbies member states to re-implement states' voting rights prior to elections if they had been revoked because the state was in arrears and pressures states to nominate qualified candidates, take into consideration gender and geographic representation, and abide by transparent voting procedures. In 2010, the CICC further expanded its electoral vetting role by establishing an unofficial Independent Panel on International Court Judicial Elections comprised of prominent, independent experts to assess the candidates put forward by states parties.[58] Immediately following the work of the Panel in the 2011 elections, the ASP decided to initiate a similar body: the Advisory Committee

---

[54] See Rules 93 and 95 of the Rules of Procedure of the ASP.
[55] Gathered from ASP official records of annual sessions. See: www.icc-cpi.int/Menus/ASP/Sessions/Official+Records/.
[56] CICC, "CICC Questionnaire to Candidates for a Post of Judge at the International Criminal Court," accessed May 10, 2011, www.coalitionfortheicc.org/documents/CICCQuestionnaire ICCcandidates_eng.pdf.
[57] Author interview with an ICC official, August 17, 2010.
[58] CICC, "Announcement to the Assembly of States Parties on the Independent Criminal Court Judicial Elections," December 2010, www.iccnow.org/documents/Judicial_Panel_Announce ment.pdf.

on Nomination of Judges. The CICC's Independent Panel discontinued its work after the ASP Committee's formation.[59]

NGOs also advocate and consult with state representatives in other ICC-related fora. NGOs provide feedback and brief the Trust Fund for Victims (TFV) Board of Directors on its strategic plans as well as liaise with state representatives at The Hague Working Group meetings.[60] The Working Group meetings are smaller deliberations in which member states regularly discuss issues of relevance to the ICC, such as cooperation, budget, governance, and victims' participation. These meetings assisted in the preparation for the stocktaking exercise that occurred at the Review Conference in Kampala in 2010. Unlike the ASP annual meetings, NGOs are not afforded observer or consultative status at these meetings, but must be invited by states. In general, diplomats approach the CICC as a sort of NGO clearinghouse, which vets and decides which NGOs will consult with the Working Group. Even without formal, permanent roles, NGOs have proven to be extremely helpful to states at the Working Group meetings, particularly with regard to outreach and victims' issues. According to a state diplomat from an ICC member state, NGOs and states have "good cooperation" and NGO personnel are professional, dedicated people who provide very helpful expertise to diplomats who are dealing with many different issues besides the ICC. This diplomat stated that the stocktaking exercise could not have happened without NGOs producing reports on the experiences in the field because embassies do not have the resources to do fieldwork for the diplomats.[61]

Naming and Shaming States for Non-Cooperation

Another critical component of state cooperation is providing support to investigations, complying with court decisions, and enforcing arrest warrants. As the ICC has no enforcement powers in the form of police, or diplomatic or economic sanctions, it needs states to require other states to comply with the Court's decisions. This means that states must exert diplomatic and political pressure on one another on behalf of the Court, either directly, through regional organizations such as the African Union (AU), or through the UNSC.[62] State cooperation in this area has been mixed. For situation countries that self-referred to the Court, states have generally provided good support and aid with investigations.[63] For situation countries that were not self-referred, and were either initiated by the *proprio motu*

---

[59] CICC, "Judges," accessed June 5, 2015, www.iccnow.org/?mod=electionjudges.

[60] Matthew Cannock, "Presentation to the Trust Fund for Victims Board of Directors," March 18, 2013, www.trustfundforvictims.org/sites/default/files/media_library/documents/pdf/CICC_Pre sentation_to_TFV_Board___180314_1.pdf.

[61] Author interview with a diplomat from an ICC member state, August 26, 2010.

[62] Author interviews with ICC officials, August 12 and 13, 2010.

[63] President Yoweri Museveni of Uganda's cooperation with the ICC is mixed. He occupies a leading role in the AU's anti-ICC campaign yet he also recently transferred LRA leader Dominic Ongwen to The Hague for trial.

prosecutorial powers or a UNSC resolution, state cooperation has been quite poor.[64] The indictments of the sitting heads of state of Sudan and Kenya unleashed a strong backlash against the Court that its selection of cases was biased against Africa.[65] President Omar al-Bashir of Sudan has regularly travelled to ICC member states such as Chad, the Democratic Republic of the Congo (DRC), Malawi, and Djibouti as well as attending AU events, even though the member states were obligated to arrest him.[66] In December 2014, ICC Prosecutor Fatou Bensouda suspended the investigation into Darfur and urged the UNSC to force the arrests of the Darfur suspects.[67] The Kenyan government has also withheld full cooperation from the ICC investigation and the AU has urged the UNSC to defer the cases against President Kenyatta and his deputy William Ruto for a year.[68] The request did not pass the UNSC.[69] In December 2014, Prosecutor Bensouda withdrew charges in the case against President Kenyatta because it was too weak to proceed. In April 2016, ICC judges terminated the joint case against Deputy President Ruto and radio broadcaster Joshua Sang because of a mistrial resulting from witness tampering.[70] In response to the Kenyan government's continued lack of cooperation with the prosecutor's investigation, the ICC Trial Chambers referred Kenya to the ASP for non-compliance with its obligations under the Rome Statute.[71] In Libya, the government refuses to surrender Saif al-Islam Gaddafi to the ICC even though the Court rejected Libya's complementarity bid to try Gaddafi in its domestic courts. Currently, there are nearly as many individuals with arrest warrants who are not

[64] Côte d'Ivoire was technically initiated through the *proprio motu* powers of the prosecutor but since President Alassane Ouattara requested the prosecutor to open an investigation because Côte d'Ivoire is not a state party, cooperation will more likely mirror a self-referral situation.

[65] BBC News, "African Union Accuses ICC of 'hunting' Africans"; Lough, "African Union Accuses ICC Prosecutor of Bias"; Birnbaum, "African Leaders Complain of Bias at ICC as Kenya Trials Get Underway."

[66] "Bashir Travel Map," Bashir Watch, accessed May 19, 2015, http://bashirwatch.org/updates/; CNN Wire Staff, "Kenya, African Union Defend Bashir Visit," *CNN.Com*, August 31, 2010, www.cnn.com/2010/WORLD/africa/08/31/kenya.bashir.visit/.

[67] Agence France-Presse in Khartoum, "Omar Al-Bashir Celebrates ICC Decision to Halt Darfur Investigation," *The Guardian*, December 14, 2014, www.theguardian.com/world/2014/dec/14/omar-al-bashir-celebrates-icc-decision-to-halt-darfur-investigation.

[68] On December 3, 2014, the Trial Chambers declared that the Kenyan government had not met the standard of good faith cooperation required by member states but decided against referring the issue of non-cooperation to the ASP. International Criminal Court, "Press Release: Kenyatta Case: ICC Trial Chamber Rejects Request for Further Adjournment and Directs the Prosecution to Indicate Either Its Withdrawal of Charges or Readiness to Proceed to Trial," December 3, 2014, www.icc-cpi.int/en_menus/icc/press%20and%20media/press%20releases/Pages/PR1071.aspx.

[69] Michelle Nichols, "Africa Fails to Get Kenya ICC Trials Deferred at United Nations," *Reuters*, November 15, 2013, www.reuters.com/article/2013/11/15/us-kenya-icc-un-idUSBRE9AE0S420131115.

[70] International Criminal Court, "Kenya: Situation in the Republic of Kenya," accessed August 9, 2016, www.icc-cpi.int/kenya.

[71] International Criminal Court, "Second Decision on Prosecution's Application for a Finding of Non-Compliance under Article 87(7) of the Statute," September 19, 2016, ICC-01/09–02/11–1037, www.icc-cpi.int/Pages/record.aspx?docNo=ICC-01/09-02/11-1037.

captured as those that have been transferred to the ICC. Even though both the prosecutors and the ICC President, Judge Sang-Hyun Song, have briefed the UNSC on the lack of cooperation regarding state obligations to arrest indicted individuals and urged strong action, the response of the international community has either been tepid or produced a backlash against the Court.[72] In recent years, multiple African member states have withdrawn or signaled their intention to withdraw from the Rome Statute due to concerns over sovereignty and the Court unfairly targeting African states. In 2016, Burundi filed a formal withdrawal with the United Nations Secretary General that became effective one year later and Gambia and South Africa signaled their intentions to exit the treaty but later reversed their decisions.[73] In early 2017, the AU called for a massive withdrawal of member states and Kenya and Zambia are considering withdrawal options.[74]

The situation in Darfur – and the necessary arrest of indicted Sudanese President Omar al-Bashir to move the case forward – was the first "hard case" of state cooperation with the ICC.[75] It tested states' willingness to cooperate with the Court when it conflicted with other interests and norms, such as diplomatic immunity and sovereignty. Failure by member state parties to arrest Bashir when he travels for

[72] Michelle Nichols, "ICC Complains of Lack of Cooperation, Wants More U.N. Support," *Reuters*, October 17, 2012, http://news.yahoo.com/icc-complains-lack-cooperation-wants-more-u-n-194348483.html; "UN News – Security Council Inaction on Darfur 'Can Only Embolden Perpetrators' – ICC Prosecutor," UN News Service Section, December 12, 2014, www.un.org/apps/news/story.asp?NewsID=49591#.VWNqU-feOdc. In 2014, the special rapporteur to the ASP issued a special report on arrest strategies. See: Assembly of States Parties, "Report on Arrest Strategies by the Rapporteur," November 21, 2014, www.google.com/url?sa=t&rct=j&q=&esrc=s&source=web&cd=1&cad=rja&uact=8&ved=0CB4QFjAA&url=http%3A%2F%2Fwww.icc-cpi.int%2Ficcdocs%2Fasp_docs%2FASP13%2FICC-ASP-13-29-Add1-ENG.pdf&ei=50dbVcncLNGvogSL-YGwDA&usg=AFQjCNEzW1CgMs8-hJyRvY2cZbUALOP8_A&bvm=bv.93756505,d.cGU.

[73] Gambia's position regarding withdrawing from the Rome Statute changed due to the election of a new president. South Africa's revocation of withdrawal was prompted by a South African High Court finding the means of withdrawal unconstitutional and invalid.
Norimitsu Onishi, "South Africa Reverses Withdrawal From International Criminal Court," *The New York Times*, March 8, 2017, www.nytimes.com/2017/03/08/world/africa/south-africa-icc-withdrawal.html; Merrit Kennedy, "Under New Leader, Gambia Cancels Withdrawal From International Criminal Court," *NPR.Org*, February 14, 2017, www.npr.org/sections/thetwo-way/2017/02/14/515219467/under-new-leader-gambia-cancels-withdrawal-from-international-criminal-court; "Burundi Notifies U.N. of International Criminal Court Withdrawal," *Reuters*, October 26, 2016, www.reuters.com/article/us-burundi-icc-idUSKCN12Q287.

[74] Rael Ombuor, "Kenya Signals Possible ICC Withdrawal," *VOA*, December 13, 2016, www.voanews.com/a/kenya-signals-possible-icc-withdrawal/3634365.html; "African Union Backs Mass Withdrawal from ICC," *BBC News*, February 1, 2017, sec. Africa, www.bbc.com/news/world-africa-38826073; Ludovica Iaccino, "Rights Groups Fear Zambia Could Be Latest African Country to Abandon the ICC," *Newsweek*, April 11, 2017, www.newsweek.com/zambia-icc-581698.

[75] According to Mills, the Darfur case was the first "hard case" of state cooperation because it forced states to choose between other interests and responsibilities and their obligation to the Court. See: Kurt Mills, "'Bashir Is Dividing Us': Africa and the International Criminal Court," *Human Rights Quarterly* 34, no. 2 (2012): 407.

diplomatic functions, not only impedes the progress of the case, but also under-mines the legitimacy of the Court as it flouts the legal obligations of member states designated under the Rome Statute. In an attempt to engender state cooperation, NGOs publicly and aggressively "name and shame" member states and non-member states that ignore their obligations to execute the arrest warrant for Bashir. "Naming and shaming," or issuing public statements, press releases, and letters decrying state inaction, is not a novel form of NGO participation. Within the NGO scholarship, this is viewed as a standard tactic for advocacy NGOs.[76] One of the reasons that NGOs engage in this participatory role is that NGOs have more latitude to pressure states regarding state cooperation than the Court does and therefore can exert more pressure or different kinds of pressure on states regarding state cooperation. Many NGOs, such as the CICC, also have strong linkages with local civil society groups that can target the government from within the country. According to a staff member of the CICC:

> We [NGOs] are free to comment in a way that the Court can't. You can actually apply that to a lot of aspects of the work of the Court, whether it is dealing with state parties directly or on an issue like cooperation. For example, after the situation with Chad and his [indicted President of Sudan al-Bashir's] non-arrest, we issued immediately a press statement galvanizing members within Chad, within the region, to basically issue statements about Chad's failure to arrest ... As far as I am aware, there wasn't a statement coming from the Court ... We are certainly free to say things that the Court may not be able to, or be forced to sanitize its message in some respects.[77]

NGOs do make provocative statements, such as states "being an insult to victims" or "tainting democracy" by allowing Bashir to travel within their borders.[78] This stands in sharp contrast to the Court's more measured actions that request states to arrest Bashir, request observations regarding states' willingness to cooperate, or inform the UNSC of non-compliance.

NGO statements are often issued days, and sometimes weeks, before the Court acts, if the Court acts at all. When Bashir has travelled to member states for various public appearances and dignitary functions, NGOs have issued public statements condemning his travel on nearly every occasion that he traveled to a member state or was issued an invitation to travel to a member state. In several cases, NGOs issued public statements regarding Bashir's travel when the Court took no action (see Table 5.2). NGOs also regularly implore non-member state parties, such as

---

[76] Emilie M. Hafner-Burton, "Sticks and Stones: Naming and Shaming the Human Rights Enforcement Problem," *International Organization* 62, no. 4 (2008): 689–716.

[77] Author interview with a CICC staff member, August 20, 2010.

[78] Liesl Gernholtz, "Dispatches: Bashir Affair Taints South African Democracy," Human Rights Watch, accessed June 17, 2015, www.hrw.org/news/2015/06/16/dispatches-bashir-affair-taints-south-african-democracy; Human Rights Watch, "Kenya: Do Not Welcome Bashir Back," accessed June 22, 2015, www.hrw.org/news/2010/10/21/kenya-do-not-welcome-bashir-back.

TABLE 5.2 *NGO and ICC Public Statements Regarding State Party Cooperation in Executing Omar al-Bashir's Arrest Warrant (2009–2015)*

Country	Date of Invitation/Travel	NGO Press Release/ Advocacy Letter	ICC Actions*
Central African Republic	December 2010	X	X
Chad	March 25–29, 2014	-	X
	May 10, 2013	X	-
	February 16–17, 2013	X	X
	August 7–8, 2010	X	X
	July 22, 2010	X	-
China**	June 28, 2011	X	-
DRC	February 25–27, 2014	X	X
Djibouti	May 9, 2011	X	X
Kenya	November 28, 2011	X	-
	October 27, 2010	X	X
	August 27, 2010	X	X
Libya***	January 7, 2012	X	-
Malawi	June 2012	X	-
	October 14–15, 2011	X	X
Nigeria	July 14–16, 2013	X	X
	June 2011	-	-
South Africa	June 13, 2015	X	X
	May 2009	-	-

Note: Data gathered from the websites of the CICC, Human Rights Watch, and Bashir Watch. Data include statements made by the CICC as well as its NGO members. ICC data gathered by searching the ICC press releases and decisions. *Italicized* dates indicate that Bashir was invited but did not attend.
* The ICC can take several actions with regard to enforcing arrest warrants: (1) Inform the UNSC and the ASP, (2) Request cooperation from the host country to execute the arrest warrant, (3) Request observations from the host country on the enforcement of warrants of arrest for individuals, (4) make a formal decision on a state's non-compliance with regard to enforcing an arrest warrant, and (5) directly inquire about the visit with state officials and remind them of their obligations.
** China is not a state party but is a permanent member of the UNSC, which referred the situation of Darfur, Sudan to the ICC.
*** Libya is not a state party to the Rome Statute but Libya is currently an ICC situation country. I include only Bashir's travel after the UNSC referral regarding Libya.

Turkey and Malaysia, to arrest Bashir – something that the Court only began doing in the last few years.[79] It is unclear whether NGO activism has narrowed the scope of countries that Bashir can safely travel to. Despite long-standing NGO activism, Chad still freely allows Bashir entry. Nevertheless, against the stated intentions of the government of Kenya to give Bashir safe passage, the local chapter of the NGO, the

[79] For example, on February 25, 2015, the Court issued a formal request to Bahrain to arrest and surrender Omar al-Bashir: www.icc-cpi.int/iccdocs/doc/doc1928185.pdf#search=Bashir%20arrest.

ICJ, initiated a domestic lawsuit that prompted the issuance of a national arrest warrant.[80]

In addition to targeting individual states for lack of cooperation in executing ICC arrest warrants, NGOs also target states or regional organizations for open hostility towards the ICC. The CICC, ICC, and other international NGOs have conducted advocacy and compiled public information and reports on the relationship between the United States and the ICC. These NGOs advocate against the "Article 98" agreements that ensure non-surrender of US personnel to the ICC as well as the American Servicemembers Protection Act that restricts foreign assistance to countries that do not sign the "Article 98" agreements.[81] Furthermore, following the AU's accusations of bias against the ICC and public pronouncements that it will not cooperate with the arrest warrant against al-Bashir, international and domestic NGOs have jointly written public letters to the foreign ministers of African member states as well as attending the AU Summit to push for greater support for the Court.[82]

Aiding Investigations

Under Article 15 of the Rome Statute, individuals and organizations can submit information or "communications" to the prosecutor about human rights abuses, which could prompt the prosecutor to submit a request to the Pre-Trial chamber to begin a preliminary investigation. This provision of the Rome Statute was absent from the first 1994 draft by the International Law Commission. NGOs, along with the "like-minded group" of states, fought and ultimately prevailed in granting the prosecutor *proprio motu* investigative powers, whereby NGOs and individuals could provide information on abuses that could prompt a prosecutorial investigation, provided the Court has jurisdiction. As of December 2013, the OTP has received a total of 10,470 Article 15 communications.[83] While the source and information of these communications are confidential, there is evidence that suggests that a substantial portion of these submissions may be from NGOs.[84] According to a 2004 discussion paper by Human Rights First: "NGOs around the world are asking

---

[80] "Kenyan Court Issues Arrest Order for Sudan's Bashir," *Reuters*, November 28, 2011, www .reuters.com/article/2011/11/28/us-kenya-bashir-icc-idUSTRE7AR0YA20111128.

[81] AMICC, "AMICC," accessed June 26, 2012, www.amicc.org/; CICC, "Bilateral Immunity Agreements," accessed June 26, 2012, www.coalitionfortheicc.org/?mod=bia; CICC, "Legislation Prohibiting Aid," accessed June 26, 2012, www.coalitionfortheicc.org/?mod=legislation.

[82] "Letter to Foreign Ministers of African States Parties to the ICC," January 26, 2012, www.hrw .org/news/2012/01/26/letter-foreign-ministers-african-states-parties-icc; CICC, "Civil Society Defends ICC at African Union Summit," accessed June 22, 2015, https://ciccglobaljustice .wordpress.com/2014/03/25/civil-society-defends-icc-at-african-union-summit/.

[83] International Criminal Court, "Communications, Referrals and Preliminary Examinations," accessed May 22, 2015, www.icc-cpi.int/en_menus/icc/structure%20of%20the%20court/office% 20of%20the%20prosecutor/comm%20and%20ref/Pages/communications%20and%20referrals .aspx.

[84] Office of the Prosecutor, "Report on Preliminary Examination Activities," December 13, 2011.

how they file information with the ICC, and the ICC has received hundreds of communications from these and other civil society members."[85] As of 2006, the Prosecutor had received over 240 communications about the situation in Iraq from "citizens and organizations."[86]

Some NGOs publically release their communications to the Court online: the Damascus Center for Human Rights Studies co-submitted an Article 15 communication regarding crimes against humanity committed in Syria; the Ghana Coalition for the ICC requested the Court to investigate genocidal statements made by a member of parliament, the Center for Constitutional Rights demanded an investigation of Vatican officials in the sex abuse scandal, and the Global Justice Center called for an investigation into Boko Haram's abduction of women and children.[87] As with most communications in general, many of the NGO communications are outside of the jurisdiction of the Court.[88] Nevertheless, the OTP sees NGO communications, or those assisted by NGOs, as high-quality and reliable and some impact prosecutorial decision-making.[89] In 2003, Prosecutor Moreno Ocampo issued a press release in which he highlighted the detailed reports communicated by two NGOs on alleged crimes committed in the Ituri region of the DRC. In the 2011 Report of the OTP on preliminary examination activities, submissions by

---

[85] Human Rights First, "The Role of Human Rights NGOs in Relation to ICC Investigations," Discussion Paper (The Hague, September 2004).

[86] Luis Moreno-Ocampo, "OTP Letter to Senders Re Iraq," February 9, 2006.

Due to the confidential nature of Article 15 communications, it is impossible to parse out what proportion of these communications are from NGOs. This lumping of NGOs into a larger civil society category that includes individuals and professional associations likely over-represents the frequency and impact of NGO participation.

[87] Damascus Center for Human Rights Studies et al., "Article 15 Communication on Crimes against Humanity Committed in Syria," accessed May 14, 2012, dchrs.org/.../Article15CommunicationOnCrimesAgainstHumanity.pdf; Emma Miles, "Ghana Petition at the ICC at The International Criminal Law Bureau Blog," International Criminal Law Bureau, May 9, 2012, www.internationallawbureau.com/blog/?p=4885; Center for Constitutional Rights, "Victims' Communication Pursuant to Article 15 of the Rome Statute Requesting Investigation and Prosecution of High-Level Vatican Officials for Rape and Other Forms of Sexual Violence as Crimes Against Humanity and Torture as a Crime Against Humanity," September 13, 2011, www.google.com/url?sa=t&rct=j&q=&esrc=s&source=web&cd=2&ved=0CFsQFjAB&url=http%3A%2F%2Fs3.documentcloud.org%2Fdocuments%2F243877%2Fvictims-communication.pdf&ei=ZP6zT9fNNoGy2QWJmLnpCA&usg=AFQjCNEQYC-b1hETAAOn4UWDngACsyWOcA&sig2=B6hqUp7gB_M-X6TPImg1Pg; Global Justice Center, "Subject: Article 15 Communication to the ICC Office of the Prosecutor Regarding Boko Haram's Targeted Abduction of Women and Children as Genocide," April 14, 2015, http://globaljusticecenter.net/index.php/publications/briefs-and-white-papers/622-subject-article-15-communication-to-the-icc-office-of-the-prosecutor-regarding-boko-haram-s-targeted-abduction-of-women-and-children-as-genocide.

[88] According to an author interview with an anonymous source with knowledge on this issue conducted on June 2, 2015, approximately 70 percent of the Article 15 communications are completely outside of the scope of the jurisdiction of the Court.

[89] Author interview with an anonymous source with knowledge on this issue, June 2, 2015; Office of the Prosecutor, "Report on Preliminary Examination Activities."

NGOs were mentioned regarding the investigations in Palestine, Honduras, Colombia, and Georgia.[90] With regard to Georgia, the report states: "The Office maintains close contacts with NGOs in the region, receiving reports from and participating in meetings with these organizations, some of which are also carrying out an assessment of relevant national proceedings pertaining to the alleged crimes committed during the August 2008 conflict."[91] In the case of the situation in Iraq, the OTP utilized press releases and investigative reports by Human Rights Watch to conclude that the crimes committed in Iraq were outside of the jurisdiction of the Court.[92]

NGOs with an on-the-ground presence in countries under investigation provide critical aid to ICC investigations by finding crime scenes, documenting evidence, gathering witness statements, and linking witnesses to the Court as "intermediaries." "Intermediaries" who are people who "work between one person and another; who facilitate contact or provide a link between one of the organs or units of the Court or Counsel on the one hand, and victims, witnesses, beneficiaries of reparations or affected communities more broadly on the other."[93] Although not mentioned in the Rome Statute or the Rules of Procedure and Evidence, NGOs use their on-the-ground knowledge of situation countries to aid the Court. Intermediaries are mostly used by the OTP and the Victims' Participation and Reparations Section and perform one of two functions. First, intermediaries provide evidence to the OTP, such as providing statements from victims and witnesses, victims' names, evidence of crimes, and other research data.[94] This information is usually not collected with the purpose of providing evidence or transmitting it to court investigators. Often, the information from local NGOs is picked up by international human rights NGOs, and possibly commissions of inquiry, who then publish reports that end up on the desk of someone in the OTP. The investigator then goes back down the chain and finally contacts the NGO on-the-ground to obtain their information.[95] Oftentimes, these NGOs require confidentiality agreements with the ICC in order to share information. Second, intermediaries serve as the "bridge between witness and court" and can help victims and witnesses participate in court proceedings and apply for reparations.[96] For example, intermediaries aid victims in completing the 19-page

---

[90]   Office of the Prosecutor, "Report on Preliminary Examination Activities."

[91]   Office of the Prosecutor, "Report on Preliminary Examination Activities," 21.

[92]   Moreno-Ocampo, "OTP Letter to Senders Re Iraq," 7.

[93]   Open Society Justice Initiative, "Intermediaries and the International Criminal Court," accessed May 16, 2012, www.opensocietyfoundations.org/publications/intermediaries-and-international-criminal-court-role-assembly-states-parties.

[94]   Human Rights First, "The Role of Human Rights NGOs in Relation to ICC Investigations"; Baylis, "Outsourcing Investigations," 122.

[95]   Author interview with an anonymous source with knowledge of this issue, June 2, 2015.

[96]   Human Rights Watch, "The International Criminal Court: How Nongovernmental Organizations Can Contribute To the Prosecution of War Criminals," September 2004, 18, www.hrw.org/legacy/backgrounder/africa/icc0904/.

form, only available in French or English, necessary to apply for reparations.[97] Local and international NGO intermediaries also create partnerships with the TFV to implement programming that provides victims with physical and psychological rehabilitation and resources.[98]

Local and international NGOs that informally share information or act as intermediaries and link victims to the Court play a "crucial role to the Court."[99] In the OTP's report on preliminary investigations, NGOs are acknowledged as helping to identify witnesses, providing leads on potential evidence as well as collecting physical evidence, witness statements, and information relevant to crime pattern analysis.[100] Prosecutor Bensouda recently praised FIDH for advancing nearly all of the OTP's investigations and providing key contact information for witnesses.[101] A CICC staff member also highlighted the crucial role that CICC members play in providing information to the ICC investigators: "The Coalition's members bring evidence to the attention of the Court. Urge the Court to take up x, y, z cases – this one and not that one, this evidence not that evidence, here are these victims, and that group of victims in this town. They point to a lot of important information."[102] According to ICC Judge Matheson, video footage of interviews with child soldiers provided by a local NGO in the DRC, Aje-di-Ka, "fill[ed] an evidentiary gap" in the case against Lubanga – who was later convicted for the use of child soldiers.[103] NGOs have also begun to pre-empt the ICC investigative process and are documenting evidence in conflict situations, such as Syria, for future use by the ICC, even if that country is not under the jurisdiction of the ICC.[104]

The use of intermediaries is not without controversy. In the *Lubanga* case, the Prosecutor's unwillingness to disclose the name of intermediaries because of confidentiality agreements resulted in two stays and threatened to derail the first case to be completed at the Court. The OTP signed confidentiality agreements with the intermediaries on the ground because the intermediaries felt that if the name of their organization was disclosed, it could jeopardize relationships with local populations with which they work.[105] The stays in the *Lubanga* case resulted in the Court and

---

[97] Human Rights Watch, *Courting History*.
[98] For the TFV implementing partners in Northern Uganda and the DRC see: www.trustfund forvictims.org/partners.
[99] Author interview with an ICC Official, August 17, 2010.
[100] Office of the Prosecutor, "Report on Preliminary Examination Activities," 31–2.
[101] FIDH, *Fatou Bensouda, ICC Prosecutor, Visits FIDH*.
[102] Author interview with a CICC staff member, July 6, 2010.
[103] Matthew Shaer, "'The Media Doesn't Care What Happens Here,'" *The New York Times*, February 18, 2015, 159, www.nytimes.com/2015/02/22/magazine/the-media-doesnt-care-what-happens-here.html.
[104] Mark Kersten, "What Counts as Evidence of Syria's War Crimes?," *The Washington Post Monkey Cage*, October 28, 2014, www.washingtonpost.com/blogs/monkey-cage/wp/2014/10/28/what-counts-as-evidence-of-syrias-war-crimes/.
[105] In the *Lubanga* case, the UN Mission in the Congo was later identified as providing the most evidence as a third-party intermediary. For more information, see: Baylis, "Outsourcing

NGOs – mostly led by the Open Society Justice Initiative (OSJI) – to draft regulations regarding intermediary use at the Court.[106] In 2014, the ICC adopted both the Code of Conduct and a model contract for intermediaries, which together seek to provide standards, monitoring mechanisms, and articulation of the protection provided by the Court.[107] The OTP still uses intermediaries and takes the Code of Conduct very seriously but is consciously trying to limit the use of intermediaries because "they were burned in the *Lubanga* case."[108] Even with the code, there are still questions about the validity and reliability of evidence collected by intermediaries and the strain it places on some local NGOs with already limited resources.[109] Since collecting information from local actors can be limited, but likely not eliminated, the Court "championed" the idea of generating standards for NGO information. In response, the OSJI again stepped in and is currently in the process of drafting guidelines for NGOs, including what kinds of information to look for and data collection methodologies.[110]

Conducting Communications and Outreach

Communications and outreach is one of the most crucial and impactful roles NGOs play with regard to the Court, as the Court is dependent on NGOs.[111] Communications and outreach involves organizing and disseminating educational information about the Court to a broad audience, sharing information with affected communities, governments, journalists and the media, and engaging with stakeholder groups, including domestic civil society organizations. NGOs provide outreach for the Court simultaneous to advocating to the ASP for greater funding for Court outreach and consulting with the Registry on strategies for effective outreach.

Investigations"; Kai Ambos, "The First Judgment of the International Criminal Court (Prosecutor v. Lubanga): A Comprehensive Analysis of the Legal Issues," *International Criminal Law Review* 12, no. 2 (2012): 115–53.

[106] Open Society Justice Initiative, "Intermediaries and the International Criminal Court."

[107] International Criminal Court, "Code of Conduct for Intermediaries," March 2014, www .google.com/url?sa=t&rct=j&q=&esrc=s&source=web&cd=3&cad=rja&uact=8&ved=0CDQ QFjAC&url=http%3A%2F%2Fwww.icc-cpi.int%2Fen_menus%2Ficc%2Flegal%2520texts% 2520and%2520tools%2Fstrategies-and-guidelines%2FDocuments%2FCCI-Eng.pdf&ei= nKxfVcWeIMvfoASu5INo&usg=AFQjCNGJ-6hHijoWlX6XEBJ_S7BXU-MVDg&sig2=zd_ b8IKtLTjySD4W99AzCQ&bvm=bv.93990622,d.cGU; International Criminal Court, "Model Contract for Intermediaries," March 2014, www.google.com/url?sa=t&rct=j&q=&esrc=s& source=web&cd=1&cad=rja&uact=8&ved=0CCYQFjAA&url=http%3A%2F%2Fwww.icc-cpi .int%2Fen_menus%2Ficc%2Flegal%2520texts%2520and%2520tools%2Fstrategies-and-guide lines%2FDocuments%2FMCI-Eng.pdf&ei=nKxfVcWeIMvfoASu5INo&usg=AFQjCNHok kOJTkc3eQTolhn8aGKcODqNCw&sig2=QuuCGcPJDIDxsogj4lArZQ&bvm=bv.93990622, d.cGU.

[108] Author interview with an anonymous source with knowledge on the issue, June 2, 2015.

[109] Beth S. Lyons, "The Intermediary Industry and the ICC," *IntLawGrrls* (blog), accessed May 22, 2015, http://ilg2.org/2014/06/06/the-intermediary-industry-and-the-icc/.

[110] Author interview with NGO personnel with information on this issue, June 5, 2015.

[111] Schiff, *Building the International Criminal Court.*

NGOs began conducting outreach on behalf of the Court because they viewed it as a critical part of the Court's work but one that was in danger of being marginalized and underfunded.[112] A CICC staff member highlights the difficulty in conducting outreach and the key role of NGOs in helping the Court draft outreach policies: "it is incredibly challenging to get the people to get the message from the Court because it takes a lot of resources, a lot of time, a lot of people, a lot of languages, village to village."[113] In 2004, when the Court first began its on-the-ground investigations in Uganda, the Registry allocated almost no resources to outreach and instead expected local NGOs to perform outreach on behalf of the Court. According to NGO reports, the strategy of solely depending on NGOs to conduct outreach generally failed because the Court did not provide information and updates to NGOs and the cost of conducting outreach was too great for many domestic NGOs.[114] Following this failure, international NGOs became more involved. In 2004, the CICC created the NGO Team on Communications to monitor, facilitate, and advocate for outreach and communications strategies.[115] In 2006–2007, the International Bar Association (IBA) and the International Center for Transitional Justice (ICTJ) also began monitoring Court outreach and communications strategies.[116] The involvement of major international NGOs resulted in a two-pronged approach to outreach: serving as a repository of educational information about the Court as well as seeking local partners to conduct on-the-ground research on behalf of the Court.

The CICC serves as the most comprehensive and accessible source of educational information about the Court, governance, and the status of current cases. The CICC produces ten electronic and print publications that cover updates and developments at the ICC, the CICC, and various regions and are available in multiple languages, including Arabic, English, French, Portuguese, and Spanish.[117]

According to the CICC, tens of thousands of these print publications have been distributed worldwide.[118] Furthermore, the CICC has compiled a book of key ICC documents and its website houses a huge repository of ICC, CICC, and other NGO documents relating to the Court. A journalist that regularly covers the ICC stated: "the ICC is producing an enormous amount of filings, an enormous amount

---

[112] CICC, "Comments and Recommendations for States Parties in Relation to the ICC and Communications," November 24, 2005, www.iccnow.org/documents/CommsTeam_ASPadvocacydoc24Nov05.pdf.

[113] Author interview with a CICC staff member, July 6, 2010.

[114] Human Rights Watch, *Courting History*.

[115] CICC, "Communications and Outreach," accessed May 11, 2011, www.iccnow.org/?mod=communications.

[116] International Bar Association, "First Outreach Report," June 1, 2006, www.iccnow.org/documents/IBA_First_Outreach_Report_June_2006.pdf; International Center for Transitional Justice, "ICTJ Launches First Report on ICC Outreach," May 9, 2007, www.iccnow.org/documents/ICTJ_PR_ReportICCOutreach9May07_eng.pdf.

[117] CICC, "Our Publications," accessed June 13, 2012, www.iccnow.org/?mod=ourpublications.

[118] CICC, "Our Publications," accessed June 13, 2012, www.iccnow.org/?mod=ourpublications.

of paperwork . . . and I think the CICC lawyers who follow the paper trail may very well be the only people outside of the ICC that read everything . . . There is no journalist that can read everything the ICC produces, it's only the CICC that has the human resources to do that. They alert us to important filings, make summaries of trial proceedings, which is most useful."[119]

NGOs also facilitate and engage in outreach with affected communities on behalf of the Court.[120] Following the establishment of the CICC's NGO Communication Team, the CICC and its members began performing outreach and facilitating relationships with local civil society groups and the ICC on behalf of the Court or in joint NGO-sponsored events with the ICC.[121] Beginning in 2004, the CICC's Kinshasa branch began distributing thousands of publications written in French for local NGOs, including texts that gave basic information on the ICC, manuals for creating public awareness, and key information for victims.[122] In Uganda, Avocats Sans Frontières (ASF) conducted outreach sessions with locally based ICC outreach personnel. The ICC personnel would speak about the Court and ASF would address any controversial issues – such as criticisms of the Court, amnesties, or domestic proceedings – that the ICC personnel felt that they could not speak to. The ICC did not ask ASF to take on this role, but it willingly worked with ASF, and it did not provide any remuneration. ASF assumed this role by "seeing the gaps in the system" and working to address them.[123]

NGOs also help facilitate outreach between the OTP and local NGOs in situation countries:

> A good example is when the Office of the Prosecutor conducts his field visits. His office conducts the field visits, investigative missions on the ground, or if they want to do outreach. They want to go to Kenya, for example, to discuss why they've initiated an investigation . . . We [the CICC] will put them in touch with local NGOs on the ground because that's also a way of doing the outreach and public information . . . We actually did it recently in the case of Georgia. The OTP did a couple of field visits to Georgia and we took the initiative of getting in touch and saying, "look there are a number of NGOs on the ground that would like to meet with you." The reasons for doing things like public information is so that local

---

[119] Author interview with a journalist that covers the ICC, August 7, 2010.

[120] Some NGO outreach activities are done with the endorsement and coordination of the Court, while others are conducted without such endorsement but in the interest of the Court.
Marlies Glasius, "What Is Global Justice and Who Decides?: Civil Society and Victim Responses to the International Criminal Court's First Investigations," *Human Rights Quarterly* 31, no. 2 (2009): 511.

[121] Human Rights Watch, *Courting History*.

[122] International Center for Transitional Justice, "Sensibilisation à la CPI en RDC," 2007, 19, www.google.com/url?sa=t&rct=j&q=&esrc=s&source=web&cd=1&ved=0CCEQFjAA&url= http%3A%2F%2Fwww.peace-justice-conference.info%2Fdownload%2F638.pdf&ei=Rr5fVbu TFsbXoASs6IKgAQ&usg=AFQjCNEZTsAon8W_b_lgKyit77YUKOxAww&sig2=_sC5PMc 1q3f8olT6IHzqhw&bvm=bv.93990622,d.cGU&cad=rja.

[123] Author interview with an NGO staff member with expertise in Uganda, June 5, 2015.

NGOs can have that access to ask questions like "what is the progress with regards to the Georgian preliminary examination? How can we help?"[124]

When ICC Prosecutor Moreno Ocampo visited Kenya in 2010, he did not leave Nairobi but met with victims who were transported to the capital by human rights NGOs.[125] Prosecutor Bensouda recently visited the offices of FIDH where she praised the partnerships between the Court and civil society and highlighted the role of NGOs, such as FIDH, in expanding outreach to affected communities by "sensitizing" to them appropriate expectations for the Court.[126]

Consulting with the Court

After the ICC's establishment, NGOs maintained and even expanded programming related to the ICC because they felt beholden to the principles articulated in the Rome Statute and wanted to see them realized in the Court. One way for their vision to be actualized was to monitor the workings of the ICC and consult with it on policies, procedures, and actions that would shift the Court more in line with how they felt it should operate. In essence, NGOs were going to act as watchdogs, not only to states, but also to the ICC itself. Over time, NGOs have consulted with the Court on outreach, universal ratification, budget, victims' issues, the use of intermediaries, the structure of the registry, general prosecutorial strategies, and specific cases, among other things. NGOs not only have formal consultative meetings but also have backdoor informal channels. In fact, established international NGOs generally have greater influence through informal meetings with the various court organs than through the formal roundtable meetings.

The formal consultative role of NGOs is at annual meetings with organs of the ICC – the Registry, the OTP, and the Presidency – as well as the Secretariat of the ASP. These consultations consist of information exchange between representatives from international and domestic NGOs and key officials from the Court organs and the ASP Secretariat on current situations and court strategies. Not any NGO or member of civil society can attend: the CICC must grant permission to attend and does so at its own discretion.[127] According to an ICC press release, these meetings are "part of a conjunct effort of both the Court and the NGOs to strengthen and

---

[124] Author interview with a CICC staff member, August 20, 2010.
[125] Institute for War & Peace Reporting, "ICC Review Conference: Taking Stock on the Ground," Institute for War and Peace Reporting, July 2010, 13, https://iwpr.net/printed-materials/icc-review-conference-taking-stock-ground.
[126] FIDH, *Fatou Bensouda, ICC Prosecutor, Visits FIDH*.
[127] The author experienced this discretion first-hand and was not granted permission by the CICC to attend the roundtable meetings due to confidentiality reasons, even though the CICC saw the author as a member of civil society.

open dialogue and maintain mutual support and understanding."[128] Since 2005, the meetings have been firmly established and regularly occur – although recently the meetings shifted from a bi-annual to an annual basis.[129]

These meetings may appear to represent a formalized venue for NGO advocacy and lobbying on court policy, but many established, international NGOs see them as more symbolic than substantive. The roundtable meetings serve not as venues of policy-making but to institutionalize the relationship between domestic civil society and the Court. This symbolic function plays out in the focus on bringing domestic NGOs from situation countries or countries under investigation to the meetings. According to a staff member of the WIGJ – a founding member of the CICC that has attended these meetings from the beginning – the meetings are not about policy, but about exchanging information and ideas. The meetings are not a space for advocacy; most of the advocacy occurs through the on-going informal conversations with the Court. The meetings are more for domestic NGOs that do not have regular access to the Court, not for established international NGOs that have continuous informal access to it.[130] During the first few years of the ICC, the CICC would select the domestic NGOs to attend and the Court would pay for their travel. Due to budget constraints, the Court recently stopped paying for this travel. Now in order to attend, local NGOs must find their own sources of money, which is quite difficult, or obtain financial sponsorship by an international NGO. During the roundtable meeting in June 2015, the OSJI sponsored the travel of civil society groups from several African countries from a one-time external grant from the Africa Trust.

In contrast to the more symbolic consultations between domestic NGOs and the ICC during the roundtable meetings, the informal, backchannel consultations are venues for tremendous NGO influence on policy. According to an ICC official, there is "an open dialogue" between the Court and NGOs. NGOs give recommendations about court strategy – what the Court is doing and what it ought to be doing. During informal meetings, NGOs exchange information and give recommendations and constructive criticism. Multiple ICC officials lauded the high level of NGO expertise and the recommendations received by the Court.[131] Even more so than the formal meetings, the backchannels to the Court are only available to a select group of NGOs, most notably the CICC and its Steering Committee

---

[128] International Criminal Court, "ICC Held Bi-Annual Strategy Meeting with NGOs," accessed May 9, 2012, www.icc-cpi.int/menus/icc/press%20and%20media/press%20releases/press%20releases%20 (2009)/pr461.

[129] International Criminal Court, "ICC – Consultations with Civil Society (NGO Round Tables)," accessed November 28, 2012, www.icc-cpi.int/en_menus/icc/structure%20of%20the %20court/office%20of%20the%20prosecutor/network%20with%20partners/consultations% 20with%20civil%20society/Pages/consultations.aspx; Kristele Younes, "NGOs Consultations with ICC Organs," *The International Criminal Court Monitor*, April 2005, Issue 29 edition.

[130] Author interview with a CICC staff member, August 20, 2010; author interview with WIGJ staff members, August 23, 2010.

[131] Author interviews with ICC officials, August 12 and 17, 2010.

members. This group includes many of the most eminent NGOs including Amnesty International, Human Rights Watch, and FIDH, as well as more issue-based NGOs such as the WIGJ and Redress.

NGO backchannels to the ICC are not limited to one court organ, but involve all organs except for Chambers.[132] In meetings with the Presidency, NGOs generally discuss the campaign for universal ratification of the Rome Statute. According to a PGA staff member, PGA collaborates with the President on where to travel (some-times PGA travels with the President or supports them on their travels) and the general strategy of promoting universal ratification as well as sharing information on specific situations regarding ratification.[133]

NGO consultations with the Registry touch on issues of outreach and victims' participation and reparations. According to an ICC official, the Registry has "many, many meetings with NGOs" and characterizes them as "frank and open dialogues." Past experience demonstrates that the Registry takes NGO feedback quite seriously. In 2014, the Registry released plans to create a single victims and defense office, which was met by sharp opposition by NGOs working on victim issues. The proposal was then placed on hold for several months due to NGO critiques.[134]

NGOs also have very strong relationships with the OTP. According to an ICC official, Bill Pace [the Convener of the CICC] had regular meetings with past Prosecutor Moreno Ocampo.[135] NGOs seek to influence the general prosecution strategy and the specifics of cases. The CICC provides input on the long-term prosecutorial strategy but does not make recommendations on specific cases. A CICC staff member details the CICC's involvement: "the Coalition and individ-ual members actually provided comments to the drafting of that [three-year pros-ecutorial strategy] document ... guidance on things like strategy with regards to intermediaries or cooperation ... We did provide comments on it but didn't touch upon whether you need to initiate an investigation in Palestine. We will take an interest and involve ourselves in things when it comes to policy and administration ... it is more about administration of the Court than the actual litigation as such."[136] While the policy of the CICC does not permit it to make recommendations on specific cases, CICC member NGOs do lobby the OTP on specific cases. In this regard, the lobbying of the WIGJ has been particularly

[132] According to an interview with a CICC staff member, some NGOs do interact with Chambers but the NGOs are very cognizant about what is off limits and that the judges maintain their independence.

[133] Author interview with Deborah Ruiz Verduzco, Senior Programme Officer, PGA, September 8, 2010.

[134] Author interview with a staff member of the OSJI, June 1, 2015; FIDH, "FIDH Comments on the ICC Registrar's ReVision Proposals in Relation to Victims," November 18, 2014, www.fidh .org/IMG/pdf/letter_registar_icc.pdf.

[135] Author interview with an ICC official, August 12, 2010.

[136] Author interview with a CICC staff member, August 20, 2010.

influential in pressuring the OTP to add indictments for gender-based crimes.[137] According to an ICC official, the work of the WIGJ is "pretty revolutionary" and has "had a visible impact." The WIGJ does not write massive reports but pushes hard on one issue and as a result all of the indictments, except the cases in Darfur, have some gender aspect to them.[138] The advocacy of the WIGJ on the prosecutorial strategy of the ICC recently resulted in a formal relationship between the WIGJ and the OTP. In August 2012, ICC Prosecutor Fatou Bensouda appointed Brigid Inder, the Executive Director of the WIGJ, as Special Gender Advisor to the OTP. The Special Gender Advisor provides the OTP with strategic advice on gender issues and prosecution of sexual and gender-based crimes.[139]

Court officials generally value the input and advocacy of these NGOs, even if they sometimes have differences of opinion and viewpoints.[140] Nevertheless, these informal channels are where NGOs provide the most criticism to the ICC and where the most potential for tension in the relationships exists. Some Court officials feel that NGOs should support, not critique, the Court or that NGOs overstep their bounds either in the severity or scope of their critiques.[141] ICC officials also worry that public NGO critiques can become weapons against the Court in the hands of some states. State diplomats are keenly aware of NGO critiques of the Court and do try to piggyback on them and use them to legitimate their own claims.[142] The tension over appropriate criticism was especially pronounced during Prosecutor Moreno Ocampo's tenure as NGOs both privately and publically critiqued the work of the OTP.[143] Only when Prosecutor Moreno Ocampo understood that they saw the Court as their child, and he the caregiver, did he understand their critical stance:

> after one meeting with NGOs he [Prosecutor Moreno Ocampo] was very frustrated because they were just really all over him, he was sort of like in this mentality of thank you for savings us from ourselves ... I said for them, all of these NGOs, it's like the biggest thing they'll ever do in their career – the most important thing for them. And it's like their baby and they handed it to you. They have to trust you with it and they may not, it's not an easy thing do. And then he got it immediately. He was like oh my god, so they're looking through the glass like, give him more milk!

[137] In addition to lobbying the OTP, the WIGJ has also trained over a hundred of the ICC staff on a gender-based perspective: author interview with WIGJ staff members, August 23, 2010.

[138] Author interview with an ICC official, August 12, 2010.

[139] International Criminal Court, "Press Release: ICC Prosecutor Fatou Bensouda Appoints Brigid Inder, Executive Director of the Women's Initiatives for Gender Justice, as Special Gender Advisor," August 21, 2012, www.icc-cpi.int/en_menus/icc/press%20and%20media/press%20releases/Pages/pr833.aspx.

[140] Author interviews with ICC officials, August 12 and 13, 2010.

[141] Author interviews with ICC officials, August 12 and 13, 2010.

[142] Author interview with a diplomat from an ICC member state, August 26, 2010.

[143] For examples of some public reports, see: Human Rights Watch, "Unfinished Business"; Human Rights Watch, *Courting History*.

Kind of panicking. Don't kill it! So, then he could kind of appreciate that very sort of personal relationship people had with the institution.[144]

Most NGOs working with the ICC reserve the right, and believe it is in their purview, to criticize the Court. Yet, organizations take different approaches as to whether to use insider channels or go public and risk state co-optation of their criticism.

Vetting and Training Legal Counsel

NGOs also provide operational support to the ICC by helping build the capacity and training of legal counsel for the defense and victims – a role designated to the ASP, but which the ASP has not implemented.[145] While the rules allow the ASP to establish an independent representative body of counsel – or a bar association for the ICC – to help link qualified, trained attorneys to victims and the defense, the ASP has not established such an organization.[146] To address the issue of legal counsel for the defense and victims, various attorneys representing national bar associations and NGOs created the International Criminal Bar (ICB) in June 2002.[147] The ICB advocates for adequate legal aid as well as establishment of a bar association for the ICC in the form of letters to the ASP and the ICC and attending ASP annual meetings.[148] The ICB also provides the services that such a bar association would provide, including giving free training in conjunction with the ICC on practicing before the Court, providing lawyers with language courses in the official languages of the Court, giving seminars and conferences to victims, and establishing lists of counsel authorized to practice before the Court.[149]

---

[144] Author interview with Jennifer Schense, International Cooperation Adviser in the Jurisdiction, Complementarity and Cooperation Division of the Office of the Prosecutor, ICC, June 3, 2015.

[145] The ICC is different from other international criminal tribunals in that victims have their own counsel in addition to attorneys for the defense and the prosecutor.

[146] Rule 20.3 of the Rules of Procedure and Evidence of the ICC.

[147] International Criminal Bar, "Objectives," accessed June 27, 2012, www.bpi-icb.com/index.php?option=com_content&view=article&id=67&Itemid=74&lang=en.

[148] International Criminal Bar, "Position Paper of the International Criminal Bar," December 25, 2011, www.bpi-icb.com/index.php?view=weblink&catid=66%3Abpi-icb-documentos-constituti vos&id=242%3Aicb-position-paper-25112011doc-icb-position-paper-25112011doc&option=com_ weblinks&Itemid=91&lang=en; International Criminal Bar, "ICB Letter to the Presidents of the ASP and the ICC," February 20, 2012, www.bpi-icb.com/index.php?view=weblink&catid= 66%3Abpi-icb-documentos-constitutivos&id=264%3Aicb-letter-to-the-presidents-of-asp-and-icc-ap&option=com_weblinks&Itemid=91&lang=en; International Criminal Bar, "Organisation," accessed June 27, 2012, www.bpi-icb.com/index.php?option=com_content&view=article&id= 61&Itemid=73&lang=en.

[149] International Criminal Bar, "Objectives"; Schiff, *Building the International Criminal Court*, 160.

Filing "Friend of the Court" Briefs

Amicus curiae, or "friend of the court," briefs are a means for non-parties to provide relevant legal or factual information to the Chambers regarding a specific case. The Rome Statute and the ICC's Rules of Evidence and Procedure – both of which NGOs provided extensive consultation on writing – have provisions that allow for NGO participatory access as amici curiae.[150] According to Rule 103(1), the Chamber can "invite or grant leave to a State, organization or person to submit, in writing or orally, any observation on any issue that the Chamber deems appropriate." Such invitations or requests can occur during the situation, pre-trial, and appeals proceedings. Non-party participation is also permitted in the reparations phase under Article 75(3) of the Rome Statute: "the Court may invite and shall take account of representations from or on behalf of convicted persons, victims, or other interested persons or interested States."

Filing amicus briefs fits with the strategies of many human rights advocacy NGOs. Amicus briefs can provide important legal expertise and information that may influence judicial decisions about prosecutorial strategies, interpretation of key legal concepts or crimes, and structuring of reparations programs. This is of particular importance at the fledgling ICC because decisions may impact future cases as well as customary international law. Although NGOs have the access and incentive to participate as amici curiae, the frequency of NGO participation differs depending on the phase of the proceedings. NGOs submitting amicus briefs under Rule 103 during the situation, pre-trial, trial, and appeals phases occurs fairly infrequently. Of the 24 cases in the ten situations under investigation, only eight out of 25 amicus applications by NGOs were accepted for filing.[151] This 32 percent rate of acceptance is low in comparison to other international criminal courts and tribunals.[152] In contrast, in the four cases that have reached the reparations phase, NGOs have successfully submitted eight briefs under Article 75 (see Table 5.3).[153]

The impact of NGO amicus briefs on judicial decisions also diverges depending on the phase of the proceeding. As best as can be measured, the influence of

---

[150] Legal experts affiliated with the CICC helped shape the Rules of Procedure and Evidence at PrepCom on a wide range of issues but it is unknown whether they specifically shaped Rule 103. See: William R. Pace and Jennifer Schense, "Coalition for the International Criminal Court at the Preparatory Commission," in *The International Criminal Court: Elements of Crimes and Rules of Procedure and Evidence*, ed. Roy S. Lee (Ardsley, NY: Transnational Publishers, Inc., 2001): 705–34.

[151] This information is current as of May 2017.

[152] The approximate acceptance rates of all amicus applications are: 8 percent at the Special Tribunal for Lebanon, 50 percent at the ECCC, 55 percent at the ICTR, and 70 percent at the ICTY. See: Sarah Williams and Emma Palmer, "Civil Society and Amicus Curiae Interventions in the International Criminal Court," *Acta Juridica* 2016, no. 1 (2016): 51.

[153] The cases are *Lubanga, Katanga, Bemba,* and *Al Madhi.* This is current as of May 2017.

TABLE 5.3 *Amicus Curiae Requests and Briefs at the International Criminal Court (2006–2017)*

Requests	Under Rule 103	Under Article 75
NGOs	25	8
Individuals	21	0
State/State Entity	9	0
Other	4	7
Total	59*	15
Accepted Briefs		
NGOs**	8	8
Individuals	5	0
State/State Entity	5	0
Other	1	7
Total	19	19

Note: Data were collected from public case documents on the ICC Legal Tools database and are current as of May 2017.

* The data do not include two invited briefs from Antonio Cassese and the United Nations High Commissioner for Human Rights in the Darfur, Sudan situation.

** The accepted request for leave to file an amicus brief by the International Criminal Bar in the *Lubanga* case was withdrawn before the amicus brief was filed.

accepted filings under Rule 103 is limited.[154] Of the eight briefs filed by NGOs, three resulted in judicial decisions by the Chambers that corresponded with the position of the brief. The first "successful brief" was submitted by the International Criminal Bar in the *Lubanga* case and argued that the Trial Chambers erred in its opinion that the prosecution is not required to share documents used by the prosecution that do not directly relate to the defendant. The other two "successful briefs" were filed by Redress and domestic partner NGOs in the *Kony et al.* and *Gaddafi* cases, respectively, and argued about the admissibility of the cases under the complementary regime of the Rome Statute.[155] Amnesty International and the

[154] Evaluating the impact of amicus briefs under Rule 103 is quite difficult as the Court rarely references briefs in judicial decisions or judgments.

[155] I use the term "successful" to designate an amicus brief that corresponds with the Chamber's decision. It does not imply that the filing necessarily contributed to the decision. In the *Lubanga* case, the decision of the Appeals Chamber was consistent with that advocated by the International Criminal Bar but came to its decision through different logic. In fact, the Appeal Chamber's decision lays out and refutes the arguments presented by the International Criminal Bar. See: International Criminal Court, "Judgment on the Appeal of Mr. Lubanga Dyilo against the Oral Decision of Trial Chamber I of 18 January 2008," July 11, 2008, 24–7, ICC-01/04–01/06–1433, www.legal-tools.org/doc/f5bc1e/. In the *Kony et al.* case, the pre-trial Chamber found the case admissible under the complementary regime of the Rome Statute. This corresponded to the information provided by Uganda Victims Fund and Redress that no domestic proceedings against the accused were underway in Uganda. In the *Gaddafi* case, Redress and the Lawyers for Justice in Libya filed a similar brief on whether Libya was "able and willing" to undertake domestic proceedings as enshrined in Article 17.

WIGJ each filed a brief in the *Bemba* case on the specific legal issues of cumulative charging and superior responsibility. Even though the Prosecutor supported the position of both briefs, the Chambers ultimately disagreed with the positions advocated.[156] The remaining three briefs did not argue for specific charges or judicial decisions but served as means to share information and expertise: two NGO briefs gave specific policy recommendations on how to implement new systems of victims' participation and another brief filed by the Africa Center for Open Governance gave detailed historical background on the post-election violence in Kenya to help understand the non-cooperative stance of the Kenyan Government. In contrast, evidence from the two cases that have concluded reparations (*Lubanga* and *Katanga*) suggests that the impact of NGO briefs on reparations' procedures may be more significant than under Rule 103.[157] In the reparations' decisions in both the *Lubanga* and *Katanga* cases, the arguments presented in the amicus briefs are thoroughly summarized and prominently featured in the final reparations' decisions.[158] In the *Lubanga* decision, the Trial Chamber even adopted the concept of "transformative reparations" presented in the submission by the WIGJ.[159]

NGO participation as amicus curiae during pre-trial, trial, and appeals proceedings under Rule 103 represents an anomaly as compared to other forms of NGO participation at the ICC: NGOs have formal access and strong motivation to shape judicial decisions but their overall levels of participation and influence is minimal. This anomaly is a result of the judicial Chambers adopting a restricted stance on allowing amicus participation.[160] The Court's restricted stance manifests in two ways: almost never requesting amicus participation and when amici request participation, to generally deny their application. The judicial chambers do not exclusively

---

[156] Regarding the amicus brief by Amnesty International, Chambers decided not to reject the provision of causality with the notion of superior responsibility as advocated by Amnesty.
See: International Criminal Court, "Decision Pursuant to Article 61(7)(a) and (b) of the Rome Statute on the Charges of the Prosecutor Against Jean-Pierre Bemba Gombo," June 15, 2009, www.legal-tools.org/doc/07965c/. Regarding the amicus brief by the WIGJ, Chambers rejected the prosecutor's application for leave to appeal the chamber's previous decision on cumulative charging that WIGJ opposed. See: International Criminal Court, "Decision on the Prosecutor's Application for Leave to Appeal the 'Decision Pursuant to Article 61(7)(a) and (b) of the Rome Statute on the Charges of the Prosecutor Against Jean-Pierre Bemba Gombo,'" September 18, 2009, www.legal-tools.org/doc/4053f8/.

[157] Because only two cases have decisions regarding reparations, it is too early to say whether NGO briefs under Article 75 will continue to be accepted and referenced in decisions.

[158] International Criminal Court, "Ordonnance de réparation en vertu de l'article 75 du Statut Accompagnée d'une annexe publique (annexe I) et d'une annexe confidentielle ex parte réservée au Représentant légal commun des victimes, au Bureau du conseil public pour les victimes," March 24, 2017, ICC-01/04-01/07-3728, www.legal-tools.org/doc/83d6c4/; International Criminal Court, "Decision Establishing the Principles and Procedures to Be Applied to Reparations," August 7, 2012, www.legal-tools.org/doc/a05830/.

[159] Williams and Palmer, "Civil Society and Amicus Curiae Interventions in the International Criminal Court," 49; International Criminal Court, "Decision Establishing the Principles and Procedures to Be Applied to Reparations."

[160] Woolaver, "The Role of Amicus Curiae Submissions at International Criminal Tribunals."

reject the applications for filing amicus briefs from NGOs; the default decision seems to be to reject all applications, including those from individuals, states, or professional organizations, unless there is an exceptional basis for acceptance (see Table 5.3).[161] The reason for the judicial Chambers to adopt such a restrictive approach is the result of a general backlash against amicus participation at all international criminal courts. When the ICC's rules of procedure and evidence were drafted in the early 2000s, granting amicus access for a range of parties, including NGOs, was expected. The provision for amici admission was included in the rules of all recently established major international criminal tribunals, including the ICTY, the ICTR, the SCSL, the ECCC, and the Special Tribunal for Lebanon.[162] Once in use, however, amici access at these international criminal courts generated controversy. The aforementioned courts not only allowed for amicus participation, but several of them were quite open to submissions and proactive in seeking amicus participation.[163] Sustained influence in trial proceedings by non-parties led to subsequent challenges of abuse and over-representation of viewpoints – challenges which complicate or even violate fair trial procedures.[164] These challenges are even more salient at the ICC due to the inclusion of another party to the proceeding: victims and their representatives. Therefore, at the ICC, amicus briefs are allowed but the judicial Chambers are reluctant to approve and use them – even though the briefs could potentially provide helpful information or legal arguments.[165] Surprisingly, the Chamber's reticence to accept amicus filings under Rule 103 appears not to extend to applications made during reparations proceedings under Article 75. It is not known why this is the case but it could be because the reparations' provisions in the Rome Statute and the Rules of Procedure

---

[161] It is unclear how Chambers denote "exceptional basis for acceptance" and whether successful applications should focus on legal or factual issues. See Chatham House, "Meeting Summary of 'Shaping the Law: Civil Society Influence at International Criminal Courts,'" 2016: 3, www.chathamhouse.org/sites/files/chathamhouse/events/160125-meeting-summary-shaping-law-civil-society-influence-international-criminal-courts.pdf. According to Williams and Palmer, the threshold of "exceptional basis" is neither an established criterion nor is consistently applied. Across Trial Chambers and sometimes even within a specific case, different standards are used to assess whether applications for amicus participation should be accepted. This varied practice suggests that some briefs receive preferential treatment – typically from Western, larger NGOs. See: Williams and Palmer, "Civil Society and Amicus Curiae Interventions in the International Criminal Court," 52–4, 56–7.

[162] Woolaver, "The Role of Amicus Curiae Submissions at International Criminal Tribunals."

[163] The ECCC and the SCSL have both extensively allowed amicus briefs and cited them in their judgments. The ICTY and the ICTR both allowed and sometimes requested amicus participation but their influence on judgment is often deemed to be more indirect. See Chatham House, "Meeting Summary of 'Shaping the Law: Civil Society Influence at International Criminal Courts,'" 4.

[164] Woolaver, "The Role of Amicus Curiae Submissions at International Criminal Tribunals."

[165] Chatham House, "Meeting Summary of 'Shaping the Law: Civil Society Influence at International Criminal Courts,'" 3.

and Evidence are vague and the amicus submissions may aid the Chambers in establishing necessary but underdeveloped guidelines and procedures.[166]

The Court's tepid response to amicus applications under Rule 103 may generate feedback whereby NGOs are less willing to file applications during pre-trial, trial, and appeals proceedings. NGOs still do file applications, and do so in the greatest number as compared to individuals, states, and other organizations. Yet, the fact that so few briefs are accepted alters the cost-benefit calculation of choosing to invest in writing a brief as opposed to pursuing supplemental or alternative strategies to influence trials, such as shaping prosecutorial strategy.[167]

There is some support for this idea. In the *Lubanga* case, the WIGJ twice attempted to file amicus briefs regarding the absence of gender-based crimes – both applications were denied. Nevertheless, the OTP was in informal communication with the WIGJ and explained to them multiple times that the absence of gender-based charges in the *Lubanga* case was an aberration and that future cases would include gender-based crimes.[168]

CONCLUSION

Predominantly international NGOs, with strong donor support and parental-like vigilance towards the ICC, continually recognized the inadequacies of the fledgling court and sought to remedy them. Without the ICC asking for help or providing financial resources, NGOs came to provide critical services to the Court, including communications and outreach, ratification, and investigative assistance. NGOs do not envision these roles as temporary. Many prominent NGOs have permanent headquarters in The Hague and see a permanent role for NGOs at the Court, even though the specifics of the roles may change over time.[169] A CICC staff member details how the CICC views its future relationship with the ICC:

> we've already established the relationship ... what may change in the future is the focus on specific issues. The elections will become a big part of our work ... which necessarily means, you could say, not establishing relationships but perhaps changing the dynamic of relationships with some of those people that we've already got that relationship with. The election process becomes less of an issue with the Court and more of an issue with states parties. So, we would have to turn our advocacy to a different entity of the Rome Statute process. But that is the very nature of the job because you are dealing with so many different issues. The issue will determine who you develop the relationship with and who you target the advocacy

---

[166] Redress, "Moving Reparation Forward at the ICC: Recommendations," November 2016: 3, www.redress.org/downloads/1611redressiccreparationpaper.pdf.

[167] Woolaver, "The Role of Amicus Curiae Submissions at International Criminal Tribunals."

[168] Author interview with an ICC official, August 12, 2010.

[169] NGOs with a permanent presence in The Hague include: The CICC, the WIGJ, and the OSJI.

towards. If the Court, the ASP, establishes new mechanisms, or sub mechanisms, like focal points, or facilitators, or working groups, then it is incumbent on us to establish that relationship with those individuals.[170]

NGOs also see a permanent role for themselves as long as the ICC struggles with funding and support: "NGOs are crucial because the Court has a limited budget. States don't want bureaucracy. There will always be a place for NGOs to support the non-judicial functions of the Court."[171]

It is likely that NGOs will always play some role at the ICC. NGOs with an on-the-ground presence in situation countries will inevitably understand domestic contexts better and have information that will be crucial to ICC investigations. In the same vein, NGOs are instrumental to ratification efforts by linking the President to prominent local actors and galvanizing domestic civil society. However, several factors may result in a more circumscribed role for NGOs in the future. First, donor funding could severely hamper the ability of NGOs to play so many participatory roles. Private philanthropic funding for ICC-related projects has declined as foundations shift away from foci on international justice to domestic level accountability mechanisms.[172] This is also true of state funding. The European Union recently stopped funding international criminal justice, which resulted in the CICC losing a large grant.[173] Funding is not yet severely hampering NGO programming, but it is becoming a much larger issue for NGOs and, in the future, may constrain the ability of NGOs to engage with the ICC on so many issues and in so many ways.[174] Second, the expertise, brand recognition, and goodwill that underpins why certain NGOs have predominant roles at the ICC may be eroding. As European universities churn out masters of international criminal law students and prominent ICC officials read academic blogs such as Justice in Conflict and Opinio Juris, NGOs no longer have a monopoly on ICC-related expertise.[175] In the same vein, as more time passes, the connection to the Rome Conference becomes less important. Fewer people associated with the Court, states, or NGOs will have attended the 1998 Rome Conference and it will seem more a historical fact than a source of authority. Recent episodes of coordinated activism for human rights and justice, such as the Arab Spring, also

---

[170] Author interview with a CICC staff member, August 20, 2010.

[171] By "non-judicial functions," the interview subject meant not relating to the judicial decision-making functions of the Court, or the process by which judges make rulings. Author interview with Deborah Ruiz Verduzco, Senior Programme Officer, PGA, September 8, 2010.

[172] MacArthur Foundation, "Human Rights & International Justice Grant Guidelines," accessed October 25, 2013, www.macfound.org/info-grantseekers/grantmaking-guidelines/human_rights-grant-guidelines/.

[173] Interview with a staff member of the CICC, June 1, 2015.

[174] Interview with a staff member of the CICC, June 1, 2015.

[175] Up to 50 of these students observe ICC proceedings every day that there is a public hearing.
Author interview with Jennifer Schense, International Cooperation Adviser in the Jurisdiction, Complementarity and Cooperation Division of the Office of the Prosecutor, ICC, June 3, 2015.

represent valid, alternative sources of civil society authority. Lastly, as the ICC seeks to become a functional, stable, and professional court, it may limit NGO roles and influence. The Court is already signaling that it may try to remedy its own deficiencies. Prosecutor Bensouda has written several op-eds that seek to explain the powers and limitations of the Court in light of political issues such as peace processes and the Palestinian referral, the Pre-Trial Chamber recently informed the UNSC of Sudan's non-cooperation, and the Trial Chamber in the *Ntaganda* case endorsed the idea of holding opening statements *in situ* in Bunia, DRC, to link the work of the Court to local communities.[176] If the aforementioned limiting factors do come to fruition, the most impactful roles for NGOs will not be for prominent, international NGOs, as is currently the situation, but for domestic NGOs with knowledge of local situations. However, as international NGOs have long played the role of coordinator, gatekeeper, and partner to domestic NGOs, it is likely that they will remain in this role as the main interlocutor between local groups and the ICC, unless the Court chooses to adopt a different approach towards civil society.

[176] The Presiding judge highlighted this factor during the Ntaganda status conference, June 2, 2015.

Fatou Bensouda, "International Justice and Diplomacy," *The New York Times*, March 19, 2013, www.nytimes.com/2013/03/20/opinion/global/the-role-of-the-icc-in-international-justice-and-diplomacy.html; Fatou Bensouda, "Fatou Bensouda: The Truth about the ICC and Gaza | Fatou Bensouda," *The Guardian*, August 29, 2014, www.theguardian.com/commentisfree/2014/aug/29/icc-gaza-hague-court-investigate-war-crimes-palestine; International Criminal Court, "Press Release: Pre-Trial Chamber II Informs the United Nations Security Council about Sudan's Non-Cooperation in the Arrest and Surrender of Omar Al Bashir," September 3, 2015, www.icc-cpi.int/en_menus/icc/press%20and%20media/press%20releases/Pages/pr1094.aspx.

Conclusion

NGOs and International Human Rights Justice

NGOs can profoundly shape the character of international human rights justice through their participation at international criminal and human rights courts. This occurs through roles normally associated with human rights NGOs, such as naming and shaming, advocacy, monitoring, and formal participation in trials. This also occurs through roles less associated with NGOs, such as consulting on issues of court governance and administration, and providing funding, outreach, and investigative services. NGO engagement has the potential to impact nearly every facet of international courts: institutional structure and rules, cases and legal strategies, financial and resource capacity, and jurisprudence.

Substantial and consequential NGO participation at international courts is not guaranteed, and is not uniform across judicial institutions. As illustrated by the case studies in this book, the breadth of participatory access, engagement, and influence are shaped by three factors. First, the institutional history of NGO engagement establishes inclusionary or exclusionary norms and perceptions by courts and member states. These norms and perceptions can shape whether courts or member states allow expanded participatory access, and demarcate the impact of such participatory access. Second, courts with significant deficiencies of resources, legitimacy, and state cooperation are more likely to allow NGO participatory access to help mitigate those deficiencies. Because NGO participatory access is granted to increase functionality, the resulting participation tends to be more substantive and impactful. Third, NGOs with the motivation and requisite capacity make claims for greater participatory access and drive subsequent participatory engagement.

The three aforementioned factors played out in distinct ways across the examined international judicial mechanisms. At the International Criminal Court (ICC), the factors operated in complementary ways, which resulted in unprecedented formal and informal access, a surge of NGO engagement, and tremendous impact on nearly every aspect of the Court. The fledgling court struggled with state cooperation and adequate financing and a well-resourced, thousands-strong network of

NGOs with pre-established legitimacy, resources, and a drive for the Court to succeed were willing to fill the Court's needs. Similarly, during the early years of the Inter-American Human Rights System (IAS), deficiencies in funding, information, and authority incapacitated both the Commission and the Court. NGOs, motivated by the urgency of human rights abuses being committed by authoritarian regimes throughout Latin America, sought participatory engagement that could build the capacity of these institutions and provide redress and accountability. Even though the Commission had no experience with NGOs, it opted to embrace NGO participation because of the functional benefits it could confer. The Court, familiar with NGO engagement with the Commission, welcomed NGO participation from the outset and even established its own NGO to provide supplemental aid. At the ECtHR, motivated NGOs have continually sought greater participatory opportunities, but access and influence is rather circumscribed. Unlike the other two courts, the European Court of Human Rights (ECtHR) has not struggled with the substantial resource deficiencies and its history of NGO exclusion has bred skepticism towards NGOs and a general reticence to further incorporate or rely on them.

This book has shown that court deficiencies, institutional history vis-à-vis NGOs, and NGO motivation and resources influence the breadth of NGO roles, participation, and impact at the ECtHR, the IAS, and the ICC. Nevertheless, the scope of the argument is limited to permanent, international, treaty-based, human rights or criminal courts. This book examined all courts that fit these criteria, save one: The African System of Human and Peoples' Rights (Commission and Court). The African system was not included in this project because both institutions were not fully functional when the research for this project was conducted – the Court had not delivered a judgment on the merits of a case. In the past few years, the African Commission and Court have gained capacity and the Court has delivered several groundbreaking judgments. Because the African system fits within the case selection criteria of this project but was not examined in the initial research, it constitutes a perfect test case of this book's argument. Subsequent investigation into NGO engagement with the African system does in fact provide additional empirical support for two of the explanatory factors: scarcity of court resources and NGO motivation and resources.[1] The young court, which struggles with legitimacy and limited jurisdiction, grants NGOs the most wide-reaching legal standing of any international court and even allocates symbolic reparations to NGO petitioners.

To further expand the purview of the theoretical argument proposed in this book, this conclusion also includes a preliminary examination of NGO participation at the Extraordinary Chambers in the Courts of Cambodia (ECCC), often referred to as the Khmer Rouge Tribunal. The Khmer Rouge Tribunal is criminal in nature

---

[1]   From the limited research available, it is unclear whether NGOs participated in the establishment of the African judicial institutions. I therefore do not include the explanatory factor of historical relationships with NGOs in this short analysis.

but falls outside of the scope of examined cases because it is temporary, not treaty-based, and hybrid in structure. The original logic for excluding ad hoc, hybrid tribunals was that their impermanent natures could deter NGOs from establishing and investing in long-term engagement strategies, especially if there were permanent courts that served as alternative sites of participation. Surprisingly, this logic does not entirely hold true, particularly with regard to local Cambodian NGOs, whose multi-pronged engagement around victims' participation proved crucial for sustained and abundant victims' involvement in key trials.[2] Much like NGO interaction with the ICC, NGOs assumed roles normally under the responsibility of the Court. This shift in roles came about because of a lack of funding to the Khmer Rouge Tribunal in these areas and a robust and well-financed network of NGOs willing to take them on.[3] This preliminary research on the Khmer Rouge Tribunal suggests that the theoretical argument of this book may be generalizable to a wider swath of international criminal courts and tribunals.

THE AFRICAN HUMAN RIGHTS SYSTEM

The African Human Rights System is the youngest of the regional human rights systems. Similar to the pre-1998 European System of Human Rights and the IAS, it comprises a Commission and a Court. The Commission, established in 1987, accepts complaints, examines country reports, and serves as a quasi-judicial filtering body for cases to the Court. The African Court on Human and Peoples' Rights (ACtHPR), which opened its doors in 2006 but did not deliver its first judgment on the merits of the case until 2013, can set down binding judgments but is limited in jurisdiction to those states that have signed an additional protocol granting it jurisdiction. The treaty undergirding the African System is the African (Banjul) Charter on Human and Peoples' Rights negotiated by member states of the Organization of African Unity, now replaced by the AU. All members of the AU, apart from South Sudan, have signed and ratified the African Charter. But as of early 2016, only 29 of the 53 AU members have ratified the Protocol that gives jurisdiction to the ACtHPR.

The African System is not only a young system with limited jurisdictional reach but it also struggles with state buy-in and financial support. National human rights institutions – which are typically better resourced and could aid with domestic implementation of Court decisions – know little of the procedures or work of the African Court

---

2   Christoph Sperfeldt, "The Role of Cambodian Civil Society in the Victim Participation Scheme of the Extraordinary Chambers of the Courts of Cambodia," in *Victims of International Crimes: An Interdisciplinary Discourse*, ed. Thorsten Bonacker and Christoph Safferling (New York, NY: Springer Science & Business Media, 2013): 345–72.
3   From the limited research available, it is unclear whether NGOs participated in the establishment of the Khmer Rouge Tribunal or if court personnel had prior relationships or experiences with NGOs. I therefore do not include the explanatory factor of historical relationships with NGOs in this short analysis.

and generally do not see their work and that of the Court as complementary.[4] Additionally, the legal aid system is grossly underfunded and the first and only contribution was made by Tanzania in 2015 in the amount of $100,000.[5] Nevertheless, the African Court holds tremendous institutional promise. For African countries, it is the only supranational court of last resort that can issue binding judgments against governments for individual human rights violations. The system is also distinctly pan-African in identity and scope and carries the legitimacy and backing of the AU.

As predicted for a young court struggling with resources and operating in a context where NGOs seek to generate human rights accountability, NGOs have a strong participatory presence in the African System. The majority of involved NGOs are domestic NGOs coming from the country before the Court; however, many prominent international human rights NGOs are also increasingly involved in the African System. Nearly 500 NGOs have observer status at the African Commission, which is necessary for legal standing before the Court, and grants them the right to prepare and present "shadow reports" on the human rights situation in their countries to the Commission. The preponderance of NGOs with observer status before the Commission are domestic NGOs with headquarters in African countries. Nevertheless, 85 NGOs from outside of Africa have consultative status, most of which are very well-resourced and have robust relationships with other international criminal or human rights courts, such as Amnesty International, Human Rights Watch, Human Rights First, the International Commission of Jurists, the World Federalist Movement, and the Center for Justice and International Law (CEJIL).[6]

The most notable form of NGO participation at the African Court, which is distinct from any other international court, is that NGOs have formal legal standing even when the organization is itself not a victim of human rights abuse.[7] Individuals and NGOs from member states can directly petition the Court if states have signed the "Special Declaration," which is a subcomponent of the Protocol that gives jurisdiction to the Court.[8] The only requirement is that the NGO must have observer status at the Commission. NGO legal standing helps transmit important cases to the Court as it allows for joint claims from individuals and NGOs that provide built-in legal expertise and resources for victims. Currently, only seven countries have signed the "Special Declaration" but there has been a sustained advocacy effort by court

---

[4] Oliver Windridge, "An Alien Institution: A Q&A with the Network of African National Human Rights Institutions," *The ACtHPR Monitor* (blog), November 24, 2015, www.acthprmonitor.org/an-alien-institution-qa-with-the-network-of-african-national-human-rights-institutions/.

[5] Oliver Windridge, "2015 at the African Court on Human and Peoples' Rights – A Year in Review," *The ACtHPR Monitor* (blog), January 25, 2016, www.acthprmonitor.org/2015-at-the-african-court-on-human-and-peoples-rights-a-year-in-review/.

[6] African Commission on Human and People's Rights, "NGOs with Observer Status: By State / Network / ACHPR," accessed February 18, 2016, www.achpr.org/network/ngo/.

[7] This is distinct from the Inter-American and European Human Rights Systems, which only grant NGOs independent standing if the organization is a victim of human rights abuses.

[8] The Special Declaration is found in Article 5(3) and Article 34(6) of the Protocol.

officials, some state officials, and NGOs to allow greater access by petition from individuals and NGOs. These efforts include sensitization visits by the Court, local NGO ratification campaigns, and a recent case at the East African Court of Justice that sought to make the additional signing of the Special Declaration to allow standing to individuals and NGOs no longer necessary.[9]

The allowance of NGO standing is not merely symbolic; NGOs have substantively impacted the burgeoning judicial cases and decisions of the African Court. In 2011, the African Court first ordered provisional measures in *African Commission on Human and Peoples' Rights* v. *Great Socialist People's Libyan Arab Jamahiriya*. These provisional measures ordered Libya to refrain from any activities that would result in loss of life or physical integrity, as it would be a breach of the African Charter on Human and Peoples' Rights. The request for provisional measures was made by three NGOs – the Egyptian Initiative for Personal Rights (EIPR), Human Rights Watch, and Interights.[10] Furthermore, two of the four judgments of the Court – all of which found states in violation of the Charter – included NGO applicants.[11] In *Zongo and Others* v. *Burkina Faso*, the Court sought to recognize the special contributions of the NGO applicant by awarding it symbolic reparations in a minor amount.

THE EXTRAORDINARY CHAMBERS IN THE COURTS OF CAMBODIA (ECCC) (THE KHMER ROUGE TRIBUNAL)

The ECCC, often referred to as the Khmer Rouge Tribunal, is a joint enterprise by the government of Cambodia and the UN to hold former members of the Khmer Rouge regime individually responsible for serious human rights violations, including genocide, war crimes, and crimes against humanity. The idea for the Khmer Rouge Tribunal originated in 1996 but the Tribunal did not become operational until 2006.[12] The Khmer Rouge Tribunal is distinct from the international courts examined in this book in several ways. First, it is ad hoc, not permanent, and therefore will cease to function after completing its prescribed mandate. Second and relatedly, there is no treaty that undergirds and serves as the mandate of the Tribunal. Its jurisdiction was demarcated in negotiation

---

[9] In 2015, the Court made sensitization visits to Lesotho, South Africa, and Chad. See: Windridge, "2015 at the African Court on Human and Peoples' Rights – A Year in Review."

    The case at the East African Court of Justice is *Democratic Party* v. *Secretary General of the East African Community and Others*. The appellate division held that signing the "Special Declaration" is necessary.

[10] Anna Dolidze, "African Court on Human and Peoples' Rights – Response to the Situation in Libya," *ASIL Insights* 15, no. 20 (2011), www.asil.org/insights110725.cfm.

[11] The four cases with judgments on the merits (not those found inadmissible) are: *Konate* v. *Burkina Faso*, *Thomas* v. *Tanzania*, *Zongo and Others* v. *Burkina Faso*, and *Mtikila and Others* v. *Tanzania*. The NGO applicant in *Zongo and Others* is Burkinabé Human and Peoples' Rights Movement. The two NGO applicants in *Mtikila* are the Tanganyika Law Society and Human Rights Centre.

[12] Extraordinary Chambers in the Courts of Cambodia (ECCC), "About ECCC," accessed March 2, 2016, www.eccc.gov.kh/en/about-eccc.

between the government of Cambodia and the UN and is territorially limited to Cambodia and the crimes committed there during the Khmer Rouge regime (April 17, 1975–January 6, 1979). Lastly, the Tribunal is hybrid in structure, meaning that it incorporates both international and domestic components in terms of staff, judges, and law.[13]

Although the ECCC is an ad hoc, hybrid tribunal, NGO interaction looks surprisingly similar to the ICC in that NGOs are performing roles that are commonly under the responsibility of the court. Local and international NGOs conduct community outreach for the Tribunal, serve as intermediaries connecting victims to the Tribunal, provide legal representation and psychosocial support for victims, monitor trial proceedings, and advocate for victims' rights.[14] The Khmer Rouge Tribunal continually relied on NGOs to perform these roles and they proved crucial for victims' participation in trials. As opposed to NGOs vis-à-vis the ICC, NGOs working on the Khmer Rouge Tribunal have not established formalized collaboration and consultation frameworks with the Tribunal or the UN.[15]

The reasons for such pronounced NGO engagement with the Khmer Rouge Tribunal in the area of victims' participation align with the broader argument of this book. First, the outreach and victims' participation programs of the Tribunal have consistently been underprioritized and underfunded. Overall, donors have contributed upward of $200 million, yet only a sliver of the funds have gone to victims' participation and reparations.[16] These resource deficiencies were even more pronounced during the Tribunal's early years. The Court's Victim Unit was established in 2007 but could not operate at a sustained level until two years later, when it received special funding from the German Foreign Office.[17] These deficiencies constituted both openings for NGOs to fulfill crucial needs of the Tribunal and incentives for the Tribunal to condone such participation, even if it did not formally cooperate with NGOs. Cambodian NGOs could take up these roles because they were part of a vibrant and well-developed NGO community, and international donors were willing to shoulder the cost. Funding partners – including the European Commission and German Development Service – provided multi-year grants and adviser expertise to Cambodian NGOs engaging with the Khmer Rouge Tribunal.[18]

FUTURE EXPANSION TO HYBRID AND ECONOMIC COURTS

The pertinence of this book's explanatory argument to NGO participation at the Khmer Rouge Tribunal suggests that the argument may be more broadly

[13] For more on hybrid courts, see: www.pict-pcti.org/courts/hybrid.html.
[14] Sperfeldt, "The Role of Cambodian Civil Society in the Victim Participation Scheme of the Extraordinary Chambers of the Courts of Cambodia."
[15] Sperfeldt, "The Role of Cambodian Civil Society," 361–2.
[16] Sperfeldt, "The Role of Cambodian Civil Society," 364.
[17] Sperfeldt, "The Role of Cambodian Civil Society," 350.
[18] Sperfeldt, "The Role of Cambodian Civil Society," 364.

generalizable than to strictly permanent, treaty-based human rights and criminal courts. Two possible avenues of research could further explore this question of applicability. First, the argument could be applied to additional ad hoc, hybrid tribunals such as the Special Court for Sierra Leone, the Crimes Panels of the District Court of Dili, and the "Regulation 64" Panels in the Courts of Kosovo. An interesting line of exploration would be to see if NGO participation at hybrid tribunals – which are based in the country where the human rights violations occurred – mostly consists of domestic, as opposed to international NGOs, as was the case at the Khmer Rouge Tribunal. Second, NGO participation could be examined at regional or subregional integration courts that have extended their jurisdiction to human rights issues. These include the ECOWAS Community Court of Justice, the East African Court of Justice, and the Tribunal of the Southern African Development Community.[19] These courts could be of particular interest to refine and test the assertions about courts as prudent and calculated actors allowing NGO participatory access to enhance their functionality. As the rules of civil society access likely reflect the economic nature and mandate of the judicial institutions, allowance of the participation of human rights NGOs could help support the notion that courts strategically seek to build their capacity in light of state hostility or lack of resources.

---

[19] Amy Porges, "Regional and Sub-Regional Human Rights Tribunals: The African Response," American Society of International Law, accessed March 4, 2016, www.asil.org/blogs/regional-and-sub-regional-human-rights-tribunals-african-response.

Interviews Conducted

The list below identifies the affiliated organizations of my interview subjects. I conducted the majority of interviews during fieldwork in the Netherlands, France, England, Costa Rica, and Washington, DC from August 2010 to January 2011. I also conducted subsequent fieldwork in the Netherlands in June 2015. All interviews were semi-structured and averaged approximately one hour in length. Most of the interview subjects requested to be identified as staff or officials of their affiliation organizations. A few individuals requested that their name and position be used, which is identified in the text. Others requested complete anonymity and their affiliated organizations are not identified in the text or listed below.

EUROPEAN COURT OF HUMAN RIGHTS

The AIRE Centre
Amnesty International
Council of Europe
European Court of Human Rights (x3)
Interights
International Commission of Jurists
Kurdish Human Rights Project
Liberty
UK-based human rights organization

INTER-AMERICAN COURT OF HUMAN RIGHTS

Americas Watch/Human Rights Watch
Center for Justice and International Law (x2)
Inter-American Commission on Human Rights (x4)
Inter-American Court of Human Rights (x2)

Inter-American Institute of Human Rights (x3)
Washington Office on Latin America

INTERNATIONAL CRIMINAL COURT

Coalition for the International Criminal Court (x4)
International Criminal Court (x7)
NGO staff member with expertise in Uganda
Open Society Initiative
Parliamentarians for Global Action
Women's Initiatives for Gender Justice (x2)

Data and Measures of Frequency and Impact of NGO Participatory Roles at the European Court of Human Rights

NGO Participatory Roles	Frequency	Impact
Representing petitioners	• Interviews with Court officials • Percentage calculated using Cichowski and Chrun's European Court of Human Rights Database	• Interviews with Court officials • Comparison of the average percentage of cases in which judgments are found versus cases where specific NGOs represent petitioners (Liberty, EHRAC, and the AIRE Centre) using NGO-provided data and court statistics • Percentages of all Grand Chamber cases of the Highest Importance from 2002 to 2012 where NGOs represent petitioners (from HUDOC)
Filing amicus curiae or "friend of the court" briefs	• Interviews with Court officials • Percentage calculated using Cichowski and Chrun's European Court of Human Rights Database	• Interviews with Court officials
Biennial meeting with Court Registry	• Interviews with NGO staff and Court officials	• Interviews with NGO staff and Court officials

NGO Participatory Roles	Frequency	Impact
Observing and advocating in reform process	• Interviews with NGO staff • Review of declarations from ministerial-level meetings for NGO attendance	• Interviews with NGO staff • Comparison of NGO advocacy documents submitted prior to ministerial-level reform conferences with conference declarations
Communications to the Committee of Ministers about execution of judgments	• Number of submitted communications as listed on the Committee of Ministers website as a proportion of pending cases awaiting execution of judgment	• *Unknown*

Data and Measures of Frequency and Impact of NGO Participatory Roles at the Inter-American Human Rights System (Commission and Court)

NGO Participatory Roles	Frequency	Impact
Representing petitioners/ Providing information on the execution of judgments	• Interviews with NGO staff and Commission officials • NGO historical activity reports	• Interviews with NGO staff and Court officials
Filing amicus curiae or "friend of the court" briefs	• Percentage calculated through search of all contentious court judgments using court database • Secondary sources	• Interviews with Court officials • Secondary sources
Advocating for funding and treaty ratification	• Interviews with NGO staff and Court and Commission officials	• Interviews with NGO staff and Court and Commission officials • Verification in archival search of US public laws
Consultants and advocates at the OAS	• Interviews with NGO staff and Court and Commission officials • NGO and OAS documents • Secondary sources	• Interviews with NGO staff and Commission officials • OAS documents • Secondary sources
Sharing information on human rights abuses	• Interviews with NGO staff and Court and Commission officials • Content analysis of Amnesty International annual reports from 1975 to 1986	• Interviews with Commission officials
Aiding Commission in investigations and cases	• Interviews with NGO staff and Commission officials • Percentage calculated by examining all court judgments from 1988 to 2000 for listed NGO advisor using court database	• Interviews with Commission officials

NGO Participatory Roles	Frequency	Impact
Providing funds for court special sessions	• Interviews with Court officials • Secondary sources	• Interviews with Court officials • Secondary sources

Data and Measures of Frequency and Impact of NGO Participatory Roles at the International Criminal Court

NGO Participatory Roles	Frequency	Impact
Filing amicus curiae or "friend of the court" briefs	• Percentage calculated through search of all cases using court database	• Comparison of the contents and arguments of NGO briefs with chamber decisions
Formal meetings with each organ of the Court and ASP Secretariat	• Court and ASP documents	• Interviews with NGO staff
Informal meetings with Court organs	• Interviews with NGO staff and Court officials • NGO documents	• Interviews with NGO staff • ICC documents
Advocating for universality of Rome Statute	• Interviews with NGO staff • NGO documents	• Interviews with NGO staff • Time lapse analysis of NGO universality campaign targets with the date of state ratification of the Rome Statute
Lobbying the Assembly of States Parties (ASP)	• Interviews with NGO staff and Court officials • Review of ASP official records of annual sessions for CICC statements • NGO documents • Secondary sources	• Interviews with NGO staff, Court officials, and a diplomat from ICC member state
Enforcement of decisions/warrants	• Constructed historical catalogue of NGO and ICC press releases following Bashir's travel to ICC member states constructed from CICC archives and court press releases	• Interviews with NGO staff

NGO Participatory Roles	Frequency	Impact
Article 15 communications	• Court and NGO documents	• Interview with anonymous source with knowledge on issue
Intermediaries and sharing information	• Interview with anonymous source with knowledge on issue • NGO documents	• Interviews with Court officials and anonymous source with knowledge on issue • NGO documents
Communications and outreach	• Interviews with NGO staff • NGO documents • Secondary sources	• Interviews with NGO staff and a journalist that covers the ICC • NGO documents • Secondary sources
Organizing legal counsel for victims and defense	• NGO documents	• NGO documents

References

Abbott, Kirby. "A Brief Overview of Legal Interoperability Challenges for NATO Arising from the Interrelationship between IHL and IHRL in Light of the European Convention on Human Rights." *International Review of the Red Cross* 96, no. 893 (2014): 107–37. https://doi.org/10.1017/S1816383115000338.

Abi-Mershed, Elizabeth A.H. "The United States and the Inter-American Court of Human Rights." In *The Sword and the Scales: The United States and International Courts and Tribunals*, ed. Cesare P. R. Romano, 185–209. Cambridge University Press, 2009.

Adler, Emanuel and Peter M. Haas. "Conclusion: Epistemic Communities, World Order, and the Creation of a Reflective Research Program." *International Organization* 46, no. 1 (1992): 367–90.

African Commission on Human and People's Rights. "NGOs with Observer Status: By State/Network/ACHPR." Accessed February 18, 2016. www.achpr.org/network/ngo/.

"African Union Backs Mass Withdrawal from ICC." *BBC News*, February 1, 2017, sec. Africa. www.bbc.com/news/world-africa-38826073.

Agence France-Presse in Khartoum. "Omar Al-Bashir Celebrates ICC Decision to Halt Darfur Investigation." *The Guardian*, December 14, 2014. www.theguardian.com/world/2014/dec/14/omar-al-bashir-celebrates-icc-decision-to-halt-darfur-investigation.

Ainley, Kirsten. "The International Criminal Court on Trial." *Cambridge Review of International Affairs* 24, no. 3 (2011): 309–33. https://doi.org/10.1080/09557571.2011.558051.

AIRE Centre, Amnesty International, and European Human Rights Advocacy Centre. "Recommendations to the Council of Europe on Implementing Judgments," May 20, 2005. www.londonmet.ac.uk/research-units/hrsj/affiliated_centres/ehrac/advocacy/recommendations-to-the-council-of-europe-on-implementing-judgments/home.cfm.

Alter, Karen J. "Agents or Trustees? International Courts in Their Political Context." *European Journal of International Relations* 14, no. 1 (2008): 33–63.

"Delegation to International Courts and the Limits of Re-Contracting Political Power." In *Delegation and Agency in International Organizations*, ed. Darren G. Hawkins, David Lake, Daniel L. Nielson, and Michael J. Tierney, 312–38. Cambridge University Press, 2006.

Ambos, Kai. "The First Judgment of the International Criminal Court (Prosecutor v. Lubanga): A Comprehensive Analysis of the Legal Issues." *International Criminal Law Review* 12, no. 2 (2012): 115–53. https://doi.org/10.1163/157181212X639644.

AMICC. "AMICC." Accessed June 26, 2012. www.amicc.org/.

Amnesty International. "Amnesty International Annual Report 1975–1976," June 1, 1976. www.amnesty.org/en/documents/document/?indexNumber=pol10%2f0001%2f1976&language=en.

"Amnesty International Annual Report 1983," January 1, 1983. www.amnesty.org/en/documents/document/?indexNumber=pol10%2f0001%2f1983&language=en.

"Amnesty International Annual Report 1984," May 1, 1984. www.amnesty.org/en/documents/document/?indexNumber=pol10%2f0004%2f1984&language=en.

"Amnesty International Annual Report 1985," May 1, 1985. www.amnesty.org/en/documents/document/?indexNumber=POL10%2f002%2f1985&language=en.

"Amnesty International Annual Report 1986," January 1, 1986. www.amnesty.org/en/documents/document/?indexNumber=pol10%2f0003%2f1986&language=en.

"Amnesty International Annual Report 1987," January 1, 1987. www.amnesty.org/en/documents/document/?indexNumber=pol10%2f0002%2f1987&language=en.

"Amnesty International Annual Report 1988," January 1, 1988. www.amnesty.org/en/documents/document/?indexNumber=pol10%2f0001%2f1988&language=en.

"Amnesty International Annual Report 1990," January 1, 1990. www.amnesty.org/en/documents/document/?indexNumber=pol10%2f0003%2f1990&language=en.

"Amnesty International Annual Report 1994," January 1, 1994. www.amnesty.org/en/documents/document/?indexNumber=pol10%2f0002%2f1994&language=en.

"Amnesty International Annual Report 2002," May 27, 2002. www.amnesty.org/en/documents/document/?indexNumber=pol10%2f0001%2f2002&language=en.

"Austria: Amnesty International Submission to the UN Universal Periodic Review," January 2011. http://lib.ohchr.org/HRBodies/UPR/Documents/Session10/AT/AI_Amnesty%20International_eng.pdf.

"Memorandum to the International Law Commission: Establishing a Just, Fair and Effective Permanent International Criminal Tribunal," July 11, 1994. www.amnesty.org/en/library/info/IOR40/007/1994/en.

"OSCE Human Dimension Implementation Meeting 2006," October 4, 2006. www.osce.org/odihr/21108?download=true.

"Venezuela's Withdrawal from Regional Human Rights Instrument Is a Serious Setback," September 2, 2013. www.amnesty.org/en/latest/news/2013/09/venezuela-s-withdrawal-regional-human-rights-instrument-serious-setback/.

Amnesty International, European Human Rights Advocacy Centre, and The AIRE Centre. "Submission Regarding Rules of the European Court of Human Rights on the Pilot Judgment Procedure," June 30, 2010. TIGO IOR 61/2010.009.

Amnesty International, Justice, European Human Rights Advocacy Centre, Liberty, Human Rights Watch, Redress, Interights, and The AIRE Centre. "NGO Comments on the Group of Wise Persons' Report." In *Reforming the European Convention on Human Rights*, 265–74. Council of Europe Publishing, 2009.

Amnesty International, The AIRE Centre, European Human Rights Advocacy Centre, Helsinki Foundation for Human Rights, Human Rights Watch, Interights, International Commission of Jurists, Justice, and Redress. "Joint NGO Input to the Ongoing Negotiations on the Draft Brighton Declaration on the Future of the European Court of Human Rights," 2012. www.amnesty.org/en/library/asset/IOR61/005/2012/en/b721f975-c545-4087-90d8-4cbc1501a5d4/ior610052012en.pdf.

"Reform of the European Court of Human Rights: Open Letter to All Member States of the Council of Europe Consideration of the Drafts of the Brighton Declaration Must Include Civil Society," 2012. www.amnesty.org/en/library/asset/IOR61/003/2012/en/24bb4499-eaeb-4381-a57b-70b912ba023c/ior610032012en.pdf.

Amnesty International, The AIRE Centre, European Human Rights Advocacy Centre, Inter-ights, International Commission of Jurists, Justice, and Liberty. "Joint Statement for the High Level Conference on the Future of the European Court of Human Rights, Izmir, Turkey, 26–27 April 2011," 2011. www.londonmet.ac.uk/londonmet/fms/MRSite/Research/HRSJ/EHRAC/Advocacy/Joint%20NGO%20Statement%20Izmir%20conference%20FINAL%2019%20APRIL%202011.doc.

Amnesty International, The AIRE Centre, European Human Rights Advocacy Centre, Interights, International Commission of Jurists, and Justice. "Recommendations Regarding the Draft Declaration for Interlaken Ministerial Conference of 11 December 2009," 2009. www.londonmet.ac.uk/londonmet/fms/MRSite/Research/HRSJ/EHRAC/Advocacy/NGOJointcommentsInterlaken.pdf.

Amnesty International, The AIRE Centre, European Human Rights Advocacy Centre, Inter-ights, International Commission of Jurists, Justice, and Redress. "Recommendations to Strengthen the Draft Declaration for Interlaken Ministerial Conference," 2010. www.londonmet.ac.uk/londonmet/fms/MRSite/Research/HRSJ/EHRAC/Advocacy/Joint%20NGO%20Comments%20on%2013%20Jan%202010%20draft%20Interlaken%20Declaration%2025011o.pdf.

Amnesty International UK. "Council of Europe: A Step Closer to a Death Penalty-Free Zone," February 25, 2002. /press-releases/council-europe-step-closer-death-penalty-free-zone.

Andersen, Ellen Ann. *Out of the Closets and into the Courts: Legal Opportunity Structure and Gay Rights Litigation*. University of Michigan Press, 2009.

Anderson, Kenneth and David Rieff. "'Global Civil Society': A Skeptical View." In *Global Civil Society 2004/5*, ed. Helmut K. Anheier, Marlies Glasius, and Mary Kaldor, 26–39. Sage Publications, 2004.

Assembly of States Parties. "Part III Resolutions Adopted by the Assembly of States Parties," 2010. ICC-ASP/9/Res.2.

  "Proposed Programme Budget for 2012 of the International Criminal Court," July 21, 2011. ICC-ASP/10/10.

  "Report on Arrest Strategies by the Rapporteur," November 21, 2014. www.google.com/url?sa=t&rct=j&q=&esrc=s&source=web&cd=1&cad=rja&uact=8&ved=0CB4QFjAA&url=http%3A%2F%2Fwww.icc-cpi.int%2Ficcdocs%2Fasp_docs%2FASP13%2FICC-ASP-13-29-Add1-ENG.pdf&ei=50dbVcncLNGvogSL-YGwDA&usg=AFQjCNEzW1CgMs8-hJyRvY2cZbUALOP8_A&bvm=bv.93756505,d.cGU.

  "Status Report on the Court's Investigations into Efficiency Measures for 2010*," 2009. ICC-ASP/8/6.

Assembly of States Parties Committee on Budget and Finance. "Report of the Committee on Budget and Finance," 2004. ICC-ASP/3/18. www.icc-cpi.int/Menus/ASP/Sessions/Documentation/3rd+Session/Third+session+of+the+Assembly+of+States+Parties.htm.

Avant, Deborah. "Conserving Nature in the State of Nature: The Politics of INGO Policy Implementation." *Review of International Studies* 30, no. 3 (2004): 361–82.

Avant, Deborah, Martha Finnemore, and Susan Sell. "Who Governs the Globe?" In *Who Governs the Globe?* Cambridge University Press, 2010.

Avant, Deborah D., Martha Finnemore, and Susan K. Sell, eds. *Who Governs the Globe?* Cambridge University Press, 2010.

Barnett, Michael. "Evolution Without Progress? Humanitarianism in a World of Hurt." *International Organization* 63, no. 4 (2009): 621–63. https://doi.org/10.1017/S0020818309990087.

"Bashir Travel Map." Bashir Watch. Accessed May 19, 2015. http://bashirwatch.org/updates/.

Bass, Gary J. *Stay the Hand of Vengeance: The Politics of War Crimes Tribunals*. Princeton University Press, 2000.

Bassiouni, M. Cherif. "Historical Survey 1919–1998." In *ICC Ratification and National Implementing Legislation*, 1–44. Saint-Agne, France: Association Internationale de Droit Penal, 1999.

Bates, Robert H. ed. *The Evolution of the European Convention on Human Rights: From Its Inception to the Creation of a Permanent Court of Human Rights*. Oxford University Press, 2009.

Bates, Robert H., Avner Greif, Margaret Levi, Jean-Laurent Rosenthal, and Barry R. Weingast. *Analytic Narratives*. Princeton University Press, 1998.

Baylis, Elena A. "Outsourcing Investigations." *UCLA Journal of International Law and Foreign Affairs* 14 (2009).

BBC News. "African Union Accuses ICC of 'hunting' Africans." Accessed May 7, 2015. www .bbc.com/news/world-africa-22681894.

"UK 'Should Cut Links to the European Court of Human Rights.'" *BBC News*, February 7, 2011.

Bensouda, Fatou. "Fatou Bensouda: The Truth about the ICC and Gaza | Fatou Bensouda." *The Guardian*, August 29, 2014. www.theguardian.com/commentisfree/2014/aug/29/icc-gaza-hague-court-investigate-war-crimes-palestine.

"International Justice and Diplomacy." *The New York Times*, March 19, 2013. www .nytimes.com/2013/03/20/opinion/global/the-role-of-the-icc-in-international-justice-and-diplomacy.html.

Bignami, Francesca. "Civil Society and International Organizations: A Liberal Framework for Global Governance." SSRN Scholarly Paper. Rochester, NY: Social Science Research Network, 2005. http://papers.ssrn.com/abstract=2031012.

Birnbaum, Michael. "African Leaders Complain of Bias at ICC as Kenya Trials Get Underway." *The Washington Post*, December 5, 2013. www.washingtonpost.com/world/europe/african-leaders-complain-of-bias-at-icc-as-kenya-trials-are-underway/2013/12/05/0c52fc7a-56cb-11e3-bdbf-097ab2a3dc2b_story.html.

Bloodgood, Elizabeth A. "The Interest Group Analogy: International Non-Governmental Advocacy Organisations in International Politics." *Review of International Studies* 37, no. 1 (January 2011): 93–120. https://doi.org/10.1017/S0260210510001051.

Bob, Clifford. "*Clashing Interests in Global Arenas: The International Battle over Small Arms Control*." San Francisco, CA, 2008.

The Marketing of Rebellion: Insurgents, Media, and International Activism. Cambridge University Press, 2005.

Bond, Martyn. *The Council of Europe and Human Rights: An Introduction to the European Convention on Human Rights*. Council of Europe Publishing, 2010.

Bonzon, Yves. *Public Participation and Legitimacy in the WTO*. Cambridge University Press, 2014.

Bosco, David. "How to Destroy the International Criminal Court From Within." *Foreign Policy*, October 10, 2014. http://foreignpolicy.com/2014/10/10/how-to-destroy-the-international-criminal-court-from-within/.

Rough Justice: The International Criminal Court in a World of Power Politics. 1st edition. Oxford and New York, NY: Oxford University Press, 2014.

Bowcott, Owen and Jamie Grierson. "Sudan President Barred from Leaving South Africa." *The Guardian*, June 15, 2015. www.theguardian.com/world/2015/jun/14/sudan-president-omar-al-bashir-south-africa-icc.

Broomhall, Bruce. *International Justice and the International Criminal Court*. Oxford University Press, 2003.

Brysk, Alison. "From Above and Below: Social Movements, the International System, and Human Rights in Argentina." *Comparative Political Studies* 26, no. 3 (1993): 259–85.

Buchinger, Kerstin, Barbara Liegl, and Astrid Steinkellner. "European Human Rights Case Law and the Rights of Homosexuals, Foreigners and Immigrants in Austria." In *European Court of Human Rights: Implementing Strasbourg's Judgments on Domestic Policy*, ed. Dia Anagnostou, 97–121. Edinburgh University Press, 2013.

Buergenthal, Thomas. "Remembering the Early Years of the Inter-American Court of Human Rights." *New York University Journal of International Law and Politics* **37** (2005): 259–80.

"The Inter-American Court, Human Rights, and the OAS." *Human Rights Law Journal* **7** (1986): 157–64.

Buergenthal, Thomas, Robert E. Norris, and Dinah Shelton. *Protecting Human Rights in the Americas: Selected Problems*. Engel, 1990.

Bürli, Nicole. *Third-Party Interventions Before the European Court of Human Rights: Amicus Curiae, Member-State and Third-Party Interventions*. Intersentia, 2017.

Burton, Steven J. *Judging in Good Faith*. Cambridge University Press, 1994.

"Burundi Notifies U.N. of International Criminal Court Withdrawal." *Reuters*, October 26, 2016. www.reuters.com/article/us-burundi-icc-idUSKCN12Q287.

Busch, M. L. and K. J. Pelc. "The Politics of Judicial Economy at the World Trade Organization." *International Organization* **64**, no. 2 (2010): 257–79.

Cali, Basak and Nicola Bruch. *Monitoring the Implementation of Judgments of the European Court of Human Rights: A Handbook for Non-Governmental Organisations*, 2011. https://ecthrproject.files.wordpress.com/2011/07/monitoringhandbook_calibruch1.pdf.

Cannock, Matthew. "Presentation to the Trust Fund for Victims Board of Directors." March 18, 2013. www.trustfundforvictims.org/sites/default/files/media_library/documents/pdf/CICC_Presentation_to_TFV_Board___180314_1.pdf.

Carozza, Paolo. "Anglo-Latin Divide and the Future of the Inter-American System of Human Rights." *Notre Dame Journal of International and Comparative Law* **5** (2015): 153.

Carpenter, R. Charli. *"Lost" Causes: Agenda Vetting in Global Issue Networks and the Shaping of Human Security*. Cornell University Press, 2014.

"Setting the Advocacy Agenda: Theorizing Issue Emergence and Nonemergence in Transnational Advocacy Networks." *International Studies Quarterly* **51**, no. 1 (2007): 99–120. https://doi.org/10.1111/j.1468-2478.2007.00441.x.

"Studying Issue (Non)-Adoption in Transnational Advocacy Networks." *International Organization* **61**, no. 3 (2007): 643–67. https://doi.org/10.1017/S002081830707021X.

"Vetting the Advocacy Agenda: Network Centrality and the Paradox of Weapons Norms." *International Organization* **65**, no. 1 (2011): 69–102. https://doi.org/10.1017/S0020818310000329.

"'Women, Children and Other Vulnerable Groups': Gender, Strategic Frames and the Protection of Civilians as a Transnational Issue." *International Studies Quarterly* **49**, no. 2 (2005): 295–334. https://doi.org/10.1111/j.0020-8833.2005.00346.x.

Cassese, Antonio. "On the Current Trends towards Criminal Prosecution and Punishment of Breaches of International Humanitarian Law." *European Journal of International Law* **9**, no. 1 (1998): 2–17.

CEJIL. "CEJIL Activities Report – 20 Years," 2011. http://cejil.org/en/publicaciones/cejil-activities-report-20-years.

Center for Constitutional Rights. "Victims' Communication Pursuant to Article 15 of the Rome Statute Requesting Investigation and Prosecution of High-Level Vatican Officials for Rape and Other Forms of Sexual Violence as Crimes Against Humanity and Torture as a Crime Against Humanity," September 13, 2011. www.google.com/url?sa=t&rct=j&q=&esrc=s&source=web&cd=2&ved=0CFsQFjAB&url=http%3A%2F%2Fs3.documentcloud.org%2Fdocuments%2F243877%2Fvictims-communication.pdf&ei=ZP6zT9fNNo

Gy2QWJmLnpCA&usg=AFQjCNEQYC-b1hETAAOn4UWDngACsyWOcA&sig2=
B6hqUp7gB_M-X6TPImg1Pg.

Cerna, Christina M. "Inter-American System for the Protection of Human Rights." *Florida
Journal of International Law* 16 (2004): 195–212.

Charnovitz, Steve. "Nongovernmental Organizations and International Law." *The American
Journal of International Law* 100, no. 2 (2006): 348–72.

"Two Centuries of Participation: NGOs and International Governance." *Michigan Journal
of International Law* 18 (1997): 183–286.

Chatham House. "Meeting Summary of 'Shaping the Law: Civil Society Influence at
International Criminal Courts,'" 2016. www.chathamhouse.org/sites/files/chatham
house/events/160125-meeting-summary-shaping-law-civil-society-influence-international-
criminal-courts.pdf.

Chazournes, Laurence Boisson de and Makane Moïse Mbengue. "The Amici Curiae and the
WTO Dispute Settlement System: The Doors Are Open." *Law and Practice of International Courts and Tribunals* 2 (2003): 205–48.

CICC. "1999." *Insight on the ICC*, no. Tenth Anniversary Special Edition (2005): 4.

"About the Coalition for the International Criminal Court." Accessed May 19, 2015. www
.google.com/url?sa=t&rct=j&q=&esrc=s&source=web&cd=2&ved=0CCcQFjAB&url=
https%3A%2F%2Fwww.iccnow.org%2Fdocuments%2FCoalition_Factsheet.pdf&ei=
wWNbVYfqKYTeoAT4voHYBw&usg=AFQjCNG9_1tlGrD6a5sfP8FJ3AZReOGMog&
bvm=bv.93756505,bs.1,d.cGU.

"Announcement to the Assembly of States Parties on the Independent Criminal Court
Judicial Elections," December 2010. www.iccnow.org/documents/Judicial_Panel_
Announcement.pdf.

"ASP Reaches Controversial Compromise on ICC Budget," December 21, 2011. www
.google.com/url?sa=t&rct=j&q=&esrc=s&source=web&cd=1&ved=0CE8QFjAA&url=
http%3A%2F%2Fwww.iccnow.org%2Fdocuments%2FCICC_PR_ASP10__BUDGET_
ADOPTION_FINAL_211211.pdf&ei=nDbqT4qAGKrhoQHvrKnTAQ&usg=AFQjC
NETwWZj9J4pp_e-YrgIzM3M5AAZDQ&sig2=0UOO376d7V86jzAF7PgVNw.

"Bilateral Immunity Agreements." Accessed June 26, 2012. www.coalitionfortheicc.org/?
mod=bia.

"Budget and Finance." Accessed June 6, 2012. www.iccnow.org/?mod=budget.

"Budget and Finance Background." Accessed June 6, 2012. www.iccnow.org/?mod=
budgetbackground.

"CICC Questionnaire to Candidates for a Post of Judge at the International Criminal
Court." Accessed May 10, 2011. www.coalitionfortheicc.org/documents/CICCQuestion
naireICCcandidates_eng.pdf.

"Civil Society Defends ICC at African Union Summit." Accessed June 22, 2015. https://
ciccglobaljustice.wordpress.com/2014/03/25/civil-society-defends-icc-at-african-union-summit/.

"Comments and Recommendations for States Parties in Relation to the ICC and Communications," November 24, 2005. www.iccnow.org/documents/CommsTeam_ASPadvoca
cydoc24Nov05.pdf.

"Communications and Outreach." Accessed May 11, 2011. www.iccnow.org/?mod=
communications.

"Implementation of the Rome Statute." Accessed May 18, 2015. www.iccnow.org/?mod=
romeimplementation.

"Judges." Accessed June 5, 2015. www.iccnow.org/?mod=electionjudges.

"Legislation Prohibiting Aid." Accessed June 26, 2012. www.coalitionfortheicc.org/?mod=
legislation.

"Our History." Accessed May 19, 2012. www.iccnow.org/?mod=cicchistory.

"Our Publications." Accessed June 13, 2012. www.iccnow.org/?mod=ourpublications.

"Ratification and Implementation." Accessed May 19, 2012. www.iccnow.org/?mod=ratimp.

"Report on the Eighth Session of the Assembly of States Parties to the Rome Statute," January 2010. www.iccnow.org/documents/CICC__ASP_8_Report.pdf.

"Steering Committee." *The MONITOR*, no. 1 (1996).

"Universal Ratification Campaign." Accessed May 5, 2013. www.iccnow.org/?mod=urc.

CICC's Budget and Finance Team. "Commentary on the Report of the Committee on Budget and Finance on the Work of Its Fifth Session (10 to 14 October 2005)," 2005. www.iccnow.org/.../CICC_CommentaryOnCBFReport_Nov05.pdf.

"Comments on the Proposed Programme Budget for 2006 of the International Criminal Court," 2005. www.google.com/url?sa=t&rct=j&q=&esrc=s&source=web&cd=1&ved= 0CE8QFjAA&url=http%3A%2F%2Fwww.iccnow.org%2Fdocuments%2FBFteam_Com mentaryProgrammeBudget_23Sept05_en.pdf&ei=_8zPT8-xMMPi2QXPpsW8DA&usg= AFQjCNG82w2fG3piAhWEiJgPzyizOhFmqg&sig2=Y4mNGUwAZrGkvBqBD8REdA.

"The 2004 Programme Budget of the International Criminal Court and the Report of the Committee on Budget and Finance," 2003. www.iccnow.org/documents/Budget_ASP_ Paper_2003.FINAL.pdf.

"The Report of the Committee on Budget and Finance Third Session, The Hague, 6–10 September 2004," 2004. www.google.com/url?sa=t&rct=j&q=&esrc=s&source=web& cd=1&ved=0CDoQFjAA&url=http%3A%2F%2Fwww.iccnow.org%2Fdocuments% 2FCICCBudgetTeam_CommentsCBFreport26Aug04.pdf&ei=asrPT9nuN8qO2wW Cy9GgDw&usg=AFQjCNHqZuiAGBfXNAGXbPOipo8a4ROBHA&sig2= vZujK9MdfQQflQI7NcVr4g.

Cichowski, Rachel A. "Civil Society and the European Court of Human Rights." In *The European Court of Human Rights between Law and Politics*, ed. Jonas Christoffersen and Mikael Rask Madsen, 77–97. Oxford University Press, 2011.

The European Court and Civil Society: Litigation, Mobilization and Governance. Cambridge University Press, 2007.

Cichowski, Rachel A. and E. Chrun. "European Court of Human Rights Database, Version 1.0 Release," n.d. http://depts.washington.edu/echrdb/.

Cleary, Edward L. *Mobilizing for Human Rights in Latin America*. Kumarian Press, 2007.

CNN Wire Staff. "Kenya, African Union Defend Bashir Visit." *CNN.Com*, August 31, 2010. www.cnn.com/2010/WORLD/africa/08/31/kenya.bashir.visit/.

Collier, David and James Mahoney. "Insights and Pitfalls: Selection Bias in Qualitative Research." *World Politics* 49, no. 1 (1996): 56–91. https://doi.org/10.1353/wp.1996.0023.

Committee of Ministers of the Council of Europe. "Supervision of the Execution of Judgments and Decisions of the European Court of Human Rights," 2014. www.coe.int/t/ dghl/monitoring/execution/Source/Publications/CM_annreport2014_en.pdf.

Cooley, Alexander and James Ron. "The NGO Scramble: Organizational Insecurity and the Political Economy of Transnational Action." *International Security* 27, no. 1 (2002): 5–39. https://doi.org/10.1162/016228802320231217.

Corey-Boulet, Robbie. "Concern over ICC Funding." *IPS Inter Press Service*, September 28, 2011. http://www.ips.org/africa/2011/09/concern-over-icc-funding/.

Council of Europe. "Participatory Status | At a Glance." Accessed January 9, 2013. www.coe .int/t/ngo/particip_status_intro_en.asp.

"Protocol 14: The Reform of the European Court of Human Rights." Accessed April 2, 2013. www.echr.coe.int/NR/rdonlyres/57211BCC-C88A-43C6-B540-AF0642E81D2C/0/CPPro tocole14EN.pdf.

"Reform of the European Court of Human Rights." Accessed December 8, 2015. www.coe
.int/t/DGHL/STANDARDSETTING/CDDH/REFORMECHR/.

"Steering Committee for Human Rights (CDDH)." 59th Meeting. Strasbourg, France,
November 23, 2004. CDDH(2004)030.

The Conscience of Europe: 50 Years of the European Court of Human Rights. Third
Millennium Publishing, 2010.

"The European Convention on Human Rights." Accessed April 11, 2013. www.echr.coe.int/
NR/rdonlyres/D5CC24A7-DC13-4318-B457-5C9014916D7A/0/Convention_ENG.pdf.

Council of Europe Committee of Ministers. "Brighton Declaration," April 20, 2012. https://
wcd.coe.int/ViewDoc.jsp?Ref=BrightonDeclaration&Language=lanEnglish&Ver=ori
ginal&Site=COE&BackColorInternet=DBDCF2&BackColorIntranet=FDC864&Back
ColorLogged=FDC864.

"Interlaken Declaration," February 19, 2010. https://wcd.coe.int/ViewDoc.jsp?id=1591969.

"Izmir Declaration," April 27, 2011. https://wcd.coe.int/ViewDoc.jsp?Ref=IzmirDeclara
tion&Language=lanEnglish&Ver=original&Site=COE&BackColorInternet=
DBDCF2&BackColorIntranet=FDC864&BackColorLogged=FDC864.

"Rules of the Committee of Ministers for the Supervision of the Execution of Judgments
and of the Terms of Friendly Settlements (Article 46, Paragraphs 2 to 5, and Article 39,
Paragraph 4, of the European Convention on Human Rights)," May 10, 2006. https://
wcd.coe.int/ViewDoc.jsp?Ref=CM/Del/Dec%282006%29964/4.4&Language=lanEngl
ish&Ver=app4&Site=COE&BackColorInternet=9999CC&BackColorIntranet=
FFBB55&BackColorLogged=FFAC75.

Crossen, Teall and Veronique Niessen. "NGO Standing in the European Court of Justice –
Does the Aarhus Regulation Open the Door?" *Review of European Community &
International Environmental Law* 16, no. 3 (2007): 332–40. https://doi.org/10.1111/
j.1467–9388.2007.00569.x.

CVCE. "Withdrawal, Expulsion and Suspension of a Member State of the Council of
Europe." Accessed April 10, 2017. www.cvce.eu/obj/withdrawal_expulsion_and_suspen
sion_of_a_member_state_of_the_council_of_europe-en-f9b31f98-f1a1-407c-97ad-
7e92363117fd.html.

Damascus Center for Human Rights Studies, The Law Firm of M. Yaser Tabbara, Chicago,
USA, YASA, International Kurdish Centre for Legal Studies & Consultancy, Union of
Syrian Kurds in the Netherlands, and INSAN, an international human rights organization.
"Article 15 Communication on Crimes against Humanity Committed in Syria." Accessed
May 14, 2012. dchrs.org/.../Article15CommunicationOnCrimesAgainstHumanity.pdf.

Danner, Alison and Erik Voeten. "Who Is Running the International Criminal Justice
System?" In *Who Governs the Globe?*, ed. Deborah Avant, Martha Finnemore, and
Susan Sell, 35–71. Cambridge University Press, 2010.

Deitelhoff, Nicole. "The Discursive Process of Legalization: Charting Islands of Persuasion in
the ICC Case." *International Organization* 63, no. 1 (2009): 33–65. https://doi.org/
10.1017/S002081830909002X.

Dicker, Richard. "Throwing Justice Under the Bus is Not the Way to Go | Human Rights
Watch." *Open Democracy*, January 6, 2015. www.hrw.org/news/2015/01/06/throwing-just
ice-under-bus-not-way-go.

Dolidze, Anna. "African Court on Human and Peoples' Rights – Response to the Situation in
Libya." *ASIL Insights* 15, no. 20 (2011). www.asil.org/insights110725.cfm.

Dothan, Shai. "A Virtual Wall of Shame: The New Way of Imposing Reputational Sanctions
on Defiant States." SSRN Scholarly Paper. Rochester, NY: Social Science Research
Network, May 3, 2016. http://papers.ssrn.com/abstract=2774040.

Drzemczewski, Andrew. "The Role of NGOs in Human Rights Matters in the Council of Europe." *Human Rights Law Journal* 8, no. 2–4 (1987): 273–82.

"The Work of the Council of Europe's Directorate of Human Rights." *Human Rights Law Journal* 11, no. 1–2 (1990): 89–117.

Dunoff, J. L. "The Misguided Debate over NGO Participation at the WTO." *Journal of International Economic Law* 1, no. 3 (1998): 433–56. https://doi.org/10.1093/jiel/1.3.433.

Dupuy, Pierre-Marie and Luisa Vierucci. *NGOs in International Law: Efficiency in Flexibility?* Edward Elgar Publishing, 2008.

Elsig, Manfred and Mark A. Pollack. "Agents, Trustees, and International Courts: The Politics of Judicial Appointment at the World Trade Organization." *European Journal of International Relations* 20, no. 2 (2014): 391–415. https://doi.org/10.1177/1354066112448201.

Epp, Charles R. *The Rights Revolution*. University of Chicago Press, 1998.

European Court of Human Rights. "Séminaire Organisé à l'occasion du 10è Anniversaire de l'entrée en Vigueur du Protocole N° 11 à la Convention Européenne des Droits de l'homme: Liste des ONGs," 2008. www.echr.coe.int/NR/rdonlyres/AF0368E7-DF14-4D5B-921D-C342C44E4C44/0/2008__Liste_des_ONG_13_10_2008.pdf.

"SURVEY: Forty Years of Activity (1959–1998)." Accessed December 14, 2012. www.echr.coe.int/NR/rdonlyres/66F2CD35-047E-44F4-A95D-890966820E81/0/Surveyapercus_19591998.pdf.

"Ten Years of the 'New' European Court of Human Rights 1998–2008 Situation and Outlook." Accessed September 20, 2016. www.echr.coe.int/Documents/10years_NC_1998_2008_ENG.pdf.

European Law Institute. "Statement on CASE-OVERLOAD AT THE EUROPEAN COURT OF HUMAN RIGHTS," July 6, 2012. www.europeanlawinstitute.eu/home/.

Evenson, Elizabeth M. "Human Rights Watch Memorandum for the Thirteenth Session of the International Criminal Court Assembly of States Parties." Accessed May 22, 2015. www.hrw.org/news/2014/11/25/human-rights-watch-memorandum-thirteenth-session-international-criminal-court-assemb.

Evenson, Elizabeth M. and Jonathan O'Donohue. "The International Criminal Court at Risk." *Open Democracy*, April 30, 2015. www.opendemocracy.net/openglobalrights/elizabeth-evenson-jonathan-o%E2%80%99donohue/international-criminal-court-at-risk.

Extraordinary Chambers in the Courts of Cambodia (ECCC). "About ECCC." Accessed March 2, 2016. www.eccc.gov.kh/en/about-eccc.

Fanton, Jonathan and Zachary Katznelson. "Human Rights and International Justice," 2010. www.atlanticphilanthropies.org/sites/default/files/uploads/HumanRightsandInternationalJustice_ChallengesandOpportunitiesatanInflectionPoint_0.pdf.

Farer, Tom J. ed. *The Future of the Inter-American System*. Praeger, 1979.

FIDH. *Fatou Bensouda, ICC Prosecutor, Visits FIDH*, 2015. www.fidh.org/International-Federation-for-Human-Rights/international-justice/international-criminal-court-icc/fatou-bensouda-icc-prosecutor-visits-fidh.

"FIDH Comments on the ICC Registrar's ReVision Proposals in Relation to Victims," November 18, 2014. www.google.com/url?sa=t&rct=j&q=&esrc=s&source=web&cd=5&ved=0CDoQFjAE&url=https%3A%2F%2Fwww.fidh.org%2FIMG%2Fpdf%2Fletter_registar_icc.pdf&ei=qzmMVfGlJISzoQSv3ZHICA&usg=AFQjCNF25lM-aOmlsa3LuSVnZS8bgdBN9w&bvm=bv.96782255,d.cGU.

Finnemore, Martha and Kathryn Sikkink. "International Norm Dynamics and Political Change." *International Organization* 52, no. 4 (1998): 887–917.

Fisher, Max. "Why Did Infamous War Criminal Bosco Ntaganda Just Surrender at a U.S. Embassy?" *The Washington Post*, March 18, 2013. www.washingtonpost.com/blogs/world

views/wp/2013/03/18/why-did-infamous-war-criminal-bosco-ntaganda-just-surrender-at-a-u-s-embassy/.

Fligstein, Neil. "Organizations: Theoretical Debates and the Scope of Organizational Theory." In *Handbook of International Sociology*, ed. C. Calhoun, C. Rojek, and B. Turner. Sage Press, 2005.

Florini, Ann. *Third Force: The Rise of Transnational Civil Society*. Washington, DC: Carnegie Endowment, 2000.

Føllesdal, Andreas, Birgit Peters, and Geir Ulfstein. *Constituting Europe: The European Court of Human Rights in a National, European and Global Context*. Cambridge University Press, 2013.

Foundation Center. "Advancing Human Rights: The State of Global Foundation Grantmaking," 2013. http://foundationcenter.org/gainknowledge/humanrights/.

Fowler, Alan. "PVO and NGO Futures: A Framework for Reflection and Dialogue," 2004. www.usaid.gov/our_work/cross-cutting_programs/private_voluntary_cooperation/conf_fowler.pdf.

Frost, Lynda E. "The Evolution of the Inter-American Court of Human Rights: Reflections of Present and Former Judges." *Human Rights Quarterly* 14, no. 2 (May 1992): 171–205.

Gerards, Janneke and Joseph Fleuren. *Implementation of the European Convention on Human Rights and of the Judgments of the ECtHR in National Case Law*, 2014. http://intersentia.com/en/implementation-of-the-european-convention-on-human-rights-and-of-the-judgments-of-the-ecthr-in-national-case-law.html.

Gernholtz, Liesl. "Dispatches: Bashir Affair Taints South African Democracy." Human Rights Watch. Accessed June 17, 2015. www.hrw.org/news/2015/06/16/dispatches-bashir-affair-taints-south-african-democracy.

Gillman, Howard. "What's Law Got to Do with It? Judicial Behavioralists Test the 'Legal Model' of Judicial Decision Making." *Law & Social Inquiry* 26, no. 2 (2001): 465–504. https://doi.org/10.1111/j.1747-4469.2001.tb00185.x.

Glasius, Marlies. "Expertise in the Cause of Justice: Global Civil Society Influence on the Statute for an International Criminal Court." In *Global Civil Society Yearbook 2002*, ed. Marlies Glasius, Mary Kaldor, and Anheier Helmut, 137–68. Oxford University Press, 2002.

    The International Criminal Court. Routledge, 2006.

    "What Is Global Justice and Who Decides?: Civil Society and Victim Responses to the International Criminal Court's First Investigations." *Human Rights Quarterly* 31, no. 2 (2009): 496–520. https://doi.org/10.1353/hrq.0.0075.

Global Justice Center. "Subject: Article 15 Communication to the ICC Office of the Prosecutor Regarding Boko Haram's Targeted Abduction of Women and Children as Genocide," April 14, 2015. http://globaljusticecenter.net/index.php/publications/briefs-and-white-papers/622-subject-article-15-communication-to-the-icc-office-of-the-prosecutor-regarding-boko-haram-s-targeted-abduction-of-women-and-children-as-genocide.

Goldman, Robert. "History and Action: The Inter-American Human Rights System and the Role of The Inter-American Commission on Human Rights." *Human Rights Quarterly* 31 (2009): 856–87.

Goldston, James. "European Court Reform: Civil Society Excluded from Debate | Open Society Foundations," April 11, 2012. www.opensocietyfoundations.org/voices/european-court-reform-civil-society-excluded-debate.

Golubok, Sergei. "The Achilles' Heel of the European Court of Human Rights." Open-GlobalRights. Accessed October 27, 2017. www.openglobalrights.org/the-achilles-heel-of-the-european-court-of-human-rights/?lang=English.

Gómez, Verónica. "The Interaction between the Political Actors of the OAS, the Commission and the Court." In *The Inter-American System of Human Rights*, edited by David Harris and Stephen Livingstone, 173–212. Oxford: Clarendon Press, 1998.

González, Felipe. "El Control Internacional de Las Organizaciones No Gubernamentales." *Revista IIDH* 25 (1997).

"Experience of the Inter-American Human Rights System." *Victoria University of Wellington Law Review* 40 (2009–2010): 103–26.

Haddad, Heidi Nichols. "After the Norm Cascade: NGO Mission Expansion and the Coalition for the International Criminal Court." *Global Governance: A Review of Multilateralism and International Organizations* 19, no. 2 (2013): 187–206.

"Judicial Institution Builders: NGOs and International Human Rights Courts." *Journal of Human Rights* 11, no. 1 (2012): 126–49. https://doi.org/10.1080/14754835.2012.648154.

Hafner-Burton, Emilie M. "Sticks and Stones: Naming and Shaming the Human Rights Enforcement Problem." *International Organization* 62, no. 4 (2008): 689–716. https://doi.org/10.1017/S0020818308080247.

Hall, Christopher Keith. "The First Proposal for a Permanent International Criminal Court." *International Review of the Red Cross (1961 – 1997)* 38, no. 322 (March 1998): 57–74. https://doi.org/10.1017/S0020860400090768.

Hansberry, Heidi L. "Too Much of a Good Thing in Lubanga and Haradinaj: The Danger of Expediency in International Criminal Trials." *Northwestern Journal of International Human Rights* 9, no. 3 (2011): 357–401.

Harlow, Carol and Richard Rawlings. *Pressure Through Law*. Psychology Press, 1992.

Harris, David. "Regional Protection of Human Rights: The Inter-American Achievement." In *The Inter-American System of Human Rights*, ed. David Harris and Stephen Livingstone, 1–30. Oxford: Clarendon Press, 1998.

Harris, David, Michael O'Boyle, Edward Bates, and Carla Buckley. *Law of the European Convention on Human Rights*. New York, NY: Oxford University Press, 2009.

Hawkins, Darren and Wade Jacoby. "Partial Compliance: A Comparison of the European and Inter-American Courts of Human Rights." *Journal of International Law and International Relations* 6 (2010): 35–85.

Hawkins, Darren G., David Lake, Daniel L. Nielson, and Michael J. Tierney, eds. *Delegation and Agency in International Organizations*. Cambridge University Press, 2006.

Hayman, Mari. "Brazil Breaks Relations With Human Rights Commission Over Belo Monte Dam." *Latin America News Dispatch*, May 3, 2011. http://latindispatch.com/2011/05/03/brazil-breaks-relations-with-human-rights-commission-over-belo-monte-dam/.

Helfer, Laurence R. and Anne-Marie Slaughter. "Toward a Theory of Effective Supranational Adjudication." *The Yale Law Journal* 107, no. 2 (1997): 273–391.

Hillebrecht, Courtney. *Domestic Politics and International Human Rights Tribunals: The Problem of Compliance*. Cambridge University Press, 2014.

"The Power of Human Rights Tribunals: Compliance with the European Court of Human Rights and Domestic Policy Change." *European Journal of International Relations*, March 18, 2014, 1354066113508591. https://doi.org/10.1177/1354066113508591.

"The Rocky Relationship between Russia and the European Court of Human Rights." *The Washington Post*, April 23, 2014. www.washingtonpost.com/news/monkey-cage/wp/2014/04/23/the-rocky-relationship-between-russia-and-the-european-court-of-human-rights/.

Hilson, Chris. "New Social Movements: The Role of Legal Opportunity." *Journal of European Public Policy* 9, no. 2 (2002): 238–55. https://doi.org/10.1080/13501760110120246.

Hilton, M., N. Crowson, J. Mouhot, and J. McKay. *A Historical Guide to NGOs in Britain: Charities, Civil Society and the Voluntary Sector Since 1945*. Springer, 2012.

Hioureas, Christina G. "Behind the Scenes of Protocol No. 14: Politics in Reforming the European Court of Human Rights." *Berkeley Journal of International Law* 24, no. 2 (2006): 718–57.

Hodson, Loveday. *NGOs and the Struggle for Human Rights in Europe*. Hart Publishing, 2011.

Hollis-Brusky, Amanda. "Support Structures and Constitutional Change: Teles, Southworth, and the Conservative Legal Movement." *Law & Social Inquiry* 36, no. 2 (2011): 516–36.

"Human Rights Act 1998." Accessed December 21, 2015. www.legislation.gov.uk/ukpga/1998/42/contents.

Human Rights First. "The Role of Human Rights NGOs in Relation to ICC Investigations." Discussion Paper. The Hague, September 2004.

"HRW and CEJIL Call on Trinidad and Tobago to Reconsider Withdrawal from the American Convention on Human Rights." Human Rights Watch, June 1, 1998. www .hrw.org/news/1998/06/01/hrw-and-cejil-call-trinidad-and-tobago-reconsider-withdrawal-american-convention.

Human Rights Watch. *Courting History*. Human Rights Watch, 2008.

"ICC: Course Correction," June 16, 2011. www.hrw.org/news/2011/06/16/icc-course-correction.

"Kenya: Do Not Welcome Bashir Back." Accessed June 22, 2015. www.hrw.org/news/2010/10/21/kenya-do-not-welcome-bashir-back.

"Q&A: The Case of Hissène Habré before the Extraordinary African Chambers in Senegal." Human Rights Watch, May 3, 2016. www.hrw.org/news/2016/05/03/qa-case-hissene-habre-extraordinary-african-chambers-senegal.

"The International Criminal Court: How Nongovernmental Organizations Can Contribute to the Prosecution of War Criminals," September 2004. www.google.com/url?sa=t&rct=j&q=&esrc=s&source=web&cd=1&ved=0CGIQFjAA&url=http%3A%2F%2Fwww .amicc.org%2Fdocs%2FHRW%2520NGOs%2520and%2520ICC.pdf&ei=aemzT_CWLubK2AWik6HpCA&usg=AFQjCNG5ui74210T4MmLurroV-GLIXSE7w&sig2=tKVwRwSXTEMrHBy8XYFjaw.

"Unfinished Business: Closing Gaps in the Selection of ICC Cases," September, 2011. www.hrw.org/node/101560.

Iaccino, Ludovica. "Rights Groups Fear Zambia Could Be Latest African Country to Abandon the ICC." *Newsweek*, April 11, 2017. www.newsweek.com/zambia-icc-581698.

ICRC. "International Humanitarian Law and International Human Rights Law," n.d. www .icrc.org/Web/Eng/siteeng0.nsf/htmlall/57JR8L/$File/IHL_and_IHRL.pdf.

Institute for War & Peace Reporting. "ICC Review Conference: Taking Stock on the Ground." Institute for War and Peace Reporting, July 2010. https://iwpr.net/printed-materials/icc-review-conference-taking-stock-ground.

Inter-American Court of Human Rights. "Inter-American Court of Human Rights Annual Report," 1982.

"Inter-American Court of Human Rights Annual Report," 2009. www.corteidh.or.cr/docs/informes/eng_2009.pdf.

International Bar Association. "First Outreach Report," June 1, 2006. www.iccnow.org/documents/IBA_First_Outreach_Report_June_2006.pdf.

International Center for Transitional Justice. "ICTJ Launches First Report on ICC Outreach," May 9, 2007. www.iccnow.org/documents/ICTJ_PR_ReportICCOutreach09May07__eng.pdf.

"Sensibilisation à la CPI en RDC," 2007. www.google.com/url?sa=t&rct=j&q=&esrc=s&source=web&cd=1&ved=0CCEQFjAA&url=http%3A%2F%2Fwww.peace-justice-conference.info%2Fdownload%2F638.pdf&ei=Rr5fVbuTFsbXoASs6IKgAQ&usg=AFQjC

NEZTsAon8W_b_lgKyit77YUKOxAww&sig2=_sC5PMc1q3f8olT6IHzqhw&bvm=
bv.93990622,d.cGU&cad=rja.

International Coalition of Human Rights Organizations in the Americas. "Pronunciamiento de La Coalicion de Organizaciones Por Los Derechos Humanos En Las Americas: Coalicion Condena Hostigamientos a Organizaciones y Defensores/as de Derechos Humanos En Venezuela," August 12, 2010.

"Request for Action to Protect the Autonomy, Independence and Impartiality, of the Inter-American Human Rights System," November 8, 2007.

International Criminal Bar. "ICB Letter to the Presidents of the ASP and the ICC," February 20, 2012. www.bpi-icb.com/index.php?view=weblink&catid=66%3Abpi-icb-documentos-constitutivos&id=264%3Aicb-letter-to-the-presidents-of-asp-and-icc-ap&option=com_weblinks&Itemid=91&lang=en.

"Objectives." Accessed June 27, 2012. www.bpi-icb.com/index.php?option=com_content&view=article&id=67&Itemid=74&lang=en.

"Organisation." Accessed June 27, 2012. www.bpi-icb.com/index.php?option=com_content&view=article&id=61&Itemid=73&lang=en.

"Position Paper of the International Criminal Bar," December 25, 2011. www.bpi-icb.com/index.php?view=weblink&catid=66%3Abpi-icb-documentos-constitutivos&id=242%3Aicb-position-paper-25112011doc-icb-position-paper-25112011doc&option=com_weblinks&Itemid=91&lang=en.

International Criminal Court. "Code of Conduct for Intermediaries," March 2014. www.google.com/url?sa=t&rct=j&q=&esrc=s&source=web&cd=3&cad=rja&uact=8&ved=0CDQQFjAC&url=http%3A%2F%2Fwww.icc-cpi.int%2Fen_menus%2Ficc%2Flegal%2520texts%2520and%2520tools%2Fstrategies-and-guidelines%2FDocuments%2FCCI-Eng.pdf&ei=nKxfVcWeIMvfoASu5INo&usg=AFQjCNGJ-6hHijoWlX6XEBJ_S7BXU-MVDg&sig2=zd_b8lKtLTjySD4W99AzCQ&bvm=bv.93990622,d.cGU.

"Communications, Referrals and Preliminary Examinations." Accessed May 22, 2015. www.icc-cpi.int/en_menus/icc/structure%20of%20the%20court/office%20of%20the%20prosecutor/comm%20and%20ref/Pages/communications%20and%20referrals.aspx.

"Decision Establishing the Principles and Procedures to be Applied to Reparations," August 7, 2012. www.legal-tools.org/doc/a05830/.

"Decision on the Prosecutor's Application for Leave to Appeal the 'Decision Pursuant to Article 61(7)(a) and (b) of the Rome Statute on the Charges of the Prosecutor Against Jean-Pierre Bemba Gombo,'" September 18, 2009. www.legal-tools.org/doc/4053f8/.

"Decision Pursuant to Article 61(7)(a) and (b) of the Rome Statute on the Charges of the Prosecutor Against Jean-Pierre Bemba Gombo," June 15, 2009. www.legal-tools.org/doc/07965c/.

"ICC – Assembly of States Parties." Accessed April 25, 2013. www.icc-cpi.int/en_menus/asp/assembly/Pages/assembly.aspx.

"ICC – Consultations with Civil Society (NGO Round Tables)." Accessed November 28, 2012. www.icc-cpi.int/en_menus/icc/structure%20of%20the%20court/office%20of%20the%20prosecutor/network%20with%20partners/consultations%20with%20civil%20society/Pages/consultations.aspx.

"ICC Held Bi-Annual Strategy Meeting with NGOs." Accessed May 9, 2012. www.icc-cpi.int/menus/icc/press%20and%20media/press%20releases/press%20releases%20(2009)/pr461.

"ICC Review Conference." Accessed May 13, 2015. www.icc-cpi.int/en_menus/asp/review conference/Pages/review%20conference.aspx#general.

"Judgment on the Appeal of Mr. Lubanga Dyilo against the Oral Decision of Trial Chamber I of 18 January 2008," July 11, 2008. ICC-01/04–01/06–1433. www.legal-tools.org/doc/f5bc1e/.

"Kenya: Situation in the Republic of Kenya." Accessed August 9, 2016. www.icc-cpi.int/kenya.

"Model Contract for Intermediaries," March 2014. www.google.com/url?sa=t&rct=j&q=&esrc=s&source=web&cd=1&cad=rja&uact=8&ved=0CCYQFjAA&url=http%3A%2F%2Fwww.icc-cpi.int%2Fen_menus%2Ficc%2Flegal%2520texts%2520and%2520tools%2Fstrategies-and-guidelines%2FDocuments%2FMCI-Eng.pdf&ei=nKxfVcWeIMvfoASu5INo&usg=AFQjCNHokkOJTkc3eQTolhn8aGKcODqNCw&sig2=QuuCGcPJDIDxsogj4lArZQ&bvm=bv.93990622,d.cGU.

"Ordonnance de réparation en vertu de l'article 75 du Statut Accompagnée d'une annexe publique (annexe I) et d'une annexe confidentielle ex parte réservée au Représentant légal commun des victimes, au Bureau du conseil public pour les victimes," March 24, 2017. ICC-01/04-01/07-3728. www.legal-tools.org/doc/83d6c4/.

"Press Release: ICC Prosecutor Fatou Bensouda Appoints Brigid Inder, Executive Director of the Women's Initiatives for Gender Justice, as Special Gender Advisor," August 21, 2012. www.icc-cpi.int/en_menus/icc/press%20and%20media/press%20releases/Pages/pr833.aspx.

"Press Release: Kenyatta Case: ICC Trial Chamber Rejects Request for Further Adjournment and Directs the Prosecution to Indicate Either Its Withdrawal of Charges or Readiness to Proceed to Trial," December 3, 2014. www.icc-cpi.int/en_menus/icc/press%20and%20media/press%20releases/Pages/PR1071.aspx.

"Press Release: Pre-Trial Chamber II Informs the United Nations Security Council about Sudan's Non-Cooperation in the Arrest and Surrender of Omar Al Bashir," September 3, 2015. www.icc-cpi.int/en_menus/icc/press%20and%20media/press%20releases/Pages/pr1094.aspx.

"Second Decision on Prosecution's Application for a Finding of Non-Compliance under Article 87(7) of the Statute," September 19, 2016. ICC-01/09-02/11-1037. www.icc-cpi.int/Pages/record.aspx?docNo=ICC-01/09-02/11-1037.

"Structure of the Court." Accessed April 25, 2013. www.icc-cpi.int/en_menus/icc/structure%20of%20the%20court/Pages/structure%20of%20the%20court.aspx.

Jean Monnet Center for International and Regional Economic Law & Justice. "Access of Private Parties to International Dispute Settlement: A Comparative Analysis – Part IV: The European Convention on Human Rights (ECHR)." Accessed December 12, 2012. http://centers.law.nyu.edu/jeanmonnet/archive/papers/97/97–13-Part-4.html#Heading48.

Kahler, Miles. "*Global Governance Redefined*." Washington University School of Law, 2004. https://law.wustl.edu/centeris/Papers/globalization/KAHLERMilesFINALPAPER.pdf.

Kaldor, Mary. *Global Civil Society: An Answer to War*. John Wiley & Sons, 2013.

Kamat, Sangeeta. "The Privatization of Public Interest: Theorizing NGO Discourse in a Neoliberal Era." *Review of International Political Economy* 11, no. 1 (2004): 155–76. https://doi.org/10.1080/0969229042000179794.

Kaye, David. "America's Honeymoon with the ICC." Foreign Affairs, April 16, 2013. www.foreignaffairs.com/articles/2013-04-16/americas-honeymoon-icc.

Keck, Margaret E. and Kathryn Sikkink. *Activists Beyond Borders*. Ithaca, NY and London: Cornell University Press, 1998.

Kelemen, R. Daniel. *Eurolegalism: The Transformation of Law and Regulation in the European Union*. Harvard University Press, 2011.

Kennedy, Merrit. "Under New Leader, Gambia Cancels Withdrawal From International Criminal Court." *NPR.Org*, February 14, 2017. www.npr.org/sections/thetwo-way/2017/02/14/515219467/under-new-leader-gambia-cancels-withdrawal-from-international-criminal-court.

"Kenyan Court Issues Arrest Order for Sudan's Bashir." *Reuters*, November 28, 2011. www
.reuters.com/article/2011/11/28/us-kenya-bashir-icc-idUSTRE7AR0YA20111128.

Kersten, Mark. "Lubanga and the Trouble with ICC Deterrence." *Opinio Juris* (blog), March
19, 2012. http://opiniojuris.org/2012/03/19/lubanga-decision-roundtable-lubanga-and-the-
trouble-with-icc-deterrence/.

"What Counts as Evidence of Syria's War Crimes?" *The Washington Post Monkey Cage*,
October 28, 2014. www.washingtonpost.com/blogs/monkey-cage/wp/2014/10/28/what-
counts-as-evidence-of-syrias-war-crimes/.

"Yes, the ICC Is in Crisis. It Always Has Been." *Justice in Conflict* (blog), February 24, 2015.
http://justiceinconflict.org/2015/02/24/yes-the-icc-is-in-crisis-it-always-has-been/.

Khagram, Sanjeev, James V. Riker, and Kathryn Sikkink, eds. *Restructuring World Politics:
Transnational Social Movements, Networks, and Norms.* University of Minnesota Press, 2002.

Kirsch, Philippe and John T. Holmes. "Birth of the International Criminal Court:
The 1998 Rome Conference, The. 1998 Rome Conference" *Canadian Yearbook of
International Law* 36 (1998): 3.

Klotz, Audie. "Norms Reconstituting Interests: Global Racial Equality and U.S. Sanctions
Against South Africa." *International Organization* 49, no. 3 (1995): 451–78.

Kontorovich, Eugene. "Sudan's Bashir Is the Palestinians' and Pretoria's Favorite Genocidal
Tyrant." *The Washington Post*, June 15, 2015. www.washingtonpost.com/news/volokh-
conspiracy/wp/2015/06/15/sudans-bashir-is-the-palestinians-and-pretorias-favorite-geno
cidal-tyrant/.

Korey, William. *NGOs and the Universal Declaration of Human Rights: A Curious
Grapevine.* Palgrave Macmillan, 1998.

Kurban, Dilek. "Strasbourg Court Jurisprudence and Human Rights in Turkey: An Overview
of Litigation, Implementation and Domestic Reform." JURISTRAS State of the Art
Report. Accessed December 13, 2012. www.juristras.eliamep.gr/?cat=7.

Lake, David A. and Wendy Wong. "The Politics of Networks: Interests, Power, and
Human Rights Norms." In *Networked Politics: Agency, Power, and Governance.* Cornell
University Press, 2009. http://papers.ssrn.com/sol3/papers.cfm?abstract_id=1004199.

Lambert-Abdelgawad, E. *The Execution of Judgments of the European Court of Human
Rights.* Council of Europe, 2008.

"Letter to Foreign Ministers of African States Parties to the ICC," January 26, 2012. www.hrw
.org/news/2012/01/26/letter-foreign-ministers-african-states-parties-icc.

Lewis, David. *Non-Governmental Organizations, Management and Development.* Routledge,
2014.

Lindblom, Anna-Karin. *Non-Governmental Organisations in International Law.* Cambridge
University Press, 2005.

Lough, Richard. "African Union Accuses ICC Prosecutor of Bias." *Reuters*, January 30, 2011.
www.reuters.com/article/2011/01/30/ozatp-africa-icc-idAFJOE70T01R20110130.

Lyons, Beth S. "The Intermediary Industry and the ICC." *IntLawGrrls* (blog). Accessed May
22, 2015. http://ilg2.org/2014/06/06/the-intermediary-industry-and-the-icc/.

MacArthur Foundation. "Human Rights & International Justice Grant Guidelines." Accessed
October 25, 2013. www.macfound.org/info-grantseekers/grantmaking-guidelines/human_
rights-grant-guidelines/.

Protecting Freedom of Expression and Enhancing Criminal Justice, 2013. www.macfound
.org/videos/379/.

Madsen, M. R. "From Cold War Instrument to Supreme European Court: The European
Court of Human Rights at the Crossroads of International and National Law and
Politics." *Law & Social Inquiry* 32, no. 1 (2007): 137–59.

Majone, Giandomenico. "Two Logics of Delegation: Agency and Fiduciary Relations in EU Governance." *European Union Politics* 2 (2001): 103–22.

Martens, Kerstin. "Mission Impossible? Defining Nongovernmental Organizations." *Voluntas: International Journal of Voluntary and Nonprofit Organizations* 13, no. 3 (n.d.): 271–85. https://doi.org/10.1023/A:1020341526691.

Mavroidis, Petros C. "Amicus Curiae Briefs before the WTO: Much Ado about Nothing," 2001.

Mayer, Lloyd. "NGO Standing and Influence in Regional Human Rights Courts and Commissions." SSRN Scholarly Paper. Rochester, NY: Social Science Research Network, April 11, 2012. http://papers.ssrn.com/abstract=2038379.

Mayerfeld, Jamie. "The Democratic Legacy of the International Criminal Court." *Fletcher Forum of World Affairs* 28 (2004): 147.

McCann, Michael W. *Rights at Work*. University of Chicago Press, 1994.

McCann, Michael W. and Helena Silverstein. "Rethinking Law's Allurements." In *Cause Lawyering: Political Commitments and Professional Responsibilities*, ed. Austin Sarat and Stuart A. Scheingold. New York: Oxford University Press, 1998.

McGreal, Chris. "Second Class Justice." *The Guardian*, April 10, 2002. www.guardian.co.uk/comment/story/0,3604,681623,00.html.

Mendez, Mario. *The Legal Effects of EU Agreements*. Oxford University Press, 2013.

Meservey, Joshua. "International Criminal Court Hurts Its Own Credibility in Africa – US News." *US News & World Report*, January 2, 2015. www.usnews.com/opinion/blogs/world-report/2015/01/02/international-criminal-court-hurts-its-own-credibility-in-africa.

Metcalfe, Eric. "The Birth of the European Convention on Human Rights." In *The Conscience of Europe: 50 Years of the European Court of Human Rights*, 16–16. Third Millennium Publishing, 2010.

Meyer, David S. *The Politics of Protest: Social Movements in America*. Oxford University Press, 2007.

Meyer, J. W., John Boli, George M. Thomas, and Francisco O. Ramirez. "World Society and the Nation-State." *The National Journal of Sociology* 103, no. 1 (1997): 144–81.

Miara, Lucja and Victoria Prais. "The Role of Civil Society in the Execution of Judgments of the European Court of Human Rights." *European Human Rights Law Review* 5 (2012): 528–37.

Miles, Emma. "Ghana Petition at the ICC at The International Criminal Law Bureau Blog." International Criminal Law Bureau, May 9, 2012. www.internationallawbureau.com/blog/?p=4885.

Mills, Kurt. "'Bashir Is Dividing Us': Africa and the International Criminal Court." *Human Rights Quarterly* 34, no. 2 (2012): 404–47. https://doi.org/10.1353/hrq.2012.0030.

Ministers' Deputies of the Council of Europe. "Notes on the Agenda, 964 Meeting, 10 May 2006," May 10, 2006. CM/Notes/964/4.4 5 May 2006.

Mohamed, Abdelsalam A. "Individual and NGO Participation in Human Rights Litigation before the African Court of Human and Peoples' Rights: Lessons from the European and Inter-American Courts of Human Rights." *Journal of African Law* 43 (1999): 201–13.

Moravcsik, Andrew. "The Origins of Human Rights Regimes: Democratic Delegation in Postwar Europe." *International Organization* 54, no. 2 (2000): 217–52.

Moreno-Ocampo, Luis. "OTP Letter to Senders Re Iraq," February 9, 2006.

"The International Criminal Court: Seeking Global Justice." *Case Western Reserve Journal of International Law* 40 (August 2007): 215–25.

Moustafa, Tamir. "Law versus the State: The Judicialization of Politics in Egypt." *Law & Social Inquiry* 28, no. 4 (2003): 883–930.

The Struggle for Constitutional Power: Law, Politics, and Economic Development in Egypt. Cambridge University Press, 2007.

Mouvement européen (Bruxelles). *European Movement and the Council of Europe.* Hutchinson & Co., 1949.

Moyer, Charles. "The Role of Amicus Curiae in the Inter-American Court of Human Rights." In *La Corte Inter-Americana de Derechos Humanos: Estudios y Documentos,* 103–14. San José: IIDH, 1986. www.bibliojuridica.org/libros/4/1996/8.pdf.

Müller, Sebastian and Christoph Gusy. "The Interrelationship between Domestic Judicial Mechanisms and the Strasbourg Court Rulings in Germany." In *European Court of Human Rights: Implementing Strasbourg's Judgments on Domestic Policy,* ed. Dia Anagnostou, 27–48. Edinburgh University Press, 2013.

Murdie, Amanda. *Help Or Harm: The Human Security Effects of International NGOs.* Stanford University Press, 2014.

Nadelmann, Ethan A. "Global Prohibition Regimes: The Evolution of Norms in International Society." *International Organization* 44, no. 4 (1990): 479–526.

Naim, Moses. "What Is a GONGO?" Foreign Policy, October 13, 2009. https://foreignpolicy .com/2009/10/13/what-is-a-gongo/.

Nelson, Paul J. and Ellen Dorsey. *New Rights Advocacy: Changing Strategies of Development and Human Rights NGOs.* Georgetown University Press, 2008.

New York Times Editorial Board. "South Africa's Disgraceful Help for President Bashir of Sudan." *The New York Times,* June 15, 2015. www.nytimes.com/2015/06/16/opinion/ south-africas-disgraceful-help-for-president-bashir-of-sudan.html.

Nichols, Michelle. "Africa Fails to Get Kenya ICC Trials Deferred at United Nations." *Reuters,* November 15, 2013. www.reuters.com/article/2013/11/15/us-kenya-icc-un-idUSBRE9AE0S420131115.

"ICC Complains of Lack of Cooperation, Wants More U.N. Support." *Reuters,* October 17, 2012. http://news.yahoo.com/icc-complains-lack-cooperation-wants-more-u-n-194348483.html.

Nouwen, Sarah M. H. *Complementarity in the Line of Fire: The Catalysing Effect of the International Criminal Court in Uganda and Sudan.* Cambridge University Press, 2013.

OAS. "Legal Assistance Fund Enters into Force," March 1, 2011. www.oas.org/en/iachr/ media_center/PReleases/2011/017.asp.

O'Donohue, Jonathan. "The 2005 Budget of the International Criminal Court: Contingency, Insufficient Funding in Key Areas and the Recurring Question of the Independence of the Prosecutor." *Leiden Journal of International Law* 18, no. 3 (2005): 591–603. https:// doi.org/10.1017/S0922156505002888.

"The Proposed 2006 Budget for the ICC: What Impact for Victims?" *Victims Rights Working Group Bulletin,* October 2005, 4th edition.

Office of the Prosecutor. "Communications Received by the Office of the Prosecutor of the ICC," July 16, 2003.

"Report on Preliminary Examination Activities," December 13, 2011.

Ombuor, Rael. "Kenya Signals Possible ICC Withdrawal." VOA, December 13, 2016. www .voanews.com/a/kenya-signals-possible-icc-withdrawal/3634365.html.

Onishi, Norimitsu. "South Africa Reverses Withdrawal From International Criminal Court." *The New York Times,* March 8, 2017. www.nytimes.com/2017/03/08/world/africa/south-africa-icc-withdrawal.html.

Open Society Justice Initiative. "Intermediaries and the International Criminal Court." Accessed May 16, 2012. www.opensocietyfoundations.org/publications/intermediaries-and-international-criminal-court-role-assembly-states-parties.

Pace, William R. "1995–2005: Coalition Celebrates Ten Years." *Insight on the ICC*, no. Tenth Anniversary Special Edition (2005): 1.

"The Relationship Between the International Criminal Court and Non-Governmental Organizations." In *Reflections on the International Criminal Court*, ed. Herman A.M. von Hebel, Johan G. Lammers, and Jolien Schukking, 189–211. T.M.C. Asser Press, 1999.

Pace, William R. and Jennifer Schense. "Coalition for the International Criminal Court at the Preparatory Commission." In *The International Criminal Court: Elements of Crimes and Rules of Procedure and Evidence*, ed. Roy S. Lee, 705–34. Transnational Publishers, Inc., 2001.

Peel, Jacqueline. "Giving the Public a Voice in the Protection of the Global Environment: Avenues for Participation by NGOs in Dispute Resolution at the European Court of Justice and World Trade Organization." *Colorado Journal of International Environmental Law and Policy* 12 (2001): 47–76.

Peskin, Victor. *International Justice in Rwanda and the Balkans: Virtual Trials and the Struggle for State Cooperation*. Cambridge University Press, 2008.

Peters, B. Guy. *Institutional Theory in Political Science*. London and New York, NY: Continuum International Publishing Group, 2005.

Pettiti, L.E. "Seminar on Extra Judicial Means of Protecting and Promoting Human Rights." Siena, Italy: Council of Europe, October 28, 1982. CDDH (82) 36 def.

PGA. "PGA ICC Campaign for the Effectiveness and Universality of the Rome Statute – International Law and Human Rights – Parliamentarians for Global Action (PGA)." Accessed June 4, 2015. www.pgaction.org/programmes/ilhr/icc-campaign-map.html.

"Programme Overview – International Law and Human Rights – Parliamentarians for Global Action (PGA)." Accessed May 19, 2012. www.pgaction.org/programmes/ilhr/overview.html.

Pinto, Mónica. "NGOs and the Inter-American Court of Human Rights." In *Civil Society, International Courts and Compliance Bodies*, ed. Tullio Treves, Marco Frigessi di Rattalma, Attila Tanzi, Alessandro Fodella, Cesare Pitea, and Chiara Ragni, 47–56. T.M.C. Asser Press, 2005.

Porges, Amy. "Regional and Sub-Regional Human Rights Tribunals: The African Response." American Society of International Law. Accessed March 4, 2016. www.asil.org/blogs/regional-and-sub-regional-human-rights-tribunals-african-response.

Posner, Eric A. and John C. Yoo. "Judicial Independence in International Tribunals." *California Law Review* 93, no. 1 (2005): 1–74.

Prakash, Aseem and Mary Kay Gugerty. *Advocacy Organizations and Collective Action*. Cambridge University Press, 2010.

"Putin Enables Russia to Overturn European Court of Human Rights Decisions." *The Moscow Times*, December 15, 2015. www.themoscowtimes.com/news/article/putin-enables-russia-to-overturn-european-court-of-human-rights-decisions/552855.html.

Quesada, Carlos. *Using the Inter-American System for Human Rights: A Practical Guide for NGOs*. Global Rights, 2004.

Quiroga, Cecilia Medina. *The Battle of Human Rights: Gross, Systematic Violations and the Inter-American System*. Martinus Nijhoff Publishers, 1988.

Raustiala, K. "States, NGOs, and International Environmental Institutions." International Studies Quarterly 41, no. 4 (1997): 719–40.

Redress. "Moving Reparation Forward at the ICC: Recommendations," November 2016. redress.org/downloads/1611redressiccreparationpaper.pdf.

Reiding, Hilde. "The Netherlands and the Development of International Human Rights Instruments." Utrecht University, 2007. http://igitur-archive.library.uu.nl/dissertations/2007-0316-202014/index.htm.

Reinsberg, Lisa. "The Future of Human Rights in the Americas: Update on the Inter-American Reform Process." *IntLawGrrls* (blog), December 10, 2012. www.intlawgrrls .com/2012/12/the-future-of-human-rights-in-americas.html.

Report of the Standing Senate Committee on Human Rights. "Enhancing Canada's Role in the OAS: Canadian Adherence to the American Convention on Human Rights," May 2003. https://sencanada.ca/content/sen/committee/372/huma/rep/repo4mayo3parti-e.htm.

Ripinsky, Sergey and Peter van den Bossche. *NGO Involvement in International Organizations: A Legal Analysis*. British Institute of International and Comparative Law, 2007.

Risse, Thomas. "Transnational Actors and World Politics." In *Handbook of International Relations*, ed. Walter Carlsnaes, Thomas Risse, and Beth A. Simmons, 255–74. Sage Publications, 2002.

Risse, Thomas, Steve C. Ropp, and Kathryn Sikkink. *The Power of Human Rights*. Cambridge University Press, 1999.

Risse, Thomas and Kathryn Sikkink. *The Persistent Power of Human Rights: From Commitment to Compliance*. Cambridge University Press, 2013.

Rivera Juaristi, Francisco. "The Amicus Curiae in the Inter-American Court of Human Rights (1982–2013)." SSRN Scholarly Paper. Rochester, NY: Social Science Research Network, August 1, 2014. https://papers.ssrn.com/abstract=2488073.

Rome Statute of the International Criminal Court. "NGO Participation in the Assembly of States Parties." Accessed May 12, 2015. http://legal.un.org/icc/asp/2ndsession/ngoinasp.2nd.htm.

   "Overview, Rome Statute of the International Criminal Court." Accessed May 11, 2015. www.un.org/law/icc/index.html.

Rosenberg, Gerald N. *The Hollow Hope*. University of Chicago Press, 2008.

Roth, Kenneth. "Africa Attacks the International Criminal Court." *The New York Review of Books*, February 6, 2014. www.nybooks.com/articles/archives/2014/feb/06/africa-attacks-international-criminal-court/.

SaCouto, Susana and Katherine Cleary. "The Gravity Threshold of the International Criminal Court." *American University Law Review* **23**, no. 5 (2007): 807–54.

Sarat, Austin and Stuart A. Scheingold. *Cause Lawyering: Political Commitments and Professional Responsibilities*. Oxford and New York, NY: Oxford University Press, 1998.

   The Worlds Cause Lawyers Make: Structure And Agency in Legal Practice. Stanford University Press, 2005.

Schabas, William A. "Why Didn't the Council of Europe Get the Nobel?" *PhD Studies in Human Rights* (blog), October 13, 2012. http://humanrightsdoctorate.blogspot.com/2012/10/why-didnt-council-of-europe-get-nobel.html.

Scheingold, Stuart A. *The Politics of Rights*. Yale University Press, 1974.

Schiff, Benjamin N. *Building the International Criminal Court*. Cambridge University Press, 2008.

Schönsteiner, J. "Alternative Appointment Procedures for the Commissioners and Judges in the Inter-American System of Human Rights." *Revista IIDH*, 2007: 195–215.

Sell, S.K. and A. Prakash. "Using Ideas Strategically: The Contest between Business and NGO Networks in Intellectual Property Rights." *International Studies Quarterly* 48, no. 1 (2004): 143–75.

Sengupta, Somini. "Omar Al-Bashir Case Shows International Criminal Court's Limitations." *The New York Times*, June 15, 2015. www.nytimes.com/2015/06/16/world/africa/sudan-bashir-international-criminal-court.html.

Shaer, Matthew. "'The Media Doesn't Care What Happens Here.'" *The New York Times*, February 18, 2015. www.nytimes.com/2015/02/22/magazine/the-media-doesnt-care-what-happens-here.html.

Shelton, Dinah. "The Participation of Nongovernmental Organizations in International Judicial Proceedings." *The American Journal of International Law* 88, no. 4 (1994): 611–42. https://doi.org/10.2307/2204133.

Sikkink, Kathryn. "Human Rights, Principled Issue-Networks, and Sovereignty in Latin America." *International Organization* 47, no. 3 (1993): 411–41.

 "Transnational Advocacy Networks and the Social Construction of Legal Rules." In *Global Prescriptions*, ed. Yves Dezalay and Bryant G. Garth, 37–64. The University of Michigan Press, 2002.

Simmons, Beth A. and Allison Danner. "Credible Commitments and the International Criminal Court." *International Organization* 64, no. 2 (2010): 225–56.

Simpson, Alfred William Brian. *Human Rights and the End of Empire: Britain and the Genesis of the European Convention*. Oxford University Press, 2004.

Skilbeck, Rupert. "Funding Justice: The Price of War Crimes Tribunals." *Human Rights Brief* 15, no. 3 (2008): 6–10.

Skocpol, Theda. "Bringing the State Back In: Strategies of Analysis in Current Research." In *Bringing the State Back In*, ed. Peter B. Evans, Dietrich Rueschemeyer, and Theda Skocpol, 3–37. New York, NY: Cambridge University Press, 1985.

Solomon, Andrew. "International Tribunal Spotlight: The Inter-American Court of Human Rights (IACHR)." *International Judicial Monitor* 2, no. 3 (2007).

Solvang, Ole. "Chechnya and the European Court of Human Rights: The Merits of Strategic Litigation." *Security & Human Rights* 19, no. 3 (2008): 208–19.

Sperfeldt, Christoph. "The Role of Cambodian Civil Society in the Victim Participation Scheme of the Extraordinary Chambers of the Courts of Cambodia." In *Victims of International Crimes: An Interdisciplinary Discourse*, ed. Thorsten Bonacker and Christoph Safferling, 345–72. Springer Science & Business Media, 2013.

Sriram, Chandra Lekha and Stephen Brown. "Kenya in the Shadow of the ICC: Complementarity, Gravity and Impact." *International Criminal Law Review* 12, no. 2 (2012): 219–44. https://doi.org/10.1163/157181212X633361.

Staton, Jeffrey K. and Alexia Romero. "Clarity and Compliance in the Inter-American Human Rights System," 2011. http://paperroom.ipsa.org/papers/paper_26179.pdf.

Stoddard, Abby. "Humanitarian NGOs: Challenges and Trends," February 27, 2009. http://dspace.cigilibrary.org/jspui/handle/123456789/22644.

Stroup, Sarah S. *Borders Among Activists: International NGOs in the United States, Britain, and France*. Cornell University Press, 2012.

Struett, Michael J. *The Politics of Constructing the International Criminal Court: NGOs, Discourse, and Agency*. Palgrave Macmillan, 2008.

Sundstrom, Lisa McIntosh. "Advocacy beyond Litigation: Examining Russian NGO Efforts on Implementation of European Court of Human Rights Judgments." *Communist and Post-Communist Studies*, Disintegration of the Soviet Union. Twenty Years Later. Assessment. Quo Vadis?, 45, no. 3–4 (September 2012): 255–68. https://doi.org/10.1016/j.postcomstud.2012.06.003.

Sweeney, James A. *The European Court of Human Rights in the Post-Cold War Era: Universality in Transition*. Routledge, 2013.

Tallberg, Jonas, Lisa M. Dellmuth, Hans Agné, and Andreas Duit. "NGO Influence in International Organizations: Information, Access and Exchange." *British Journal of Political Science*, September 2015, 1–26. https://doi.org/10.1017/S000712341500037X.

Tallberg, Jonas, Thomas Sommerer, Theresa Squatrito, and Christer Jönsson. *The Opening Up of International Organizations: Transnational Access in Global Governance*. Cambridge University Press, 2013.

Tarrow, Sidney. *Power in Movement: Social Movements and Contentious Politics.* Cambridge University Press, 2011.

Teitel, Ruti G. *Humanity's Law.* Oxford University Press, 2011.

Tilly, Charles and Sidney Tarrow. *Contentious Politics.* Oxford University Press, 2015.

Tisdall, Simon. "Omar Al-Bashir Case Suggests South African Foreign Policy Is Going Rogue." *The Guardian,* June 15, 2015. www.theguardian.com/world/2015/jun/15/omar-al-bashir-south-africa-sudan-international-criminal-court-icc.

Tretter, Hannes, Barbara Liegl, Kerstin Buchinger, and Astrid Steinkellner. "Strasbourg Court Jurisprudence and Human Rights in Austria: An Overview of Litigation, Implementation and Domestic Reform." JURISTRAS State of the Art Report, March 2007. www.juristras.eliamep.gr/?cat=7.

Treves, Tullio, Marco Figessi di Rattalma, Attila Tanzi, Alessandro Fodella, Cesare Pitea, and Chiara Ragni eds. *Civil Society, International Courts and Compliance Bodies.* Cambridge University Press, 2005.

True, Jacqui and Michael Mintrom. "Transnational Networks and Policy Diffusion: The Case of Gender Mainstreaming." *International Studies Quarterly* 45, no. 1 (2001): 27–57.

Ubeda de Torres, Amaya. "Strasbourg Court Jurisprudence and Human Rights in France: An Overview of Litigation, Implementation and Domestic Reform." JURISTRAS State of the Art Report, February 2007. www.juristras.eliamep.gr/?cat=7.

"UN News – Security Council Inaction on Darfur 'Can Only Embolden Perpetrators' – ICC Prosecutor." UN News Service Section, December 12, 2014. www.un.org/apps/news/story.asp?NewsID=49591#.VWNqU-feOdc.

"United Nations Diplomatic Conference of Plenipotentiaries on the Establishment of an International Criminal Court, 1998 - Volume II," 1998. http://legal.un.org/diplomatic conferences/icc-1998/vol_II_e.html.

United Nations Human Rights Office of the High Commissioner. "Human Rights Treaty Bodies." Accessed September 13, 2016. www.ohchr.org/EN/HRBodies/Pages/WhatTBDo.aspx.

Van den Eynde, Laura. "Amicus Curiae Briefs of Human Rights NGOs at the European Court of Human Rights." Stanford University Law School, 2011.

  "Amicus Curiae Briefs of Human Rights NGOs before the European Court of Human Rights." Stanford University Law School, 2011.

Van der Vet, Freek. "Seeking Life, Finding Justice: Russian NGO Litigation and Chechen Disappearances before the European Court of Human Rights." *Human Rights Review* 13, no. 3 (2012): 303–25. https://doi.org/10.1007/s12142-012-0226-2.

Viljoen, Frans and Lirette Louw. "State Compliance with the Recommendations of the African Commission on Human and Peoples' Rights, 1994–2004." *The American Journal of International Law* 101, no. 1 (2007): 1–34.

Voeten, Erik. "The Politics of International Judicial Appointments: Evidence from the European Court of Human Rights." *International Organization* 61, no. 4 (2007): 669–701. https://doi.org/10.1017/S0020818307070233.

Washington Post Editorial Board. "The International Criminal Court on Shaky Ground." *The Washington Post,* December 28, 2014. www.washingtonpost.com/opinions/the-international-criminal-court-on-shaky-ground/2014/12/28/8d11a3d6-815c-11e4-81fd-8c4814dfa9d7_story.html.

Weiss, Thomas George and Leon Gordenker eds. *NGOs, the UN, and Global Governance.* Lynne Rienner, 1996.

Whitlock, Craig. "Detention of African Warlord Raises Legal Questions for Pentagon." *The Washington Post,* January 13, 2015. www.washingtonpost.com/world/national-security/

detention-of-warlord-raises-legal-questions-for-pentagon/2015/01/13/3839c43e-9b4b-11e4-96cc-e858eba91ced_story.html.

Williams, Sarah and Emma Palmer. "Civil Society and Amicus Curiae Interventions in the International Criminal Court." *Acta Juridica* 2016, no. 1 (2016): 40–65.

Wilson, Bruce M. and Juan Carlos Rodríguez Cordero. "Legal Opportunity Structures and Social Movements The Effects of Institutional Change on Costa Rican Politics." *Comparative Political Studies* 39, no. 3 (2006): 325–51. https://doi.org/10.1177/0010414005281934.

Windridge, Oliver. "2015 at the African Court on Human and Peoples' Rights – A Year in Review." *The ACtHPR Monitor* (blog), January 25, 2016. www.acthprmonitor.org/2015-at-the-african-court-on-human-and-peoples-rights-a-year-in-review/.

"An Alien Institution: A Q&A with the Network of African National Human Rights Institutions." *The ACtHPR Monitor* (blog), November 24, 2015. www.acthprmonitor.org/an-alien-institution-qa-with-the-network-of-african-national-human-rights-institutions/.

Wolf, Hans Dieter. "Private Actors and the Legitimacy of Governance beyond the State." In *Governance and Democracy: Comparing National, European and International Experiences*, ed. Arthur Benz and Ioannis Papadopoulos, 200–27. Routledge, 2006.

Wong, Wendy. *Internal Affairs: How the Structure of NGOs Transforms Human Rights*. Cornell University Press, 2012.

Woolaver, Hannah. "The Role of Amicus Curiae Submissions at International Criminal Tribunals." International Judicial Monitor – Special Report, Spring 2016. www.judicialmonitor.org/spring2016/specialreport2.html.

Younes, Kristele. "NGOs Consultations with ICC Organs." *The International Criminal Court Monitor*, April 2005, Issue 29 edition.

Zagorac, Dean. "International Courts and Compliance Bodies: The Experience of Amnesty International." In *Civil Society, International Courts and Compliance Bodies*, ed. Tullio Treves, Marco Figessi di Rattalma, Attila Tanzi, and Alessandro Fodella, 11–39. T.M.C. Asser Press, 2005.

Index

For EU product safety concerns, contact us at Calle de José Abascal, 56–1°, 28003 Madrid, Spain or eugpsr@cambridge.org.

www.ingramcontent.com/pod-product-compliance
Ingram Content Group UK Ltd.
Pitfield, Milton Keynes, MK11 3LW, UK
UKHW020352140625
459647UK00020B/2422